My Father's Shadow

UNCOVERING THE STORIES BETWEEN THE LINES

I0211486

SONDERHO PRESS

A MEMOIR

SARA AHARON

Sonderho Press, Prescott, Ontario K0E 1T0
Copyright © 2025, Sara Aharon.
All rights reserved. Published 2025.

Published by Sonderho Press.

Printed in Canada.

ISBN: 978-1-7386952-9-4

This book is printed on acid-free paper.

To my father,

I see you (more)
clearly now.

PRAISE FOR
My Father's Shadow

"*Sara Aharon draws on her unique training as a psychologist and trauma specialist to bring to light the fabled life of her father, Ran Kislev, the Holocaust survivor and acclaimed Haaretz journalist responsible for exposing the Israeli mafia and other aspects of Israel's shadow. Just as her father took a deep dive into the Israeli underground, Aharon takes the reader into the depths of her father's life: his idiosyncratic history as well as the far-reaching implications of his personal and professional choices, especially on those nearest to him.*"

> — Tanya Bellehumeur-Allatt, author of
> *Peacekeeper's Daughter: A Middle East Memoir and Carrying War*

"*Sara Aharon's memoir of her journalist father, a complicated man—courageous, noble, selfish, deceitful—is also a look back at an Israel that was maturing into the country it is today. Written with love, scrutiny, and incredulity, in this book Sara works hard to understand herself, her father, and a people and country that is much misunderstood today.*"

> — David Bezmozgis,, author of
> The Betrayers, a 2014 Giller Prize Finalist

"*Many of us remember the devastating moment when we realized that a parent is but a unique, flawed human being. The narrative of one's childhood must be rewritten from a new perspective, and in her memoir, My Father's Shadow, Sara Aharon does so with grace, empathy, and brutal honesty. Charting life 'before' and 'after' that moment to understand her accomplished but controversial father, we join her in a gripping, page-turning journey of history, mystery, and transformation.*"

> — Alexandra Risen, author of
> *Unearthed: Love, Acceptance, and Other Lessons from an Abandoned Garden*

"*Constructed of personal recollections and meticulous research, My Father's Shadow is an important and compulsive read for anyone interested in the evolution of Israel's identity. It deals with one woman's quest to understand her father and to make sense of the political events that shadowed her unique and often harrowing childhood. My Father's Shadow is not only the story of an important and courageous journalist who risked everything to bring truths to light, it is also the story of a brave and resilient daughter who seeks to make sense of the secrets that shrouded her childhood.*"

> — Julie Hartley, author of
> *The Promise She Made*

"Someone I loved once gave me

a box full of darkness.

It took me years to understand

That this too, was a gift."

— Mary Oliver,
The Uses of Sorrow
(Thirst: Poems, 2007)

"In the midst of darkness,

Light persists."

— Mahatma Gandhi

Author's Note

As a psychologist, I've learned that writing a memoir involves weaving together two elements: narrative and recollection. My process of research and memory excavation was very much like sewing patches into a quilt—one filled with holes. I have done my best to verify details of past experiences and events through research and interviews. The rest is my story, to the best of my recollection. Dialogues in this memoir are not transcripts, but rather reconstructions based on the essence of the memory. Aside from direct quotations from articles or books, this memoir reflects my emotional truth. Most of the written source material was in Hebrew and I had translated it myself. I paid a professional to translate from French to English. The names of certain individuals have been fictionalized, including Dina, Nira, Jonathan (The Source), Magda, Dalia, her son Ari, Officer Katan, and others.

CONTENTS

Prologue

My father may be at peace now, but I am unsettled. Questions swirl in my head. I look at his vacant body, a tiny smile on his face. Is that what "taking secrets to the grave" looks like?

I've just spent the last ten days in the archive of the newspaper he worked at for forty years, *Haaretz Daily*. Truthfully, I was avoiding more unpleasant daughterly activities, such as holding his grey and emaciated hand. He was comatose during his final days, and while waiting for the inevitable, I chose to look through some of the thousands of articles and editorials he'd penned over decades. I'd never read any of them. My father could no longer speak, but this way, I could hear his voice. The scope of his work was astounding. I had no idea.

While going over a small sample of his articles, opening the mini brown envelopes, unfolding the yellowing articles one at a time, I had flashbacks to the years in which some of them were written. As if I had slid through a wrinkle in time, forgotten memories came into full view.

I realize now that I've known so little about the journalist who was famous enough that I grew up as "the daughter of". While I was prancing in flower fields, that version of my father, Ran Kislev, became highly influential in Israel, politically and socially. He remained so for several decades.

My father was known for shining light on what Carl Jung called "the shadow" of Israel. Just like the individual's shadow, which refers to aspects of the self that we repress and deny, society has a shadow, too. From organized crime to organized religion and cults to the Arab-Israeli conflict, politics, institutional corruption of all types, and many other investigative pieces, my father exposed it all at a critical time in Israel's history. The word "courage" was often associated with him.

His respected public persona helped keep my father's personal shadow hidden.

I was startled by how much his articles revealed about him and about my strange childhood. As a psychologist, I recognize that doing this involved an excavation of traumas I had buried deep enough that they stayed in the shadows for decades. Shining light on all of it raised many questions. I am mad at myself for not reading his life's work sooner.

Too late.

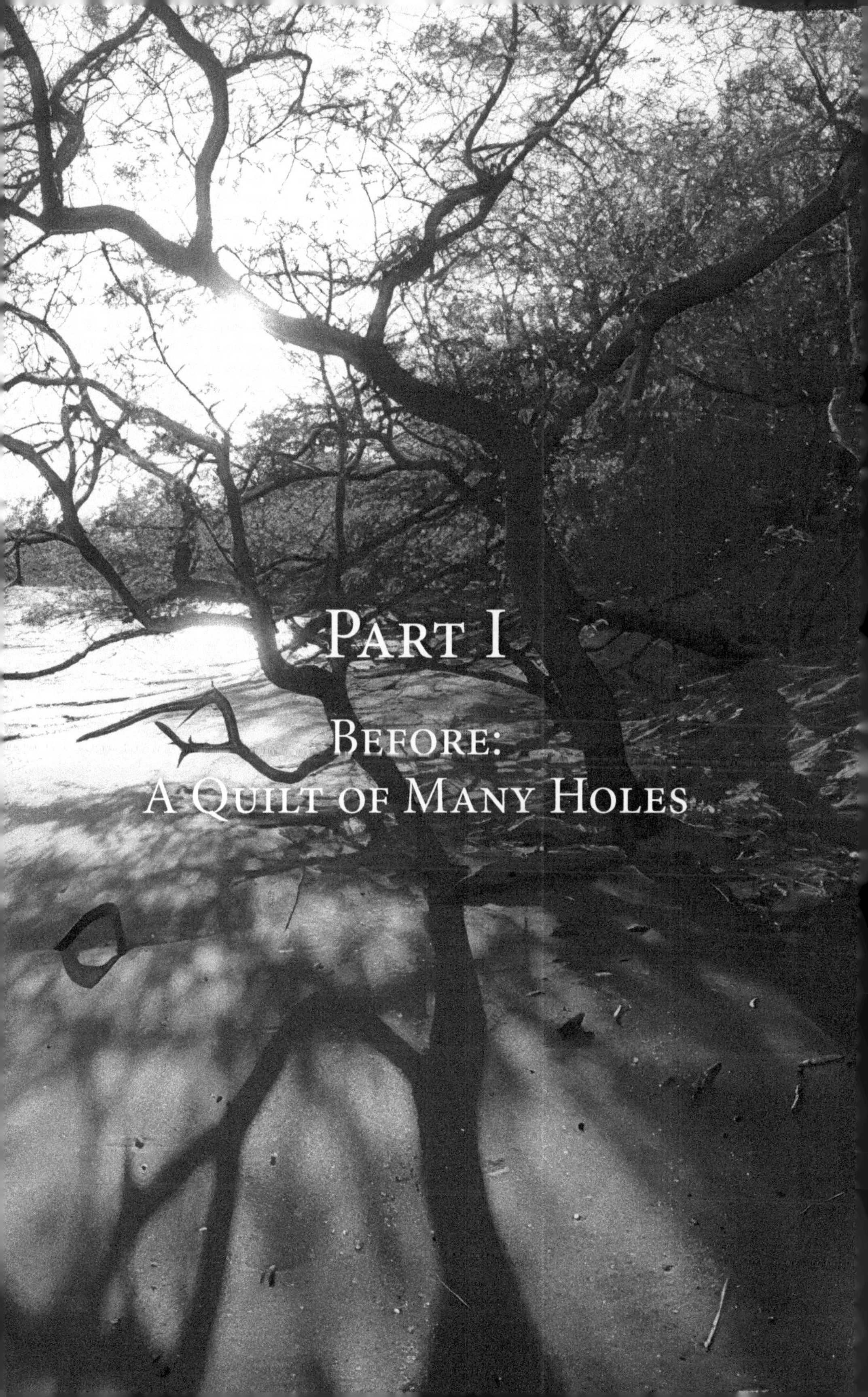

Part I

Before:
A Quilt of Many Holes

1974—
WE NEED TO TALK

My parents had a poor sense of timing.

On the first day of middle school, I hurried, eager to start the day, only to find them waiting for me on our worn-out beige sofa in the living room, serious expressions on their faces. In a synchronized gesture, they each took a cigarette from their packs. My mother moved a strand of her blonde hair that covered one eye and elbowed my father. The grooves on his forehead deepened and he looked away.

"Sit down, we need to talk to you," my mother said.

With the new leather schoolbag resting on my knees, I bounced my feet. At age twelve, I had little patience for my parents' lectures and was anxious to head to school, excited to meet new friends.

My father began, "You know how I've written articles about criminals and organized crime?"

Three years earlier, in 1971, our lives had changed drastically after my father published his series on organized crime in *Haaretz Daily*. The memory of the two men following me everywhere who turned out to be detectives, the appearance of pistols which my father still had, the strange phone calls and intense conversations between my parents, were still fresh on my mind.

So yes, I did know.

"Yes. and…," I said.

"About these…," he paused and drew deeply on his cigarette.

"Remember the names of the criminals at the top of Israel's organized crime?" my mother asked.

"Yes, like Danoch and Mentesh. What about them?"

"Well, a few of them live nearby," my father said. He hesitated before adding, "some have children."

"Okay. Why are you telling me this?"

"A couple of their kids are close to your age. They will be at your new school."

I sighed.

"The one you need to worry about the most is the son of Danoch," my mother said.

Wait, what?"

I remembered hearing them talk about a Danoch who threatened my father, more than once. Sweat was building up under my arms and in the palms of my hands.

"Our advice is that you keep a low profile," my father said as he pulled

the overflowing ashtray close and flicked the ash.

"And don't let anyone know what your last name is," my mother said.

My father nodded his balding head enthusiastically.

"So why are you sending me to that school?" My eyes darted between them.

"We don't have a choice because of the integration rules," my father said.

"Students have to go to designated schools for three years before they can switch elsewhere."

"You're kidding me, right?"

"Sadly, no. And recently members of the Israeli mafia tried to kill someone who was investigating them." My mother stared hard at my father as she said that.

My tummy twisted.

I'd heard about the bomb that exploded outside the door of the person who was in charge of investigating a criminal's tax evasion case. It had been all over the news.

"So, like when they take attendance at school and call 'Sara Kislev' like what exactly do you think I should do? Look around, pretend it's not me?"

Crossing her arms, my mother said, "Okay. You're being ridiculous. Maybe just don't say who your father is," and she turned her head away, towards the window.

"And the fact there is no other Kislev in *all* of Tel Aviv is not going to give it away?"

It used to amuse me that there were no other Kislev's in the phone book in those days. Suddenly, it didn't feel like such a cool thing.

"Well, let's hope not," my father said.

That wasn't much of an answer.

All I could do was imagine my head being pushed into the toilet in the school restroom. And worse.

It wasn't until that morning that I'd become fully aware of the danger I was in as a result of my father's work. The earlier flutter of excitement in my belly, in anticipation of the first day in a new school, transformed into frantic butterflies flapping for their lives.

Kislev, for the parents of several future schoolmates, was the Devil's last name. I didn't doubt they heard this name at home, just like I'd heard their last names.

Had my father not realized this would happen when he moved us to Bialik Street? He knew that some of the criminals lived close by. Why was he making it easy for criminals to find us and hurt us? How long would it take their kids to figure out who I was?

My father, the man whose job was to keep me safe, had done the opposite. As I dragged my feet towards my new school, the first seeds of resentment towards him were planted. In the coming years, my contempt for and disappointment in him would grow.

My father's long and dark shadow followed me.

1967—
Magical Adventures

Crime was only one of my father's favourite subjects to investigate and write about. As I would learn over time, his journalistic career was a quest for him, full of excitement and often danger. He traipsed into other minefields as well—politics, religion, social injustice of all types and the conflict with Arabs in Israel and those who identified as displaced Palestinians. He always wanted to check things up close before writing about them. This meant putting himself in risky situations and occasionally my mother and I accompanied him.

Many early experiences seemed at the time like magical adventures—but they involved day trips to places my friends' parents would not have dreamed of taking a child.

I am grateful I remained oblivious to the danger for so long.

When my father was around in my early years, it meant that something exhilarating was always about to happen.

I leaf through my memory folders and land in June of 1967, when I was five years old. At that time, large swaths of Israel were still covered with the detritus of war and my father decided it was time for a family road trip. As soon as the sirens of the Six Day War stopped making us sprint to the shelter in the day and crawl out of bed like drunken zombies at night, we headed out of town. Live ammunition rounds, burnt army vehicles, and missile shells were scattered everywhere on the land Israel won control over. There were warnings to stay away from these areas until the army cleared them. But my father, a hungry freelance journalist at various tabloids, chased any potential scoop—and war was a big one.

Since my father drove exclusively clunkers he resurrected from places where cars go to die, my parents recruited their friends Gadi and Edna and their much healthier car for our trip. And so it was that on a hot mid-June day, all four adults and five-year-old me headed out of the city. As always before long car rides, my mother fed me enough anti-nausea medication to sedate a camel. My parents were tired of cleaning my vomit during drives, often multiple times, so any drive longer than fifteen minutes required rendering me unconscious, door to door.

By the time I woke up we were very far from home, and I found myself in a place where you might expect to meet the Little Prince if your plane crashed there.

I squinted in the bright desert sun and pivoted on my skinny legs. In front of us were rows of single-story houses. Not a single human or animal could be seen among them. The silence was disrupted only by the sound of the car door slamming and the gravel crunching under our sandals as we moved around the car. My father cleared his throat and said, "We should look around." He lit a cigarette, took out his camera and fished a new roll of film out of his pocket. He crouched low and looked at me with half a smile as I watched his fingers manipulate the film that stuck out of a plastic cylinder. The burning cigarette hung from the corner of his mouth, and I wondered how he could manage to do so many things while always having a cigarette dangling from his lips.

Gadi and Edna had already moseyed away from the car and my father called out to them to wait. In the meantime, my mother fixed her lipstick using a small mirror she always had with her. She ran her fingers through her shiny blonde hair to make sure every strand was in place.

We were near the ancient town of Jericho where, according to a book called *The Bible*, Joshua and his soldiers made the walls of the city crumble by walking around them and blowing their trumpets. As my mother explained this to me, her hair blew in the desert wind. She took big steps like a marching soldier, walked in circles and pretended to blow a trumpet with great flair.

"Come, let's look around," my mother said when she finished trumpeting. With a slight push to my back, she guided me up the dirt road where the others were already exploring.

Perched on the edge of Jericho, the houses beckoned us as if saying: *take a closer look and remember.*

In silence, we strolled on small, unpaved streets between once-white one-story houses and shacks. Doors creaked and banged in the wind. Thin curtains blew in and out of windows like lonely ghosts, searching for something or someone. The tiny hairs on the nape of my neck stood on end. The grown-ups peered through open windows and doors. I followed my mother everywhere but stayed on the thresholds, feeling uneasy about crossing them. The adults who were milling around this village gasped and said things I didn't understand. I didn't know why we had come to this place, and I wanted to go back home.

Then, my mother pulled me into a house that would haunt me for years.

A crooked painting on the wall, flies hovering over plates that still had food on them, toppled chairs, a broken glass on the floor. This image etched itself deep into my psyche along with the eerie silence. I felt as if we'd shown up mere moments after the family that lived there ran out the door for some mysterious reason. I could feel their presence yet couldn't see them.

I smelled it.

Fear.

It lingered in the center of the room like fog so thick it was hard to move through it.

"Mommy, my tummy...," I whispered.

I turned my head towards a child's bed and noticed a small blanket on the floor. Next to the child's bed lay a doll with her arms outstretched towards the door. My eyes were an overflowing pond.

My father stood in the middle of the room, holding the camera with both hands in front of him. Frozen. Not taking pictures.

"Where is the girl?" I asked.

"Everyone in this village left overnight, thinking they'd come back in a day or two," my father said in a quiet voice.

"Is that why the girl didn't take the doll?"

"Must be," he said.

"What happened to them?"

"We don't know. We think they're staying in tents somewhere. Hopefully, they'll be able to come back soon and there'll be some peace and quiet in this country."

The confidence in his voice made me believe these families were going to return to their homes shortly and the girl who lived in that house would get her doll back. My sadness transformed to relief.

Soon after the trip to the abandoned village near Jericho, which my father turned into a long article in the tabloid he worked for, we made a pilgrimage to another place that the Israeli army conquered in the war, this time from Egypt.

The drive was long, and we stopped overnight to sleep in the town of Beer Sheva. The next day, my parents woke me at dawn, gave me my pill, and we got on the road again. I woke up too early to the loud singing of victory war songs. *Nasser is waiting for Rabin* and *The Tiran Straights* songs produced very enthusiastic screams from everyone. With the car swerving left and right as Gadi banged on the horn, singing in ecstasy, I ruined the party by puking to all four winds.

By mid-afternoon, we arrived at the end of the earth. Or at least the end of the country.

Standing outside the car, I was struck by a world that lost all its colours and was now painted brown. My eyes landed on a brown fortress wall in front of an enormous, jagged brown mountain. I saw the face of an old man in the mountain, but my father said it was a mirage. We walked slowly towards a gate. My mother lagged behind.

"What's a mirage?" I asked.

"It is something that happens when the heat and sun of the desert can make you see things that are not there."

"But there *is* a face there."

"How can there be a face on a mountain? It's your imagination."

"What's imagination?"

My father chuckled.

"Imagination is what helps you make up stories and see things that are not there," my mother said as she caught up with us.

This was confusing because I saw not only a face in the mountain, but everywhere in nature and many trees looked human to me. In time, I'd capture them in photographs and paintings so others could see them, too.

Dust blew into my eyes and mouth while we stood waiting at a gate, so I had to stop talking and spit out the dust. Finally, a man came, and my father showed him a card that said he was a journalist. Inside, we stood in front of a crumbling building. Looming close behind was the mountain, and it looked ominous. At that late afternoon hour, the sky seemed as if it was on fire.

"This place is called Saint Catherine's monastery and the mountain behind is Mount Sinai, where God gave Moses the Ten Commandments," my mother said with conviction while pointing at one of the mountain peaks around us. I hadn't read *The Bible* yet, so neither God nor Moses meant anything to me, but they sounded important.

"Oh, stop it. There is no God. But yes, that's what's written in *The Bible*," my father corrected my mother. He did that often.

"Let's move it. We don't have much time to see this place before Israel gives it back," my father said, so I pulled his hand as I tried to run towards the entrance.

"It's not going to happen right now, silly," my father said and squeezed my shoulder lightly.

A man wearing a cassock, a long black robe and a funny hat came to greet us.

Out of my father's earshot, my mother explained that there was another reason it was worth visiting this place before it was too late and told me about the weirdest thing—a bush that kept burning and burning.

"Show me, show me," I said pulling on the hem of her skirt.

"I think this place was built were the bush once burned," she said quietly.

My father put one finger to his lips and motioned us and their friends to follow him. We entered the monastery together. Everyone inside spoke in low voices. Not much light streamed through the windows, but you could see well enough with many burning candles all around. Giant paintings covered the walls, and they sparkled. There was a lot of gold in them. I gasped. My mother whispered that they told the stories of *The Bible* and of Joshua, the same guy she'd talked about before when she blew an imaginary trumpet. One painting mesmerized me. Against a background of gold, people were climbing up a ladder while some evil-looking creatures tried to pull them down. I stood in front of it for a long time until my mother bent down to tell me it was about the struggle between good and evil. Many years later, as a student of Art History at Tel-Aviv University, I looked up the image and learned it is called *The Ladder of Divine Ascent*.

When we came out of the monastery, my father took photos of the building while my mother and I squatted in the shade by the gate. She handed me my pills and lukewarm water. I gulped it and she explained that the place was named after Catherine, a woman who suffered greatly because of something she had, called The Christian Faith, and people tried to beat it out of her. What was left of her was buried under the floor we'd just walked on. I leaned my head into my mother's lap. To brighten my mood, she told me more about the Ten Commandments. Before I had the chance to ask what Thou Shall Not Commit Adultery meant, my father caught up with us. He scowled at my mother.

In the car, after lighting a cigarette, my father turned to me and said, "Religion is nonsense. *The Bible* is mostly made-up fables like the ones in your La Fontaine and Aesop's Fables books." I loved these books because they had the most incredible pictures, next to the words which I couldn't yet read. My mother turned her head away to look out the window and I knew she didn't like what my father said. It was on that trip that I had the first inkling as to how annoyed my father was with the words *Bible* or *God*. The word God alone unleashed tongues of fury in the form of harsh words and condemnation.

What stayed with me from that trip was a distinct impression that the Sinai Mountain Range and the monastery were special. It turns out that I was born in a country full of special places.

And that's not always a good thing.

Nature personified or my pareidolia.

OMAR

Even after it stopped being safe for Israeli Jews to do so, my father was welcomed into any Arab community.

Loud "Salaam Aleykum" hollers from the men in long white galabias and the children who trailed them, greeted us as we stepped out of our car in the center of a village or town.

"Salaam, shalom," my father returned the wishes for peace on everyone.

While my father drank coffee from a carved copper pot, with a long handle, set on a low round table in the center of the Arab town of Qualqilia or Tul Karem or other towns and villages, my mother visited the kitchens of their wives. Under the cover of grapevines, I played with local kids. We tossed marbles or peach pits and ate the juicy, sweet cactus fruit or dug seeds out of pomegranate halves. These were fun-filled Saturday afternoons. We spoke the universal language of children.

Back then, I hadn't realized the significance of our trips. They were nothing like the weekend shopping trips to the Arab markets that other Israelis made in the 1960s and even part of the '70s. They were work trips for my father. The conversations he had with the men involved a complex reality. He listened to their complaints in the deepest sense of the word. He heard them and he told their stories in his articles—articles I didn't read until 2013.

Before going back home we'd stop at the markets to buy fresh pitas and I was allowed to choose souvenirs: a plain terracotta vase I could paint over, embroidered sachets or any trinket that caught my eye. I painted the vase bought on our last trip to an Arab town in the early '70s in cheerful hues of red, yellow, purple, and orange. It sat proudly for several years atop my closet, and it was the first thing I saw in the mornings when I opened my eyes.

Like the chances of peaceful co-existence between Arabs and Jews, along the Syrian-African fault-line, one day an early morning earthquake toppled and shattered my beautiful vase into a million little pieces.

While visiting and shopping in Arab communities was not unusual for Israeli Jews in the 1960s, inviting them to stay at your home was. But at age five, I didn't know that.

One day in the summer of 1967, I spent the afternoon climbing trees, running between sprinklers to cool down, and looking for turtles and snails with friends. As the sun was setting, my friends went home, answering their mothers' calls from the balconies. Eventually, I too went home, carrying a box with snails I picked up around a leaky sprinkler. Stepping into our apartment, I heard loud laughter and an unfamiliar man's voice. In the living room, I saw my parents and a stranger who wore a red and white scarf on his head with a black hoop on top like some men in the villages we'd visited. He rose slowly, walked towards me and said, "Korim li Omar," bending down to meet my eyes.

"Tell him your name too," my mother said.

"Sara," I blurted out and scurried to my bedroom hoping my parents won't ask about the content of my box. In my room, I was surprised to find a suitcase and some other items that didn't belong to me. My mother followed me and said, "Our friend Omar is going to stay in your room. Our home will be his home for a week."

"Hmm… huh, why?" I said as I tried unsuccessfully to use my foot to push the shoebox behind a pile of toys on the floor.

"He'll sleep on one of your sofas," she said, frowning in the direction of the shoebox.

I didn't have a bed in my room, just two ancient sofas—one green and one yellow. Everything in our apartment was rented and we had to make do with whatever furniture was there.

I tried hard to come up with a reason why a stranger shouldn't sleep in my room but couldn't find the right words. My mother, on the other hand, had a strong argument why I'd have to take the snails out when she lifted the lid: "The poor things will die if you keep them here. They need fresh air, food and moisture." So, I released them the next morning, while my parents kept a human in my room for a whole week.

At night, before he went to sleep on the green sofa in my room, Omar folded his head scarf neatly. On the first night, sitting across from him on the yellow sofa, I asked him if I could touch it. He laughed and said "Aywa" which I knew meant 'yes' in Arabic. He told me it was called a keffiyeh and let me hold it. I passed my fingers across it, enjoying the lumpiness of the stitches, wrapped it around me like a robe, and rolled it like a scarf. Omar was sprawled on the sofa he slept on, reading a book with squiggly letters. He lifted his eyes now and then to peek at me, winking and grinning.

Throughout his stay, our guest made my parents strong black coffee in the shiny blue coffee pot he brought with him, which he gifted them upon leaving. Every morning, he left the apartment with my parents and every evening, sometimes very late, the three of them returned in good spirits.

Why did my parents invite him?

What was he doing all day with my parents?

At the end of the week, I watched as Omar packed his clothes and prepared to leave.

Turning to me, he said, "Thank you for letting me sleep in your room."

"I didn't mind it. Why did you come here?" I asked, not realizing this was a rude question to ask a guest.

"Your parents invited me to see Tel Aviv."

"Where do you live?"

"Near Jerusalem."

"Oh."

"That's nice of your parents to invite me. Good people your parents."

Omar picked up his bag and was about to leave my room when he hesitated and took off his keffiyeh. He folded it neatly and laid it flat in the open palms of his hands.

"Here. You like this very much, you keep it."

"Really? Thank you."

I immediately wrapped myself with it and jumped up and down on my sofa. Dazzled by this beautiful fabric, I was delighted that he gave it to me.

Omar laughed, reached over to give me a pat on the head, and left with my parents.

"I'll see you again soon," he said.

I hoped he'd return soon.

And this was how I became the owner of an authentic red-and-white keffiyeh used by Muslim men (not the smaller cheap imitations sold in tourists' shops as scarves). I used it gleefully over the years as a robe, scarf, skirt, bed throw and in the summer, a blanket. The fabric held many wonderful memories for me.

One evening, a couple of years after this peculiar visit, I found my parents chain-smoking in the living room and heard them mention the name Omar.

"I wonder if we achieved the opposite outcome of what we hoped for Omar," my mother said to my father.

I interrupted and asked, "Are you talking about Omar, the nice man who stayed in my room and gave me his keffiyeh?"

The silence and frown on my mother's face and my father's pale face suggested it was that same Omar.

"What happened?"

"Nothing Kooka. Go to your room," my father said and turned back to my mother. Kooka was his nickname for me. He said my curious eyes reminded him of the Kukulka bird (Polish for Cuckoo bird).

In the months to come I heard my parents nervously mention Omar's visit a few times. It remained one of many confusing memories from my childhood, one of many holes in the quilt that needed to be patched.

SPECIAL PLACES

For a good chunk of my childhood, both my parents were freelance journalists for tabloids, chasing scoops and getting paid poorly, or not at all. While my mother wrote about children's beauty pageants and other fun subjects for *This World*, my father reported about the bad stuff for tabloids and later for *Haaretz Daily*. Whenever he needed a break from all the upsetting things that happened in Israel, he looked for spots outside the city for us to escape to. Most Saturdays he loaded my mother and me into the car and off we went. When we didn't visit Arab villages, he drove us to pretty parks, caves, rivers and streams, archaeological digs, and picturesque churches and mosques. He wanted to experience it all and to share it with us.

After Jerusalem was unified in the Six Day War, my father took us on a tour. I can still recall the sights and smells of the old city. The scent was a cacophony of pines, spices, coffee, and fresh baked pitas. Fragments of memories from this time include picking pinecones in a grove and walking between gnarly olive trees on a mountainside. There are also memory bits involving men peddling their goods in the market of the old city, a kind old man who gave me a bag full of candies, a golden dome, and one long wall made of giant uneven stones and the people who stood in front of it and wept.

In one memory snapshot, I sit on the window ledge of an abandoned building and the song "Jerusalem of Gold" is playing in the background. Where the music came from is unclear and maybe it is simply an association my brain made after this trip. The song was written after this war when Jews were able to return to Jerusalem. The lyrics speak of a city captive in a dream, that sits alone, and about a wall in its midst. There are lines in this song that stir something deep inside me. They lament the cisterns that had dried up, the empty marketplace and the fact no one visits the Temple Mount. Listening closely to the lyrics now, I notice how the city is personified as an abandoned and lonely woman. The slow and sad music, the violins, magnify the emotions. Maybe it had always made me sad because the words evoke a sense of abandonment and loss, an all too familiar feeling from my childhood.

The old city of Jerusalem, 1967.

My father took photos of us in the old city, one just outside a place called El-Aqsa.

"This place is important to Jews, Muslims and Christians. We are standing where the second temple once was. The Muslims believe their prophet Muhammed rose to heaven from there," my father explained.

I still recall the eerie silence around us, the blue and gold tiles on the walls. I had a distinct feeling there was something different about this place. When I look at the photos from this trip now, my chest tightens a little, knowing that it has become a source of deadly conflicts.

Yet another "special" place in the land I was born.

As we walked towards a church called The Church of Resurrection, my father pointed at an old white building with a pointy tower and said, "The Jews have synagogues, the Christians have churches, and Muslims have mosques. This is the Mosque of Omar."

"Do you mean the mosque belongs to our friend Omar?" I asked while pulling hard on my father's arm.

"No, it's a different Omar silly. It's someone who lived and died many years ago."

El-Aqsa mosque, with my mother, 1967.

Another year, on a cold December evening, we visited the Church of Nativity in Bethlehem.

As we stepped out of the car my father said, "This is one of the oldest cities in the world. Jews believe that King David was born here."

"Oh," I said, not knowing yet anything about King David.

For what seemed to me like hours, we waited in line to be let into the church so we could watch something called a Midnight Mass. I was shivering from the cold and at the same time was mesmerized by the colourful lights all around us.

"Christians believe Yeshu was born here," my father said as we walked into the church.

"Who is Yeshu[1]?"

---

1. Israelis call Jesus Yeshu, short for his Hebrew name Yehoshua.

"A wise Jewish man who became a famous rabbi."

"Why didn't I hear him about him?"

My father laughed and then said, "After Yeshu died, his followers started a religion called Christianity, so it's not the main religion in Israel. I just want you to see how other religions celebrate holidays. This holiday is called Christmas."

My eyes followed the walls and ceilings and what I remember is a lot of red and gold. At first it was quiet inside, until suddenly priests in long robes and funny hats came out waving objects, red and purple smoke all around and candlelight surrounding them. I was in awe and felt waves of excitement around me. And at age seven, I was particularly happy that I got to see a ceremony involving bringing out a doll from a hole in the floor.

My father raised me for a moment above the grownups so I could see that.

"What is happening?" I asked him.

"They are showing us now the birth of Yeshu," he whispered and even then, it seemed a bit strange to me.

It amuses me to realize that I had been to a church and a mosque in Israel before I set foot inside a synagogue. That's what growing up with a father like mine meant, among other unusual things.

In retrospect, I realize my father had a profound love for Israel, for the polarities of the country's geographical, religious, and cultural landscapes. As I would discover, Israel's complex history mirrored his own.

A Road Trip
to Remember

On one of our many road trips to northern Israel, I woke up before we made it to our destination. That day, it was the Banias River, which Israel secured access to on the sixth day of the Six Day War.

My father left skid marks on the road when he heard me moan. Once we fully stopped, my mother lifted me out of the car before I could puke. We had to wait until I felt better so that I could take another anti-nausea tablet. My father raised the hood of the car to cool the engine, and my mother lit cigarettes for each of them. As I started to feel better, sitting on the side of the road and taking in the fresh air, my mother gave me the tablet. We had to wait fifteen minutes before it knocked me unconscious again.

Looking around, I stood at what was surely an undiscovered part of paradise. It started past an opening in a thick barbed-wired fence. Touching the horizon was a tapestry of red and orange poppies and anemones, pink, red and white daisies, and many other flowers I couldn't name. I bounded with joy into the field, singing and whirling. White butterflies hopped from petal to petal, like me, unable to pick their favourite. Up in the blue sky, a single fluffy cloud floated. It was a perfect moment, one that you'd only experience if you lived in the heavenly garden.

A scream pierced the air and snapped me out of my reverie.

When I turned around, I saw my parents in the distance flailing their arms and pointing at the fence. Something was terribly wrong. I didn't know what, but I felt it in every cell of my body. My arms dropped to my sides, and I went limp. As my parents' shouts grew increasingly louder, my insides tightened into a fist. I couldn't understand what they were saying, yelling over each other. I began running towards them because I didn't know what else to do.

"Noooo! Stop! Kooka Stop!" I heard my father and heard fear in his voice for the first time in my life. From a distance, I thought I saw my mother pull him back while he tried to walk forward.

What? I stopped, confused. I saw my father raise his hands up while he yelled words slowly, "Do---not---move! I---am---co-ming to-get you."

I froze.

Befuddled, I watched him walk very slowly and deliberately. He was looking down as if trying to avoid stepping on pretty flowers or ladybugs. The wrinkles on his face seemed deeper, and his skin whiter, by the time he reached me. Sweat was pouring profusely down his neck, although it wasn't terribly hot that day. He scooped me up, but not like he always did, in one swoop. Instead, he did it slowly as if I was a fragile flower vase. Lucky for him, at age seven I weighed more like a four-year-old. He turned us around and walked back. It looked like he was re-tracing his steps until we reached the car.

Dripping sweat and breathing heavily, my father lowered me to the ground. I stared at him as he shook violently. Suddenly, he lost his balance and collapsed onto the side of the car, struggling to steady himself.

"Let's get outta here," my mother said to my father with great urgency in her voice.

"Okay, Chip," my father said in an unusually weak voice. He gave my mother the nickname Chip because she liked the cartoon Chip' n Dale, featuring the adventures of two chipmunks, although her name was Tsipora. My mother helped to steady him so he could get into the car.

Once in the car, my father struggled to light a cigarette with his trembling hands.

What's happening? I'd never seen him like that.

"Why, why are you like that?" I began sobbing.

"You're okay now," my mother said and, white like the butterflies, she explained what just happened. In a high-pitched voice she said, "Sara'le, we didn't notice the sign on the fence," and she pointed at the big sign that had a red skull with an X across it. "This field has not been cleared of landmines yet."

My school had shown us scary short films warning about wandering into fields which could be full of landmines, but until that moment I didn't make the connection between the carpet of flowers and butterflies and danger. My heart thumped so loud I couldn't hear the rest of what she was saying.

From the back seat I stared at my parents while they faced each other. There was an intensity I'd not seen before. With trembling hands, my father lit a new cigarette and drew deeply. Tears rolled down my mother's face in slow motion.

Soon, my eyes felt heavy as the pill took effect and I curled into a ball in the back seat and fell asleep.

When we finally arrived at the Banias River, I spilled out of the car. My father and I climbed down a steep and rocky path to swim in the ice-cold water while my mother napped in the shade. We never spoke of that trip again. The lesson in suppressing and moving on was over.

At the time, I didn't understand the full extent of my father's heroism, and because I didn't understand, he scored no points with me to offset the ones he'd lose in coming years.

It would be years before I'd fully grasp what almost happened that day, in a war-torn corner of the Garden of Eden. When you suppress memories, both the good and the bad are hidden from view.

The fist that clenched in my stomach that day wouldn't unravel for decades.

GOD SCHMOD

For a long time, I didn't understand why my family didn't celebrate Jewish holidays. If I mentioned the Bible, or, God forbid, said "God", my father would scrunch his nose. He despised anything religious and reserved his harshest words for Orthodox people. His dislike was palpable and uncompromising. I heard him say big words like doctrine and dogma and that "they" had no right to tell him how to live his life. But I didn't understand then what he was talking about. The religious people I saw on the street never told me how to live my life.

I didn't know what to make of his attitude, especially since it was clear that celebrating the New Year, Hanukkah, and Passover with families was a fun time for all my friends who were just as secular we were.

"Why do you hate religious people so much?" I asked him once in my teens.

"Just because someone is wearing a yarmulke or a black coat and hat and studies or teaches the Torah all day, doesn't mean they are good people. Sometimes corrupt people think they can hide behind these religious symbols," my father said.

"But not everyone is corrupt, right?"

"You're right, but I loathe the fact that the religious parties force their rules and way of life on me, kosher rules, not allowing buses on Shabbat. Secular people should have a choice in everyday matters."

And he tried to explain to me something about separation between state and religious institutes, but none of this made sense to me and he gave up.

"Just don't let anyone brainwash you and tell you how to dress, what to eat, who you can marry."

"Okay, Aba."

It also annoyed him to no end that the government gave yeshiva students money to study the Torah and that they didn't have to serve in the army or work. This anger was shared by many secular Israelis.

My father's feelings about Orthodox people were secrets I had to keep. As a journalist, he couldn't show a clear dislike to any political or social group; he was supposed to be neutral. But in time, I'd discover he wasn't very good at hiding his opinion, and in fact wrote many articles criticizing these groups.

Although I sensed that his aversion to religion was unusual, I couldn't have imagined there were far deeper roots to it. So intense was my father's disgust for religion, that for years my mother and I had no choice but to participate in his civic acts of defiance.

Before Passover, Israeli grocery stores emptied their shelves of bread, flour and other *chametz*—anything that might have leaven in it. From the first night of Passover, Israeli Jews started a week-long national *lent* from leavened bread, pastries and pasta, eating for one week a constipating dry cracker called matza. In anticipation, my father stocked our fridge and freezer with pita bread, challahs, baguettes, cakes and buns, enough to feed a small brigade of infidels.

On the night of the Seder, the ceremonial Passover meal, most Jews in the country sat down with friends and family to enjoy the holiday feast. When they recounted the story of Passover during the Seder, I could hear from all the apartment buildings around us the singing of beautiful holiday songs, followed by the sound of forks and knives clinging against plates. Rather than take part in this shared ancient tradition, my father insisted that we'd have a baguette smeared with butter and a thick slice of Schinke (sliced cooked pork), violating three kosher rules all at once. To drown the sound of holiday songs from our neighbours, he turned the volume up on television as we watched whatever movie our little antenna picked up from a neighbouring country.

When school was back after the three-week Passover school holiday, everyone in class asked, "What did you get for the Afikomen?" Other kids bubbled over about the ransom they'd received for finding this special matza the adults hid. One asked for a doll, another for roller skates. I lowered my head and mumbled something, too embarrassed to admit I spent the evening like a non-Jew. Sometimes I lied and said I asked for LEGO˚ or other wonderful presents.

My father worked hard at convincing me there was no God (if there was one, we would have seen it), that religious customs were all nonsensical, and that organized religion was a way to control ignorant masses. Still, I didn't understand why we were the only family not participating in traditions shared by millions of non-religious people.

"Can we just light the Hanukkah candles, Aba?" I asked every year even though we didn't own a menorah.

"No," he'd answer with a scowl. He'd throw away the crude menorahs I made at school in art class from cardboard and foil smeared in acrylic. They were quite ugly too and into the trash they went.

"What harm will lighting a Menorah do to us?" my mother asked him once.

"What harm? Taking part in brainwashing our daughter, for one thing. I won't permit superstitious phooey in my home." He banged his fist on the dining table.

What harm would lighting colourful skinny candles, eating latkes and donuts have done to him, beyond gaining a couple of pounds?

When I got older, my father told me there was no God worth worshipping, because if there was one, how could he let the Holocaust happen? This was a common response of Jewish survivors of WWII.

Years later, I wondered why he had taken up so many causes and agreed to help many people yet didn't defend his family's right to follow his people's ancient tradition, a right that millions of Jews have died defending. It would turn out to be a far more complicated issue than I could have imagined.

There was another intense and puzzling aversion my father had: to corn. In my teens, I made popcorn once, not knowing it was so repugnant to him. When he entered our home, he raged and yelled for me to open all the windows. Slamming the apartment door behind him, so hard the entire building quaked, he disappeared for several hours until the smell was gone. I'd never seen him act like that before.

My father reacted to anything religious the same way, with visceral disgust as if he could smell God. Corn and God were not allowed in our home. Why? I didn't know.

After years of my begging and pleading through my mother, he agreed to start marking holidays, albeit in the most secular way. When he finally agreed to have a Seder, it was at a very small scale. With my aunt and uncle, Seder was long and boring. But, at the Lidskys, my parents' very secular lawyer friends, it was a riot. My father would scoff and scrunch his nose every time the word God was mentioned in the Haggadah, the book that tells the story of the exodus from Egypt. He couldn't wait for the formal part to be over so he, my mother, Nira and Tzvi Lidsky could drink the real stuff, not just the wine for the blessings. They became louder and rowdier, sometimes putting a record on and dancing and laughing while I and the Lidsky daughters, Galit and Osnat, went upstairs to play.

At the end of these nights, we made our own exodus and once we were in the car, my father would say, "God Schmod, let's go home and eat some baguette with Schinke."

QUE SERA SERA

"You can choose anything you want in the store," my father said.

"Anything?" This had never happened before.

"Yes."

My feet barely touched the ground.

In May 1970 I turned eight, and for my birthday, the busy journalist Ran Kislev found the time to take me to the toy store in the shopping plaza of our neighbourhood Maoz-Aviv.

I picked the biggest, coolest-looking LEGO® box, possibly the most expensive toy in the store. I wouldn't have to lie to friends anymore about getting a LEGO®. With a wide grin, my father paid by cheque, and I hugged him as hard as I could and hopped and pranced all the way home. When we opened the box together, I jumped into his lap and said, "I love you sooo much."

"Me too, Kooka," he replied and ruffled my curly head.

A week later, the store owner began calling us. My parents trained me to ask who was on the phone by starting with "Hello who is it?" and repeating the name I'd hear out loud.

"Hello Mr. Landau from the toy store," I said the first time he called.

"Tell him we are not home," my mother mouthed while waving her hand in an urgent *No* gesture.

Another week passed and Mr. Landau called again, "Tell your father the cheque bounced and he has to bring me the money tomorrow." I didn't understand how a cheque could bounce or even move on its own, but I didn't ask. The tone of his voice told me he was unhappy about it.

One evening, the store owner knocked on our door. My parents installed a chain on the door of our rented apartment, and I had to put it on before opening the door, while they hid in their bedroom.

"Are your parents home?" Mr. Landau asked.

"I will check," I said, and went to ask my parents if they were home, the way they had taught me to.

"No, say we are at work and will be home very late," my mother said quietly while my father nodded and looked away. They were in bed, under their blanket, holding it up to their necks.

The nice man at the door frowned when I repeated that and he yelled, "I know you're there." I jumped back.

We never went back to that store. In fact, I was scared to walk near the plaza with my friends after that, in case the owner might see me. Since then I felt bad every time I played with the LEGO° and wished my father would take it back.

The same thing happened with the supermarket, the garage where my father took our clunker for repairs, and other stores my parents visited. Many angry calls and loud knocks on the door followed and it was up to me to keep the furious vendors away from my parents.

For decades after, knocks on doors and the ring of a telephone triggered dread in me.

During those same years, electricity often went out.

"Great! Get our candle bottles, Chip!" My father called out to my mother. His cheery voice eliminated my momentary fear of darkness.

Empty wine bottles lined the floor along our living room wall, each covered in colourful wax from all the candles we lit during these nights. My parents would pick out three bottles and place them at the center of the coffee table. They'd let me light the candles while my father took out the guitar he had borrowed from a friend but forgot to return. We'd sing songs starting with quiet ones like "Que Sera Sera" and "Jerusalem of Gold", followed by a couple of fast children's songs like "Run Little Horse". We concluded the evenings with "Guantanamera". My mother led the singing as my father and I hummed along. We burst out singing the chorus: "Guantanamera Guafira Guantanamera, Guantanamera Guafira Guantanamera" and screamed the final chorus in bliss. I'd roll on the floor laughing, so out of breath I could sing no more. If his mood was right, my father sang his favourite Polish or Russian tunes, usually after he drank a couple of glasses of a clear drink that smelled awful.

I didn't let my parents peel the wax off the bottles because I loved looking at the rivers of different colours and feeling their textures. These power-outage nights were the best indoor family times of my childhood, and the bottles were the mementos, reminders of laughter and cheer-filled nights with my parents.

"How come we no longer have these fun singing nights around bottles with candles?" I asked my mother a few years later, as I caressed the last bottle left from that special era.

She laughed and said, "Oh, because now we can pay the electricity bills."

"I had no idea we were so poor," I said.

"You know when the direness of our situation first hit me too?" my mother asked.

"When cheques bounced?" I suggested.

"No, when you commented on the fact that our clothesline only had one set of your clothes while the neighbours' were full of children clothes. You only had two outfits and we couldn't let you dirty them both at the same time."

When it came to his personal affairs, my father lived by the motto "que sera sera"—just like the song—whatever will be will be. He didn't mind being in debt, or driving and transporting us in unsafe cars.

Back in those days, it didn't seem strange to me that once a week, we feasted at restaurants while the fridge was empty. When I asked several years later how we could afford to eat out, I learned that my parents submitted the bills every two weeks as expenses and received the money back. They never said no to a free meal.

Being the free spirited Pippy Longstockings that I was, on days when we didn't eat at restaurants, I munched on edible plants I found in the flower fields. Picking the sweet and ripe carob pods from the ground, I'd happily chew on them. There also was the Arab Bread plant, (a.k.a. Malva), which satisfied my barely noticeable hunger. For a long time, I was unable to read signals from my body that I needed to eat.

In the meantime, while I was roaming about freely and without a care in the world, my father fought for this or that cause, exposing problems and demanding action. And he made a big name for himself doing just that in 1971, when a series he wrote was published in *Haaretz*. The words "Organized Crime" were repeated at our home and on television and radio after that. I didn't understand what it meant, and I certainly didn't grasp the full impact his work had on Israel and our lives until years later.

BAD PEOPLE

Before April 15, 1971, we were an unremarkable, struggling Israeli family. After that day, Ran Kislev became a household name, and the series he published starting that day became fodder for intense controversy. The eight-year-old me was oblivious to this.

"Organized Crime in Israel" was the title of the first instalment of my father's investigative series and it was followed by twelve more articles spelling out what he believed was taking place in Israel's underworld. He shone light on what Carl Jung called The Shadow—the shadow of society, in this case.

My father named key players and shocked the country when he claimed they had connections to police and politicians. He worked on this series for a long time. My mother worked hard, too. She was a journalist at *This World* and had written different articles, some of which she'd talked about. There was the one she did on how housekeepers were overcharging and under-cleaning or the one where she became a bait for purse snatchers on motorcycles. When I did see my parents, they were always excited about what they were working on, and I could tell they had fun doing it.

And so it was that in 1971, when I was in Grade Three, my parents were too busy to realize this was the third year in a row that I was mostly *not* attending school. This meant a carefree existence, unsupervised and unconstrained. I spent most days climbing trees and playing with neighbourhood cats. I set off to school with other children each day but ducked behind the pine trees and waited until my parents had left our apartment building. Only then I'd emerge from behind the bushes. I spent most of my days wandering about in the fields. Occasionally, I showed up at school to avoid my absences being flagged. I knew that this was an offence, and if caught, they'd sentence me to serve time in school, indefinitely.

So, when I noticed one sunny morning, while prancing in the flower field, two men with dark sunglasses watching me from some distance, I grew nervous. Maybe the school was checking up on me? Or maybe my parents heard about my delinquency and wanted to know what I was up to?

On the balcony in Maoz Aviv. My Garden of Eden in the background, 1968.

Maoz Aviv, 1969.

It became very uncomfortable. I attempted to trick them by rolling down on the ground to disappear from their view. I lay there for a while, tickled by ladybugs and butterflies, as I watched them looking for me. When they walked in the opposite direction and I was sure they couldn't see me, I ran and climbed into my trusted friend, the old Sycamore tree. But when I came down an hour later, the men were still there, in the distance, watching me.

Since my first plan hadn't worked, I figured they'd leave me alone if I started going to school regularly. So I did. But they continued to trail me, standing just outside the schoolyard fence.

At that point, I decided to tell my mother about them. She was getting ready to go out to a party and wore a shiny green blouse and short black skirt. Her shiny hair looked even shinier.

"Mom, there are men following me everywhere…"

"Oh, those guys. They're police detectives who are there to protect you," she said and smacked her lips a few times as she applied bright red lipstick.

"From what?" I said after a while, standing behind her at the entrance to the bathroom while she fixed her hair.

"Aba wrote about some bad people and they are making threats trying to make him stop." Now she was applying green eyeshadow and kept stepping back and forth in front of the mirror, looking at herself.

"What bad people?"

"Criminals, robbers, murderers."

"So why are the detectives following *me*?"

"To make sure these people won't hurt any of us."

"Oh. Is Aba scared?"

My mother turned her head towards me and squinted her blue eyes and said, "Aba is not scared of anything. He will do what he thinks is right." I wasn't sure whether she was angry when she said that.

After my parents left the apartment I sat on their bed for a while, confused. Oddly, I was relieved that I wasn't caught neglecting my only duty, showing up at school. I wondered if the detectives would report my delinquency to my parents, so for a while I graced my Grade Three classroom with my elusive presence. During recess, one girl began bothering me, pulling my hair and calling me mean names. She yelled that I was poor and wore dirty clothes. As I left the school grounds another day, a boy called to me in a singing voice, "Your mother is a whore, your mother is a whore." I sensed that his taunt was bad but I didn't know what he meant.

All the while, the two men with dark glasses stood behind the school fence and did nothing. So much for being there to protect me.

When I asked my mother why the boy called her a whore, and what did it mean anyway, she said, "A whore is…well, hmm… he said this because those bad people took one of my modelling photos, cut my head and glued it to a photo of a naked woman."

"That's very mean. But how did the boy in my school see it?"

"Right, that's because they made copies of a photo and put my name and our phone number on it and plastered it all over the neighbourhood."

I was actually not surprised that the bad people found a photo of my mother and changed it as she said. We had all kinds of photos of her at home from when she modeled clothes, bathing-suits and make-up. Every once in a while, she showed me new photos and sometimes an ad in a newspaper.

"But what's a whore?" I asked.

"Don't worry about that now."

These incidents did not make me want to give school a chance. And not too long after that, I resumed my errant ways, playing in the fields instead of attending classes, even though the two men in dark glasses had become my sticky shadows.

One time after the boy called my mother that bad name, I came home from playing outside and our apartment was full of people I didn't know. They were doing something with my mother in the kitchen.

"Sara'le!" she called to me from the kitchen. "Stay in the living room until we finish here."

I couldn't help myself, and quietly snuck into the kitchen, crawling between the men's legs. My mother was folded inside a big fridge wearing a fur coat. Both the fridge and the coat were things we didn't have before, and I was in awe of these items yet confused by the spectacle. I jumped onto the kitchen counter, sat down and hugged my skinny knees so I wouldn't be in the way, and watched. The strangers told my mother to move this way or that way, look up, look down, to the side, smile, not smile, and when she finally came out, I saw that she was wearing nothing but underwear and a bra under the coat. Later, my mother explained that they took a photo of her inside the modern fridge with a fur coat to show how much room it had inside and how cold it got. They let her keep the coat and fridge, and the landlord said we could throw out the old ice box.

After that day, I was worried that kids from school would see the photo of my mom sitting inside the fridge in the paper and would say the bad word about her again. As it turned out, there were worse things to worry about, but thankfully I would remain oblivious to them for quite some time.

Modelling a bathing suit in Tel Aviv with The Shalom Tower in the background.

Mother's modelling photo, Not sure what she was modelling.

Fire at *This World*

Howling winds rattled the lone tree outside my bedroom window one late November night in 1971. A branch knocked repeatedly on the glass. There was something unsettling in the air. It took me a long time to fall asleep.

In the early morning, the phone rang and shook all of us out of our slumber. I heard shuffling and "Hallo" followed by several Oys, gasps and "how bad?" Curious, I came out of my room and saw my parents huddled in the living room, lighting one cigarette after another. They didn't notice me.

What were they talking about?

A fire? And why did they mention the tabloid my mother still worked for?

From the hallway, I saw my mother bury her head in my father's chest. She was whimpering. I knew better than to ask and went back to my bedroom.

Over the next few evenings, I overheard my parents repeat the word 'fire.' The way they talked about it made my stomach twist in knots.

"What are you talking about?" I asked my mother finally.

"There was a fire at the offices of *This World* a few nights ago."

My mother looked pale and trembled when she said that. She was still working there, although my father had moved on to *Haaretz Daily* by then.

"Does this mean I won't be able to go there with you anymore?"

I liked going with my mother to the tabloid office on Karlibach Street because the cafeteria in the building had the world's best grilled-cheese sandwich. Their cheese stretched the longest.

"I don't know yet," my mother said with a frown.

Over the next few years, my parents occasionally mentioned the fire, but they always stopped talking about it when I entered the room. I figured they thought it was a grownup thing that I shouldn't have been bothered with. Another thing to add to the ever-growing list of grown-up things I was excluded from.

Organizing the books in my mother's office at the tabloid *This World* 1969.

In time, it turned out that the fire *would* have been of great interest to me. Decades passed before I'd learn the entire shocking story.

GROWNUPS ARE CONFUSING

In 1971, I saw very little of my parents and I often had dinner with neighbours. Sometimes, they would even bathe me or have me stay at their apartment for days. One time I even stayed with my classmate Rutti for a whole week and got to play with her pink Barbie house and had a special thing called a bubble bath.

Since my parents were absent all day, almost all the time, after the first few articles on organized crime came out in 1971, they hired a baby-sitter, Ettie. She was supposed to feed me when I (faked) returning from school. One afternoon when I entered our apartment, Ettie came out of my bedroom looking like she had just woken up. Her hair was messy, and her face was frazzled. Inside my room, I found a man sitting on my green sofa buttoning his shirt.

"This is my boyfriend," she told me. "He is helping me."

Ettie's boyfriend came every day to "help" her. She made me terrible meals, always too spicy although I told her the food burned my mouth. Even the spaghetti and vegetable soup were too spicy. I flushed her food down the toilet. It was easy to do, since she'd put the plate on the kitchen table and go back to my bedroom with her boyfriend and close the door. She stayed there until it was time for her to go home. If I called her to ask for anything, like permission to go into my room, she yelled at me to go away. I told my friend and next-door neighbour Irit about her. She was a year older than me, and she hatched a plan to get rid of Ettie—we found broken pieces of a mirror near our building, and we stood outside the kitchen window to try and blind Ettie when she stood at the sink. It didn't work. A couple of days passed and Irit showed me a booklet she made. She stapled together several pages with drawings of a man and a woman kissing and lying together in bed in funny poses. She wrote "Ettie" above the female and "Boyfriend" above the man. The next day, we entered the apartment quietly and slid the booklet under my bedroom door. After that, Ettie stopped coming, but not before she showed the booklet to my parents, crying. My parents' eyebrows rose high and their mouths quivered. After Ettie left, they burst out laughing. I didn't fully understand the whole thing but was relieved she was gone.

Irit (Linur) grew up to be a famous journalist, author, and television personality. It's not surprising, as she is smart and talented. She also has a sharp tongue.

I wasn't yet aware of it then, but from April of 1971, my father became famous and everyone in Israel knew who Ran Kislev was. When we were out in public, people sometimes stopped him on the street like they knew him from somewhere, but many times he didn't know them. A few were nice and said things like "bravo" and "thank you". Others said words I didn't understand but I could tell they were bad because my parents pulled me away.

On a warm spring evening, not too long after the first articles were published, I sat in our living room, rivetted to the black-and-white television screen by Sami, who was talking to his puppet Susu[2] in melodic Arabic. I was startled when the phone rang, and I answered as I always did.

A man's voice barked, "Hello!"

"Hello, who is it?" I asked.

"Do you want a number?" he asked.

"We have a phone number already," I said politely. My mother was in the kitchen and within earshot, since there was a window between the kitchen and dining area to pass plates through.

"No, do you want a number?" he said in an irritated and louder tone.

"Oh, you mean an identity number. I don't need one yet. I'm only eight."

"No. Dooo-you waaaa-nt a nuuuum-ber!" He repeated slower and much, much louder. It made my tummy feel funny and I pulled the phone away from my ear and looked at it.

My mother dashed from the kitchen and grabbed the phone from my hand.

"I'm calling the police," she yelled into the receiver and slammed it.

I was confused.

She told me not to answer the phone anymore.

I didn't know what any of this was about, but I assumed it was not good to discuss numbers with people I didn't know.

Shortly after, my mother asked me to go to my room because she had to

---

2. Sami and Susu was a popular children program in Arabic broadcast on Israeli television from 1968-1974.

make an important phone call. I was intrigued and put my ear against my bedroom door. I could hear words like "threat", "Sara'le", and "danger". When my father came home, he gave me an unusually long hug. Through their bedroom door later that night, I heard only muffled voices, but by the tone of my mother's voice, I could tell she was upset.

As I discovered years later, asking a woman (in Israel) if she wanted a number was a rude way of asking her if she wanted to have sex.

From that day on, and for a long time, whenever I did see my parents that year, they didn't look right, always serious and whispering to each other. When the phone rang, they jumped, and they told me to lock the door if I was home alone. No one locked their doors in our neighbourhood then, but I went along with my parents' new habit.

The biggest issue in my life in those days was figuring out how to stay out of school without getting caught and how many days I had to make an appearance to be allowed to advance to the next grade. My parents were far too busy in their grown-up world to notice.

One thing did finally get their attention.

Nocturnal Surprise

The first time it happened I woke up in the middle of the night feeling wet. I was nine years old and still occasionally had "accidents", but I knew this wasn't pee. My pajama bottoms were dry but the top and my hair were wet.

Bleary eyed, I stumbled over broken toys that covered my floor and turned on the light. My pajama top, which had been white with yellow flowers when I went to sleep, was now red. I'd never had a nosebleed like that before and it dripped as I moved around the room. I looked at my bed and it had a large red stain on the pillow that continued to the sheets. Not sure what to do, I went to my parents' bedroom and turned on their light. My mother screamed when she looked up at me.

"Who did that? Call the police!" she yelled to my father.

I jumped back.

"Calm down, it's just a nosebleed," my father said and put his hand on her shoulder.

Swiftly, my father acted, taking me to the bathroom and asking my mother to wash me while he changed my soaked sheets. My mother was breathing fast as she washed my now lumpy hair in the sink, turning the water bright pink. She had a hard time buttoning my top after that, as her hands trembled.

In my room, my father was frantically trying to clean the big blood stain on the sofa we didn't own. He said they couldn't afford to replace it. I felt bad.

"How did this happen?" my mother asked.

"I don't know, I was asleep."

"Leave her alone and go back to bed," my father snapped at my mother. He placed a clean sheet on my other sofa and tucked me in.

"Thank you, Aba," I said. He kissed me on the forehead, and I drifted back to sleep.

I didn't feel good the next morning and wasn't in the mood to prance around in the flower fields, so I decided to go to school. Not ten minutes into the first class, the teacher stopped and stared at me.

"Your nose is bleeding, Sara," she said.

All heads turned and I heard gasps.

"Oh." I took out a handkerchief from my school bag and held it against my nostrils. The square piece of cloth became soaked within seconds.

"Stop moving," my teacher said and came over to my desk. She tilted my head back but the tap kept dripping. She led me with my head titled back to the school nurse and I spent the rest of the morning in her office. The nurse had me lie down and by the time my nose stopped dripping, the bell rang, and it was time to go home.

The whole thing repeated the next day, me bleeding during the night and the next day at school. The teacher said I should stay home. After several days of uncontrollable nosebleeds, I had a hard time standing on my feet and my mother called a doctor. In the meantime, she plugged my nose with cotton balls which got soaked every time I moved.

A half-bald man in thick rimmed glasses and a white coat came to our apartment. He pricked my arm and drew blood into little glass bottles and told my mother I should stay home until the nosebleeds stopped.

I felt nauseous all the time. My mother tried to make me eat but I flushed most of the food down the toilet or threw it out the window for the birds and the neighbourhood cats. I slept most hours of the day. When I opened my eyes, sometimes my mother wasn't there. After a few days the half-bald doctor returned. He said I had something called anemia. He brought red and black capsules and said I had to take two a day and eat lots of spinach.

The nosebleeds continued on and off for weeks.

In total, I missed twelve consecutive weeks of playing in the fields. And of school.

"Sara will grow out of the nosebleeds," the doctor assured my parents. While they became less frequent, they'd still happen a lot and usually at the worst moments; at a birthday party, while playing with friends in their homes, and sometimes in my sleep. It made me quite weak and for a while, my wild and adventurous spirit was replaced by one that needed to nap a lot.

Looking back, it occurs to me now that both bed-wetting and nosebleeds in children can be caused by stress or chronic anxiety. Is it possible that my nosebleeds during the early months of the organized crime series were a result of the fact I saw even less of my parents? Did I pick up on their high level of stress due to repeated threats by criminals and the mysterious fire? Did the fact I was bullied by some kids, along with the chronic absence of my parents, play a role in it?

From what I now know about how the body manifests psychological distress, this explanation seems most plausible. Especially since both the nosebleeds and bed-wetting recurred until we moved to another apartment and my mother stopped working.

But before we moved, a beautiful woman in great distress visited us.

VERA GRAN

S urely, she'd leapt out of one of those Hollywood oldies we caught on television with our little antenna. Standing in the middle of our living room, I looked up at this magnificent creature. She wore a white blouse and blue skirt and walked very straight on heels that made clickety sounds. She was so fancy.

"Halo, my name is Vera. Da you speek Ployish or Anglish?" she asked in a deep, velvety voice with an accent just like my father's, only thicker.

"English," I said. I recognized her voice, as I'd talked to her once on the phone when she called my father.

"Dobjie. Vat is your name meidele?" She bent down to shake my hand and smiled but there was no crease in the corner of her eyes. When the smile went away, I saw that her full lips curved downward. Long black eyelashes fanned her big, dark, sad eyes. When she turned her head sideways and opened her glittery purse, I stared at the perfect bun of her shiny black hair. She took out a doll in a clear plastic package and handed it to me.

"D'his is a Polyish doll."

I thanked her, but I wasn't too excited.

The doll's torso could swivel, which Vera demonstrated as she took it out of the container. She handed it to me, and I held it up in front of my face. I adjusted its pleated skirt, which had all the colours of the rainbow, moved my finger along the sleeves of its white blouse and over the red kerchief that was glued to the black hair. Vera must have asked my father for my age before bringing this gift. Had she asked him what his eight-year-old daughter liked to play with he would have surely told her, not dolls. Dolls interested me in one way only. I was curious how they were put together and usually removed their limbs and heads within less than a day then put the body parts back together over and over. Even the expensive Barbies my mother's best friend bought me in America didn't escape this fate. Quite often, I couldn't put dolls back together properly and ultimately ended up with a pile of torsos and limbs scattered about in my room. In time, I'd choose a career in which I'd be trying to put people together—not their limbs, but their minds and hearts.

Vera patted my head and turned away when my father said something to her in Polish and they sat down on the sofa. As I headed out of the living room, my mother came in carrying our white plastic tray with orange juice and pretzels. My father and Vera sat for hours talking in a cloud of blue smoke, while my mother and I made ourselves scarce.

After Vera left, my father told me, "Vera is a great singer and very famous in Poland and France." He showed me a record with a big photo of her on the cover and played it for me on our record player. I thought it was weird. It was full of *pshe psha* and *voche dvoche* sounds and the music was boring. I moaned and my father frowned. Sometime later, he brought another record and played a song with a familiar melody. My father loved to dance with me and my mother to his favourite tunes, and this clearly was one of those. At the first notes, my father closed his eyes and swayed to the melody. He took my skinny hand and twirled me around in our small living room. Vera sang in Polish, and he understood the lyrics. When the song ended, he said the song was called "La Vie en Rose" and it was originally sung in French by Edith Piaf. We had one of Piaf's records, which was why I recognized the tune.

"This song is about seeing the world through pink glasses as a way to survive hardship, like the hardship of war." My father wanted me to be smart, so he told me things like that.

"Hmm…" was all I said.

When I listened again to Edith Piaf singing "La Vie en Rose," I realized I liked Vera's version better. I didn't understand either language but there was something haunting about Vera's singing that made my spine tingle.

Vera suffered greatly during the Holocaust, my father said, but I didn't ask what that meant. I knew it was a terrible war and involved a bad man called Hitler and that no one who'd lived through that war wanted to talk about it. I also knew that all the people I'd seen with tattooed numbers on their arms—neighbours, parents of friends, friends of my parents, teachers, doctors—had all survived that awful war.

I recall Vera's second visit, too. She seemed different then. She still donned the perfect bun, and she still wore fancy clothes, but her mouth only curved down and she moved more slowly.

"Hallo Sarinka," she said and mindlessly handed me a record with her photo on the cover. The image was of her face with the palms of her hands placed on her cheeks. Big letters were scribbled on it—her autograph and a dedication to my father. Later he told me that it said in Polish: "To Dearest Henyek with deepest gratitude, Yours Vera Gran". (Polish people who knew my father called him Henyek.) After giving it to me, she turned away and they began a very long conversation in our living room. I put the album on top of our dining table and went out to play checkers and pickup sticks with Irit next door. My mother soon followed me to the Linurs' apartment, as Mira, Irit's mother, was her friend, too. Sometimes, the best place for my father to interview people was at our apartment, he said.

After a few hours, my mother and I returned, and Vera was still there. My mother busied herself in the kitchen and I went to my room. Behind my closed bedroom door, I could hear Vera talking in high tones, but since it was in *pshe pshe* and *voche dvoche dvoche*, I understood nothing.

A few days later, when I came back home after playing with friends, I opened the front door and heard what sounded like a puppy whimpering. But when I looked into our living room, I saw it was Vera again. She was slumped on our sofa as my father stroked her arm. My father's wrinkles looked deeper. Vera quivered when she noticed me, and I saw that her eyes were red. Her eye make-up streaked horribly on her face, making her look spooky. Her formerly neat bun was now in disarray. I went to my room quickly. I was confused.

Months after Vera's visits, I overheard my parents talking about her.

"These bastards are vicious. They won't let her be, like dogs with a bone," my father said.

"I don't understand this at all. Why do they do that?" My mother said. "They are destroying her."

I suddenly felt cold as if ice flowed in my veins. I didn't ask my parents to explain this and tucked those words into a mental folder titled *Grown Up Stuff I Don't Understand*.

That folder was getting thick.

WE MOVE

After the success of the series on organized crime that transformed my father from an unknown journalist into a celebrity, it was time for us to move up in life. On December first of 1971, my parents came home early from work while I was playing outside with friends. My mother found nine-year-old me in the field near our building.

"Run home and pack your things quickly. We are moving."

"What? Why?"

"We are going to live somewhere else. Just get your things. We don't have a lot of time."

"But, but, what about my friends?" I said as tears streamed down my face.

"You need to come now," she grabbed my arm.

Inside our apartment, she gave me a sack and said to throw in it whatever I wanted to take with me. I did so, then dragged the sack to the car, sobbing.

Clouds of gray fumes surrounded our baby-blanket-blue Skylark clunker. It was full of boxes, suitcases and bags. All our life's possessions fit in the car—mostly, my mother's clothes. She had given me half of an anti-nausea pill before we left the apartment, and I had to lie down flat on top of boxes in the back seat. It was only a half-hour drive, but my parents didn't want to take a chance. My cat Kiki was just as unhappy, hollering inside a box at my mother's feet.

"I don't want to leave, please let me stay...," I whispered over and over as I drifted into unconsciousness.

It was Gershom Schocken, the *Haaretz* newspaper owner, who persuaded my father to move out of our rented apartment in Maoz-Aviv. He wanted to help lift us out of poverty, as well as have my father closer to the *Haaretz* offices. Schocken gave my father a large bonus and a loan, which was enough to purchase sixty percent of an apartment in downtown Tel-Aviv, in what was called Key Money³ ownership.

For my parents this may have been moving up, but for me it meant the end of my tenure in the Garden of Eden.

And why did we leave in such a hurry? I never thought about it until after both my parents had died, so I couldn't ask them. I wonder if they'd skipped the rent. They had a rich history of leaving unpaid accounts in grocery stores and "bouncing" cheques. Skipping rent seems like a strong possibility.

Stepping out of the car at our new address, Nine Bialik Street, I found myself in an entirely new world.

"Is this a palace?" I asked my father as he brought me to the entrance to our building. It had an arch and a round window and the two columns in front made it look majestic.

"No it's not, but it kind of looks like it, doesn't it?"

"Yeah." I looked up and saw that the building had three floors and two balconies on each floor.

"Which one is ours?" I asked.

My father pointed at the third floor to the right.

The neighbourhood we left was a bubble on the edge of the big city, designed for families and especially kids. The rows of apartment blocks were separated by lawns and pine groves. I didn't have to cross any roads to visit a friend on the other side of the neighbourhood. It was the closest thing to a kibbutz, but in a city. Parents looked out for each other's kids, and everyone knew everyone. All apartments in the long blocks were three-storeys-high and identical, which eliminated distinctions in social class. When we moved there in 1967, the buildings were about thirteen years old. Built originally to accommodate army families, non-army families had to go through an interview to be accepted. The criterion was being a good person. It had everything a family needed right there: a grocery store, a toy store, a bakery, a post office, and safety. Bialik Street was the opposite in every way.

Our new home was a decaying apartment in a rundown street in the historic downtown of Tel Aviv. It was surrounded by a dense jungle of soot-covered buildings with the occasional and very sad trees that no kid wanted to climb.

---

3. Key money ownership means that the buyer owns sixty percent of the property and landlord owns forty percent and receives some rent. It was a way to help people who didn't want to continue to pay rent move toward ownership when they couldn't afford the full price of a home or business.

Here and there grew a bush that struggled to bloom in the spring.

Rather than the eyes of caring parents, I felt the stares of predatory men directed at me. Especially the one who leaned against the wall near the garbage bins and wanked off while looking up towards our third-floor kitchen balcony hoping my mother or I would come out to hang laundry or take it down. There was the man who followed me into the building and pinned me against the wall—he didn't achieve his goal only because I managed to scream. And there was the neighbour in the next building whom I thought loved to wipe his windows but was actually jerking off with much gusto looking towards our windows. On the street, the leers and cat calls only got worse as I got older.

But I didn't notice these shortcomings right away. At first, I was in awe of the façade of the building and the design of our apartment. Every room had differently patterned tiled floors—a permanent carpet unique in its colour scheme. From all four corners of the earth, light streamed through big windows and broken shutters. My bedroom was in the back, the closest to the sea, and the tall ceilings swallowed my broomstick figure. My room had once been an open balcony, so windows covered three of the four walls. Through them, between two buildings, I could see a sliver of the blue sea in the distance. And when I opened the window wafts of intoxicating salt air blew in. Our new home was a ten-minute walk to the Mediterranean Sea and a world away from the old life I had.

Almost all the thirty-two buildings on Bialik Street are part of Tel Aviv's White City, a collection of more than four thousand UNESCO-protected buildings which, starting in the 1930s, were built in the unique Bauhaus/International style. They were designed by Jewish German architects who had immigrated to British Mandate Palestine after the rise of the Nazis. Bialik Number Nine was built in the International style and in its heyday was home to well-off families. Most of the buildings on Bialik are now heritage-protected and cannot be torn down. The one we lived in was bought some years ago by a wealthy family from England that restored it tile by tile and turned the six apartments into a one-family dwelling. Every visit to Israel, I'd check out the changes in the building and, like the rest of the country and the people in it, it kept evolving, not always for the better. But the sea remains in its place, as old as time. That was where I found solace during the tough times that followed our relocation. Its turquoise expanse, the comforting sound of waves, and the gales that mimicked internal storms would swallow my pain.

When we moved in, our building was but a shadow of its glorious past and decades away from its rebirth as a swanky mansion. About half of the units were turned into offices including a publishing house on the ground floor. It took a while, but within a year or so, I began to notice how terribly run-down the building was. Years of neglect were showing. One time, I walked down the metal fire-escape in the back, and under my skinny body the stairs shifted downward, separating from the wall. After I ran back home, the whole staircase collapsed. The landlord refused to pay for proper maintenance including, for a fresh layer of tar needed to seal the flat roof above. So, with the first heavy downpour, puddles slowly found their way in. The first time this happened, a year after we moved in, I woke up in the middle of the night to the sound of water dripping close to my ear. My blanket was wet, not inside, but out. I turned on the light and stopped breathing when I saw the ceiling above me was cracked and water was dripping everywhere. One of the walls was wet as well. I heard my parents shuffling about. Their bed was soaked, and we spent the rest of the night in the living room.

"I'll call the landlord tomorrow," my father said. But nothing came of it, the landlord ignored the calls.

At the end of each long and wet season, behind the soot-covered façade, we were hard-pressed to imagine the past splendour of this architectural wonder. Camping out in the living room when the bedrooms were flooded was something I learned to expect every winter.

That apartment on Bialik Street would become the landscape of certain nightmares for the rest of my life. To this day, waking up at night to the rhythmical drip of rain takes me back

9 Bialik Street, Tel-Aviv, before restoration, Our apartment – top right.

to the puddles and soaked mattress and induces dark existential dread. The part of my brain that is hard-wired to watch out for dangers refuses to let go of that fear.

That's the nature of trauma.

CAMPING

While I learned to expect camping in the living room every winter, in the summers I looked forward to camping outdoors. My father arranged it and was as excited as I was about it. For reasons I didn't understand in those days, we were poor despite both of my parents working all the time. I know now that they weren't always paid for their work and that camping in tents was the cheapest type of vacation, one step up from staying home.

But I felt lucky.

From Grade One until the summer before middle school, every August, I jumped for joy each time we left the city to camp on the shore of the Sea of Galilee. For a whole week we slept under the stars, in a tent in kibbutz Maagan Michael's camping site. These trips forged some of my fondest childhood memories.

It was only my father and I who took pleasure in minimal separation from nature. We didn't mind sleeping on a thin mat or in sleeping bags, flicking creepy crawlies off our bodies or dealing with a few insect bites. Each morning, at dawn, he woke me up to swim in the clear sea before anyone else in the campsite got into the water.

We could see all the way to the bottom—the shiny silver fish, the sparkling shells, and the pebbles. We swam together far toward the horizon until our tent was but a speck, and if I was too tired to swim back, my father carried me on his back while I wrapped my arms around his neck and talked his ear off. Maybe I've always been drawn to bodies of water because I was born by the sea at the port city of Haifa.

My mother, on the other hand, hated everything about camping, especially the general lack of amenities. You had to walk half a kilometer to get to a decent washroom, and showers were just cold water from a rusty pipe. I preferred to wash in the sea, but my mother refused to go in, saying she hated the slimy feeling of the little fish touching her feet. At the time I didn't realize how unhappy she was there.

When leaving for that week, we would pack tins of spam and sardines, a coffee pot, a Primus stove, and plastic plates and mugs. The camping site had coal grills, but we never grilled anything because my parents couldn't afford to buy meat of any kind. Other campers sometimes offered us hotdogs or shish kebabs.

The best meal was breakfast. After our early morning swims, my father walked a kilometer to the farmers' store that sold buns straight out of the oven, fresh butter, and milk. The memory of that meal—the freshest and purest butter on earth spread generously on the sweet and aromatic bun—still makes me salivate. To this day, butter tastes for me like blue sky, clear water and the beginning of an adventurous day. Occasionally, my father used the portable stove to make scrambled eggs when the farmer's store had them. And he made café botz, coffee that looks like mud, which my parents sipped slowly from plastic cups with great pleasure.

After our breakfast, my father went back to the tent and probably rolled in the sleeping bag with my mother while I chased peacocks, collected shells, and made friends among the other young tent dwellers. I'd come back to the tent only when it started to get dark. After eating dinner, a can of spam, we sat on a blanket to watch a movie on a large screen with other campers.

It was difficult to keep anything cool. Other campers who had extra liras could rent a cooling cubby in a large fridge, but it was quite a trek to get there. My parents may have stored alcohol there, since my father brought a bottle every night and they poured whatever was in it into little glasses when the sun disappeared behind the trees. My mother seemed a lot more relaxed with one of those, and her constant complaining about the army of bugs and mosquitoes stopped.

By the end of each of these camping weeks, I'd amass a large collection of mussel-shells, peacock feathers, and memories that are stored in every cell of my body. I'd be severely sunburned and beginning to molt, yet I would cry inconsolably when it was time to go back to the city. My mother yelled, hurrying us to get in the car already, while I tried to steal a few last moments circling the car but not getting in. My father also walked around for a while, supposedly to make sure we didn't leave any trash or belongings behind. Maybe he was trying to store in his inner generator a little bit of the peaceful calm and beauty of this part of Israel, where they say Jesus walked on water.

After moving to Bialik and clawing our way out of poverty, my mother campaigned hard against camping. The last time we camped was in the summer of 1974. My mother, who was six months pregnant with my little brother

Mickey, whined even louder the whole week. My father and I knew it was the last time she would agree to sleep outdoors, and so we cherished every last moment. On that final trip in mid-August, we swam in the mornings and at night. Far from the shore, on the penultimate mid-August evening, we marveled at the shimmering sky, counting falling stars. If not for my mother's hollers for us to come back to shore, we might have stayed there forever.

When Mickey was a year and a half, we glamped. My father convinced my mother to try four nights at Tantura beach. The accommodation he booked was an igloo-shaped, air-conditioned room on the Mediterranean Sea north of Tel Aviv. Despite the relative luxury of the igloo, she refused to entertain any form of camping or glamping after that year. I appreciated my father's futile effort to keep the tradition I so enjoyed.

All of this happened before I noticed any of my father's flaws.

RETURN TO SCHOOL

L ife was hard enough in downtown Tel Aviv. Missing my old friends and the familiar corner of paradise, I cried myself to sleep every night for weeks. My black-and-white cat Kiki that moved with us from the old neighbourhood disappeared the moment we opened the door of the new place. I was horrified when my parents said he might have been run over by a car while looking for his old stomping grounds. I could understand his yearning to return to greener pastures. If I had his homing ability, I'd have done the same. Thankfully, Kiki returned after two weeks, minus part of his ear and the tip of his tail.

A new neighbourhood also meant a new school. I was a little nervous but decided that in the new school, I'd be like everyone else. I wanted to be a pupil who does her homework, a student who studies for tests, a kid who generally knows what's going on in class. It was as if something awakened in me—the need to be part of a group, to fit in.

Since I was expelled from paradise and there were no more wildflower fields and good trees to climb, I had let go of my identity as Pippy Longstockings. In the old neighbourhood, some kids called me the girl Huckleberry Finn, which I appreciated just as much as Pippy. But I didn't want to worry anymore at the end of each school year if I'd advance to the next grade. My mother said she wouldn't show my new teacher my old (and embarrassing) report cards. "I lost them, on purpose," she told me.

I was ready for a fresh start.

But even before I set foot in my new school, the kids decided to hate me. While I didn't know a single soul, they'd already heard all about me. I know this because, decades after my first day in the school, Yonit, a lifelong friend whom I met in that class, revealed to me what went down before I entered that classroom.

"Children, I have something very exciting to tell you. You want to know what it is?" my new teacher Dina told the class. "We are very lucky because the daughter of a very important person is going to join us."

"Who? Who?" Some kids asked, surely hoping it would be a daughter of a famous singer or actor.

"She is the daughter of the important journalist Ran Kislev."

The Grade Four students shrugged.

Thanks to the teacher, my new classmates were convinced that the new girl, me, was going to be a pompous snob who'd look down upon them. Without any objective reference point, I had no idea that anything about me or my father was special. At that age, I didn't yet realize that my father was so famous, or that the parents of my peers knew who he was. It was still three years before I started middle school and was told to hide my last name.

"During recess, after the teacher told us about you, the kids decided that no one was going to play with you," Yonit told me all these years later.

"How come I never heard about this?" I asked her. "There's nothing in my recollection of that day or afterwards that suggests this is how other kids felt."

"That's because when you walked into the classroom, so shy and super cute with those two braids, it was clear you were not the show-off we thought you'd be. So we just forgot to hate you."

I made an important discovery that year and it did not involve roaming in flower fields or climbing trees. It involved books.

My father, who was married before he married my mother, had a son and a daughter. They visited us a few times a year. My stepbrother Yoram was six years older than me and Irit was twelve years older. One day, Yoram dropped off a series of encyclopedias he no longer needed. Three hardcover volumes bound in dark blue fabric caught my eye. I organized the books neatly on my mostly empty bookshelves and took out the first blue volume. In that moment, a door to a vast and exciting world opened, just as the door to my old life had closed.

Once a latchkey wanderer who felt like a butterfly, I now entered a cocoon stage and in a reverse metamorphosis, became a bookworm.

In one chapter, I encountered a tribe in some African country whose notion of beauty involved expanding their lower lip by stretching it with a wide cylinder or plate. In another chapter, I read about people who had strange beliefs, like those who pricked dolls with needles thinking it would hurt their enemies. Within weeks, my eager little brain had amassed a mountain of trivia.

More importantly, each day I judiciously completed my homework and in class I raised my hand enthusiastically to participate. Then came time to study for a test. I went over all the information about the history of Tel Aviv. The name of the first mayor, the original name of the city and many other useless facts, all of which I memorized perfectly. Excited, I sat down to write the test and eagerly awaited the results.

Having studied so hard for the first time in my short academic career, I frolicked all the way home and waved the page with the one-hundred-percent mark in red at the top.

"Look, look!" I yelled as I burst into our apartment. My mother came out of the kitchen wiping her greasy hands on her apron and was all smiles when she took the perfect test from me. I watched as her eyes scanned my brilliant answers. For some reason, her smile turned to a frown.

"What's wrong, Mom?"

She looked up at me.

"What's this?" she said in a low voice and sat at the avocado green table, on the avocado green vinyl chair.

"What do you mean? I got a hundred! On my first test!"

"No darling. The test was about Haifa, not Tel Aviv, you see the question at the top?" And she placed it close to my face.

I crumpled like the test my mother squished into a ball in her hand.

"So why did the teacher give me a hundred?"

"Well, maybe because you are new to the school she gave you full points for getting the right answers about another city. I don't know…".

Soon enough it became clear that Sara Kislev couldn't do anything wrong even if she tried. In Dina's class, I never got anything below ninety percent, including on math tests, where my answers looked like the hieroglyphs I saw in the blue encyclopedia.

What was the point of doing homework or studying for tests?

There was none, as it turned out.

And so it was that I gave up becoming a normal kid, a student who cares. Out of boredom, to pass the afternoons when my friends were doing their homework and napping, I read all the volumes of the used encyclopedias and dictionaries that my stepbrother continued to bring to our apartment. In class, I was often the only kid who raised a hand when the teacher asked about obscure facts. And the Grade Four teacher, Dina, praised me as the genius daughter of the important journalist Ran Kislev.

I skated effortlessly to the next grade.

Occasionally, I had moments of fear of being found out—this time not because I skipped school, but because I was getting marks I didn't deserve.

But, in Grade Five, a new teacher arrived, Yael Agmon. She was a tall woman with blonde hair tied in a ballet dancer's bun and piercing blue eyes that saw right through me. She seemed nice at first, until my first test: she gave me fifty-five percent.

I dragged my feet home after school. When I showed my mother the test and wiped my tears on my sleeve, I declared: "My new teacher hates me. Look what she gave me."

One of the things I appreciated about my mother was how she always had my back when dealing with teachers. The next day she went to talk to the evil new teacher. I waited on our third-floor balcony, impatient to find out the outcome of this visit. Surely, she'd admit her error and give me the one hundred percent I deserved. By then, I believed I had somehow earned the spectacular report card in Grade Four.

"What did she say? Did she correct my mark? Did she?" I asked as soon as my mother walked through the door.

"No, deary. Sit down, we need to talk." I sank into our fraying living room sofa as my mother sat down next to me. Turning towards me she said, "Now here's the thing. Your new teacher asked me to relate a message to you."

Uh oh…

"She wants you to know she doesn't care one bit who your father is. She made it clear she is going to give *you* the grades, not *him*."

"What do you mean?"

"In case you didn't realize, the report cards Teacher Dina gave you last year were really for Aba."

"Huh?"

"Remember that test on Haifa that you got all wrong but still got a hundred percent?"

"But you said…" My mother raised her open hand to signal I should be quiet.

And with that came the sad realization that I couldn't get high grades just by showing up at school and gracing the teacher with my effervescent presence and the last name Kislev. I had to work for it.

So I did.

By the second term, my marks approached the grades I had received but didn't earn the year before.

Yael Agmon, who was both my Grade-Five and -Six teacher, later shared with my mother how annoying it had been to hear Dina go on and on in the teachers' lounge about her amazing student, the daughter of.

Of all the teachers I had growing up, Yael was the one who had the greatest positive impact on me. Caring about my education and not about my father's celebrity, she got me back on track. This experience in elementary school was the first time I had an inkling that having my particular father meant people might treat me differently. It became a joke in our family to say that my father was repeating elementary school. For a while I thought it was funny, but eventually, being *the daughter of* was an unwelcomed identity.

In time, frustration built up as I moved through life unsure if people wanted to be my friend or date me (or kill me) because of who my father was.

My father's shadow was long, wide and sticky, and because of that, for a long time, I couldn't see my own.

Dis-Integration

P arents often give a pep-talk to their kids prior to the first day at a new school. In September of 1974, my parents prepared one too, before I started Grade Seven at Geula school. It was the wrong pep-talk, though. Not because it didn't involve words of wisdom about making new friends, the challenges of dropping to the bottom of the food chain or strategies to cope with the heavier workload—all of which would have been helpful for me to hear. No—it was wrong because it was about gangsters' children. It would have been far more helpful if they had told me about ethnic tension and bullies.

Geula means "salvation" in Hebrew. If ever there was a misnomer, this was certainly it. The antonyms provide a perfect description of my experience at that school: damnation, loss, destruction, harm, desolation, injury, downfall, and endangerment. Especially endangerment.

As it turned out, there were no mafia kids in my class, at least none that I knew of, and when the teacher called out "Sara Kislev", no one batted an eyelash.

My real problem at Geula would be my ethnicity.

While I am of Ashkenazi (Eastern European) descent, my friends in elementary school were Sephardi or Mizrahi, with my closest friends being of Egyptian, Yemenite, and Moroccan descent. To me, the different ethnic roots of my friends simply meant they had better food at home and their parents spoke melodic languages like Arabic or French rather than the ear-bending Hungarian my mother spoke with her sister and the ancient-sounding Polish my father spoke with his friends.

Prior to the first day at Geula, I was blind to any other implications of one's ethnic background. But that changed when, on a hot September day in 1974, I joined thousands of adolescents who were thrown into the biggest (failed) educational experiment in Israel's history.

As of that year, students were no longer allowed to choose which middle school to attend. The "Integration Program" was supposed to be the cure for the socio-economic divide between the two big Jewish ethnic groups in Israel, Sephardi/Mizrahi and Ashkenazi.

To achieve "proper integration", it was decided to bring students from neighbourhoods with different socio-economic and ethnic backgrounds together. It was thought that this would increase the odds for disenfranchised kids to attain a high-school diploma and have better chances to succeed in life.

The concept seemed strange to me. My small class in elementary school was already ethnically diverse. Students of all ethnic and socio-economic backgrounds were there, and I was unaware of any difference in their academic performance.

Nothing in my experience until Grade Seven alerted me to the problem. But within days in the new school, I became schooled on the subject. While I was oblivious to it, my pale skin symbolized everything that afflicted some of the Mizrahi kids' lives. Their parents' deep and very real social alienation, the entrenched discrimination they experienced in society, the blocked opportunities—all due to their different backgrounds, darker skin tones, accents, and last names—trickled into their children's lives through poverty and bitterness.

The haphazard Integration Program resulted in very uneven situations. Most of the students in my Grade Seven class were not Ashkenazi, coming mainly from Kerem Ha-Teimanim neighborhood. Their previous school experiences were drastically different than mine and several had a knack for preventing teachers from imparting any knowledge. Most teachers gave up and simply sat in front of us, told us to read from a book, and buried their own heads in a book. Teachers who dared to turn their back on the class to write on the blackboard risked being hit by objects some students tossed across the classroom, sometimes at them.

No counselling or support for students or teachers was put in place at the start of the Integration Program. The whistle sounded and we jumped into the pool. It was sink or swim.

I sank.

My plan to be a studious pupil disintegrated.

Boys, some who were kept behind and were much bigger and older, looked at me in ways that made me feel extremely uncomfortable.

During recess, a few of the girls, also older and hence several sizes bigger, made it an Olympic sport to beat me up. They didn't like the way boys looked at me, either.

On the first day, I had a first taste of their hatred.

"Hey, blondie," a tall and wide-shouldered girl called. Her name was Nira, and she was the ringleader and my nemesis. She had dark skin like some of my friends from elementary school. My hair was still blonde that year, so I turned to look just as her friend hurled a crumbling half-sandwich with jam at me that stained my new school uniform. Laugher erupted and they congratulated each other.

I was terrified to walk the school halls alone. Fortunately, when a girl became physical with me at recess, boys usually appeared to defend me. The girls had to be clever if their murderous plot was to succeed. If I dared enter the bathroom alone, I was sure to get pushed, pinched, kicked, or have my hair pulled.

The best chance to pounce on me presented itself during field trips to a farm for Agriculture class. Boys were sent to do hard labour in the fields, while the girls were allowed to putz around in the shade and pick up a few vegetables between long naps. But there was no snoozing for me—I was on high alert.

Given the exuberance certain girls demonstrated, I presume they had waited all week for the opportunity the field trip presented. As soon as we arrived at the farm and the teachers left, they jumped on me in what looked like a well-choreographed war dance. While most girls just relaxed in the shade and enjoyed a lazy hour of gossip, two house-sized girls stomped on me, punched me, and provided me with new shades of skin colour. When it was time to get back on the bus, they instructed me to say that I just fell and hurt myself if the teacher asked. But the teachers were oblivious or chose to ignore signs of violence, unless blood was gushing, or bones were broken.

Very quickly, I gave up on studying and my grades plummeted. I started missing school, pretending to be sick while I nursed bruises. I knew I wouldn't be able to get out of that hell until Grade Nine, and I didn't think I'd survive.

"Can't you pull strings and get me out of here?" I asked my father after two months in the Alcatraz of Geula.

"No," he said, "you have to stay in that school until the end of Grade Nine, like everyone else."

By then, my father was a big-shot journalist. In 1971, he won the Journalist of the Year award and his name, my mother's, mine, Yoram, and Irit's were all entered in the fancy *World's Who's Who* book starting in 1972. My mother said it was a big deal and displayed the red-covered book in our living room.

By 1974 when I started middle school, my father was writing mostly about politics. I knew that because all the big political parties engaged in serious ass-kissing manoeuvres and competed each holiday over who'd send us the biggest, most expensive gift basket. We feasted for weeks on fancy chocolates, candies, cheese, anchovies, cookies, and nuts. My parents savoured the expensive wines and fancy French Camembert that came in the baskets. With Shimeon, Yitzchak, Menachem, and even Golda all calling and asking to speak or leave messages for my father, it was clear to me that he had connections in all levels of government, including the Ministry of Education, and if he didn't, he surely knew someone who did.

On a cold winter evening a few months into the school year, I brought up the subject again. My father was getting ready to watch the eight o'clock news and lit a cigarette. My mother was in the kitchen preparing his Earl Gray tea with milk, and his favourite thick meat slices on half a baguette, lathered in butter. Knowing I only had a few minutes before the news started, I stood in the living room doorway and asked for his help.

"I would move you, but I am in a pickle," my father said. He avoided my gaze, looking at the muted television.

"What pickle? They are going to kill me. It shouldn't be that hard to see that." I stepped forward and rolled my pants and shirt sleeves to show him the latest bruises.

"Ze lo tov," he said. It's not good.

The grooves on his forehead deepened, and he took a long drag on his Marlboro. My neck and back tightened and tears gathered in the corners of my eyes. At that moment, my mother walked in with the tray and placed the sandwich and tea in front of him.

"Nuuu…" I said. I wasn't going to let up.

"The problem is that I am the chair of the Ethics Committee of Israel's Journalists' Association, and I have to model the highest ethics in everything." I stared at him and left the room in a huff.

Had I known then what I discovered later about his personal ethics, I might have challenged him. But I was ignorant and so I let it go, feeling hopeless and abandoned.

A Useless
(Powerful) Father

Early in Grade Seven, my father gave me a speech about the Integration Program possibly to justify his refusal to pull strings and transfer me to another school.

"It brings Ashkenazi kids like you who are encouraged by their families to study hard with kids whose parents don't do that," he said. "This can help change the trajectory of the Sephardi kids' lives."

"What do you mean?" I asked, staring hard at him.

"Many of the Sephardi parents don't have even a high-school diploma and they don't value that like we do. This way, kids like you can inspire the disenfranchised pupils to do well in school and give them a better chance to do well in life."

The unfairness of this situation and how it made my life hell was the only thing I cared about. I completely missed the racist aspect of his statement. It turned out that there were many highly educated Sephardi and Mizrahi parents in Israel. And as I learned over time, some were so disadvantaged they needed their children to bring income which meant that several of my high-school peers dropped out to find whatever low paying jobs they could get and tried to complete their education in evening schools while working. My father saying that their parents didn't value higher education reflected his prejudice and that of many of his Ashkenazi peers.

In my class at Geula, the Integration Program seemed to achieve the opposite of its intended goal. My first report card reflected that. My grades dropped from the high eighties and nineties in elementary school to low sixties.

"Sara seems distracted," my home-room teacher told my parents.

Yup. My focus was on survival.

"What's happening?" my parents asked after the first parent-teacher interview.

"Really? You're surprised?"

I had learned sarcasm from my father, and it was all I had to fight back with. I stopped talking about the beatings by the girls—it's called "learned helplessness". But certain things were so confusing that I had to ask my parents to explain them—such as the time I overheard a conversation between two older boys who sat in front of me. Leaning into each other, I could hear them as they discussed a plan.

"I'll tell her I wanna show her something and get her into the abandoned house."

"Yeah, bring the kloroforn, I'll wait inside."

They laughed and demonstrated to each other with their fingers how they would put their something into her something, in and out many times.

I asked my parents to translate what I heard and saw.

"This is bad, this is really bad. Just stay away from them," my mother said, looking at my father.

"It's not 'kloroforn', it's chloroform and it's an anaesthetic drug. How will they even get it?" my father rightly asked. To my knowledge, he never investigated it.

"I don't want to go to this school at all and worry about these things all day," I pleaded

"You don't have a choice; it's the only way integration can work."

If the situation was so bad as my mother said, why didn't it convince him to take me out of Geula? I was fuming.

"It's not working! Get me out of there," I said and ran out of the room sobbing.

Thinking about this today, I wonder why my parents didn't report such incidents to the school. If my daughters experienced any level of bullying and violence, I'd do whatever was necessary to make sure it stopped and keep them safe. Instead, my parents let me languish in that place. Was it misguided "White guilt"?

Or selfishness and neglect?

Or all the above?

Meanwhile, my father's power and influence only grew. He was *Haaretz's* parliamentary correspondent and covered all aspects of politics. The election at the end of 1973 was still on people's minds in 1974. The Labour party led by

Golda Meir lost several seats to Menachem Begin's right-wing Likud party and to the religious, Arab, and other small parties. Almost every day, long articles by my father were published, analyzing and critiquing this or that politician or policy. I didn't know the full extent of it then, but since *Haaretz* was considered in those days the most influential daily, his articles had great impact on Israeli politics. There were attempts to bribe him to support this or that party, and I remember my mother getting upset that he once declined an offer of a new apartment in a fancy new building.

"Why do you have to be so stubborn? Why can't you just once think of us?" she yelled.

I put my ear against the wall and heard my father say, "So you think I should accept bribes? And an apartment? Are you insane? If you think I will ever accept a bribe, you'll be sorely disappointed."

"I have been sorely disappointed for a long time now. All your fame and look where we live. Look at the cracked and wet ceilings. We can't buy an apartment that doesn't rain on us in the winter or new furniture with your fame."

I heard my father storm out of our dilapidated apartment. He came back close to midnight and afterwards they both pretended that conversation never happened.

A part of me—my shadow—wished he would quietly accept a nice apartment with dry ceilings in a nice neighbourhood. Another part of me understood it was wrong and would be a legally risky, career-ending mistake to do so.

Unpaid utility bills printed in red ink stacked up high in our kitchen, and if I wanted brand name clothes or art supplies, I had to work for them. Since age twelve, I babysat and tutored children in the neighbourhood and delivered flowers on my bike. I didn't mind—all I wanted was for my father to use his power and influence to help me get out of Geula. I resented him for failing to do so.

To his credit or discredit, he bought me the bike for my Bat-Mitzva with one of those bouncy cheques he continued to use from time to time.

Over time, I'd noticed that my father selectively practiced what he preached. For example, he scowled when I started dating and brought home Mizrahi, dark-skinned boys with the "wrong" last names, ones that didn't end with -berg or -stein, and he interrogated me about their families. He was all for social equality and integration, just not in his home. He beamed when my first "real boyfriend" was blonde and blue-eyed. He scowled again when subsequent boyfriends were every kind of non-Ashkenazi.

But when in 1986, at age twenty-four, I introduced my then-boyfriend and future husband, Roni, whose parents were born in Iraq, I was surprised at my father's positive response.

"He's a keeper," he told my mother.

"Oh, how come?" she asked.

"He dresses smart, and I like how confident he is and that he shook my hand when he entered our apartment."

The day before they met, Roni had sent me a big bouquet of flowers for my birthday and my father beamed when he saw it. A man who sends flowers, dresses well and shakes the hand of a parent scored points with him, yet his overall view of non-Ashkenazis remained biased. And it was hard for him to hide or suppress it. In the early days of my marriage, my father let slip infuriating comments that led to loud exchanges, like the time he overheard me arguing on the phone with Roni about the pressure by his family to visit his many uncles and aunts during our brief trip to Israel. My father grabbed the phone, slammed it down and yelled, "Enough with this tribal mentality."

I stormed out of the apartment and walked up and down the street until I calmed down. When I came back, I found him making tea. Folding my arms at the entrance to the kitchen, I said, "If you can't deal with the fact I married an Iraqi guy, just tell me and I won't be staying here anymore."

"Cool your jets. I just hate seeing you get so upset each time you visit, and Roni's family put such unreasonable demands on you. You have one aunt, and he has what, fifteen aunts and uncles? You're only here for a couple of weeks…"

I ignored the dig and, for the sake of peace, said, "Aba, I can manage this on my own and if you have concerns, please keep them to yourself. I'm an adult."

With great effort, I refrained from blasting him over the many racist comments he had made over the years. But I didn't forget. In fact, I took secret pleasure in seeing him struggle to be polite when served what he considered to be spicy food that my Iraqi mother-in-law cooked. Having suffered greatly through the bland meals he had forced my mother to cook for us, I found this to be a delicious revenge.

My generation experienced various degrees of prejudice held by our parents, and we rebelled by marrying across ethnic lines in large numbers.

My Twelfth Year

M y twelfth year sucked. My father, despite being a rising star in the world of Israeli journalism, continued to drive cars resurrected from the place where dying cars go to make organ donations. The blue Studebaker Skylark was a massive creature and seemed invincible. However, one day in late 1974, my father drove onto the highway the wrong way—he didn't notice the signs indicating a reversal of lane direction due to construction. It was the 'Lark's final voyage. By that age, I refused to take the anti-nausea pills, and I usually travelled with my head down or stuck out the window. My mother's scream made me look up and, in that moment, my father crashed at full speed into a concrete median. The headrest of my mother's seat hit my throat and everything went black.

From what seemed like a great distance I heard my father's voice calling me and my mother to get out. Smoke was everywhere and I coughed hard. I managed to open the door and at the same time my mother, who was eight months pregnant, wiggled herself out with my father's help. Her feet were badly bruised, trapped by the whole front of the car, which had been squished like an accordion. Later my father said that when he realized he was driving into oncoming traffic he tried to brake but the brakes failed so he veered into the concrete median to avoid crashing into other cars.

"Can you walk, Chip?" my father asked.

"Yes, yes, I can," my mother said as she leaned on him.

"And you Kooka?"

"Yes, I'm fine," I lied, placing one hand on the front of my neck.

We limped away from the wreck and never looked back. Shuffling at varying speeds, we eventually made it to the nearest gas station and my father called a taxi to take us home. Hospitals were for sissies.

Soon after, in November of 1974, a thirteen-year-old boy I was infatuated with, Shimeon Almakyas, disappeared. Earlier that evening, he had joined our group when we played hide-and-seek, and I may have been the last person to see him before he vanished. His disappearance was never solved, and I have never forgotten him.

Not too long after the crash and Shimeon's disappearance, my mother had something important to tell me. It was early December of 1974, and she was nine months pregnant.

Facing me in the kitchen after she set a plate in front of me, she opened the conversation with, "You know your uncle Yoav…"

I loved Uncle Yoav. I was introduced to him at age six. He used to pick me up once a week to do fun things or we'd go to his apartment where he tried to teach me chess or read to me from science books, describing cool things like black holes and cosmic storms.

"Yes, what about Uncle Yoav?"

"Well … he is not really your uncle."

"Oh."

"And your father…"

"Huh?"

"He's not really your father."

I was stunned into silence and sat for a while trying to take in these revelations.

When I recovered, I asked how it was possible.

"I divorced Yoav when you were very little, so you didn't remember that he was there before Ran," she said.

"Obviously," I said as a balloon formed in my throat. "And how come you didn't tell me before?"

"We didn't want kids to tease you over this," my mother said.

Parents in those days thought they were protecting their children by keeping divorce a secret, as it was seen as shameful.

For years, everyone had told me I looked more like Ran and nothing at all like my mother. Ran was the only father I had a conscious recollection of, so learning that he was not actually my biological father turned my world upside-down.

My parents must have figured it was the right time to let me know that my gene pool was somewhat different from that of the sibling whose arrival was imminent.

"Oh, and you have a four-year-old sister. Her name is Haley. You'll meet her next week," my mother added before she shut down the conversation.

For the next hour I was unable to move.

For months after, I believed I was fully adopted and searched for proof in my parents' closet. I found none, but I wasn't convinced. I didn't look like my mother, the beautiful blonde, blue-eyed woman, and now I knew that Ran wasn't my biological father. Had I known then that it's nearly impossible to have brown eyes when both parents have blue eyes, I might have suspected something earlier. I lost trust in both my parents for their deception.

After the revelation, I began correcting people who said I looked more like Ran than my mother. I'd laugh and say, "Actually he is not my real father."

"Why are you saying that?" my father asked me the second time he heard that.

"But Aba, they don't know," I was so obsessed with truth-telling that I missed the hurtful aspect of my words.

"Why does it matter? I am your real father in all the important ways. I don't want to hear you say that again." His mouth curved down and I thought I saw tears forming in the corners of his eyes. Later, my mother told me that he was deeply hurt. I never corrected people again in front of him.

He *was* my father. I had no recollection of life with my biological father Yoav. Even after learning the truth, Ran remained my psychological father, flaws and all. In fact, I believe I lowered the bar of my expectations for him once I learned that it wasn't his sperm that had fertilized my mother's egg.

But what was left of my assumption of a knowable world had shattered.

THE ROOT OF INSOMNIA

T he best thing that happened in my twelfth year was the birth of my little brother Mickey. This blue-eyed bundle of joy, always smiling and good natured, arrived in December of 1974. My father tried to spend more time at home and my parents appeared happier and more affectionate with each other.

With the used camera I received for my Bat-Mitzva from a photojournalist friend of my father's, and film I bought using money I saved, I took dozens of photos of him. I loved him to bits. But that couldn't protect me from the calamity that was my twelfth year, especially from what happened next.

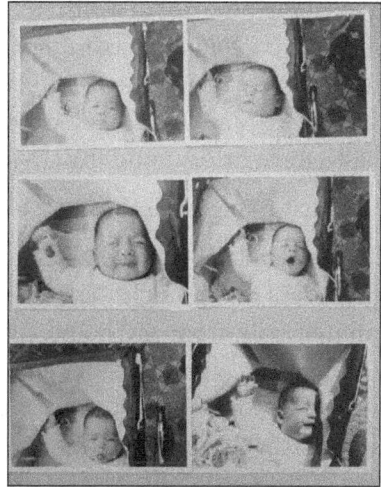

All of us (looking so happy), 1975.

While children and babies were massacred in terror attacks in other parts of Israel, sometimes in schools, some even in their beds while they slept, I was always able to lull myself to dreamland feeling safe from this distant danger. I think my parents had something to do with this idea, having told me these attacks would never happen in Tel-Aviv.

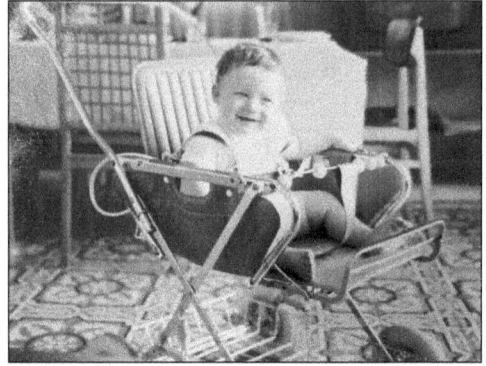

Mickey (Carpet-tiled floor in living room visible).

Just like in *Star Trek*, I felt like we had a force field around the city.

That changed on the night of March 4, 1975.

Two inflatable boats loaded with eight terrorists, automatic weapons and grenades, got through. They landed at the bottom of Allenby Street, a ten-minute walk from my home. The terrorists took hostages in Savoy hotel on Geula street, trying to negotiate the release of other terrorists from Israeli jails. As a rule, Israel did not negotiate with terrorists then, so gun and mortar fire were exchanged all night lighting up the night sky. Somehow, I slept through the battle. Apparently, it was so loud that people living on the other side of town woke up—but not me.

What woke me up was the sound of our radio blaring at seven o'clock in the morning. It was unusual.

"What's happening?" I asked my mother half asleep and exceedingly annoyed in an adolescent kind of way. She was in the kitchen with the radio on, listening to news reports.

My mother broke the news to me.

"Oh my God. Anyone killed?"

"They didn't give numbers, but I think several people are dead and a few were injured."

In that moment, my imagined force field around Tel Aviv disintegrated.

"Wait, it's near my school? My friend Carol lives right by the school. I hope she is okay," I said.

"I'm sure she's fine. Don't cry," my mother said when she saw me wipe tears with my pajama sleeve.

"Your father is crazy," my mother said after a pause. "We heard explosions at night but didn't know what it was. The news said that terrorists entered Tel-Aviv near here, so he decided to be a cowboy and took his pistols and went down there to check it out."

My heart thumped wildly.

"But he came back soon after because he said bullets were flying around him and police officers and soldiers told him to leave. He saw wounded people treated on the street and lots of ambulances too."

"So where is he now?" I asked, and my mind raced as fast as my heart, playing horrific bloody images like those I'd seen on television in other parts of Israel.

"He put on his army uniform and went back. I tried to stop him. The terrorists took hostages, and they just said in the news that the army stormed the hotel and killed them."

It was a lot to process—that the attack happened right by my school and a few minutes' walk from our apartment, and that my father could be so reckless. What if he was hurt or killed? This was the first time a dent appeared in his all-knowing persona for me. I was old enough to understand that it was a stupid thing to do.

I studied my mother's face as she continued to sit at the kitchen table, smoking and flicking ashes into an overflowing ashtray.

At that moment, our front door opened. I walked to the hallway and saw my father enter in his dusty army uniform. He smiled when he saw me and went into the living room with a pile of morning papers under his arm.

"Can you get me coffee here, Chip?" he called out.

He lay down the newspapers in front of him as he did every morning. I stood, planted in the corridor between the kitchen and living room, unable to speak.

Banging sounds from the kitchen echoed as my mother prepared his coffee.

Minutes later, she called out to me, "Here, take him his coffee. I don't want to talk to him after what he put me through."

With shaking hands, I brought my father his coffee and sat it on the table. His eyes scanned the early morning editions. I stared at him in horror, noticing the large sweat stains under his arms.

He could have been killed, and for what? Curiosity? A good story? In my mind's eye, I could see him running behind buildings with his pistol raised high by his ear, jumping between buildings the way it's done in movies. Only this wasn't a movie. There were live bullets and grenades.

When he raised his eyes from the paper, he said, "I don't think you'll be able to go to school today."

But to my disappointment, a news update later announced that Geula school would open after all.

During the long ten o'clock school recess, a group of us went down to look at the aftermath. It was a different world at the bottom of Geula Street, where a part of the Savoy hotel was in ruins. Buildings near the school were covered in bullet holes and windows were shattered. We stood for a while in silence. Today, we would say that it felt dystopian. Back then, we were simply stunned by the level of destruction and how close it was to where we lived. The impact would reverberate in my psyche for decades.

Minutes after we returned to our classrooms, sirens sounded, and we ran to the school shelter. It turned out that one of the terrorists had emerged from the rubble. I was told by friends that they saw me in the evening news that night, standing very close to where he had been. Shock at the sight of the rubble had prevented me from noticing the local and international television crews that surrounded the place. The sighting of the terrorist was the reason sirens went off near the school.

At school, teachers talked about how Israel had the best army in the world and reminded us that one day we'd be able to serve in it and protect our country and the children of Israel. Patriotism and admiration of Israel's Defense Forces (the IDF) were everywhere we looked—in movies, images, even on greeting cards.

In the days after the attack, it was reported that eight civilians and three IDF soldiers were killed in the attack and the Palestinian Liberation Organization (PLO) claimed responsibility. I tried to come to grips with what happened. Everyone I knew, even friends who lived across town, woke up from the gunfire and explosions. How could I have been so unaware? What if the terrorists had made it to our apartment building and started shooting everyone? I'd seen reports in the news about previous terror attacks and how those terrorists searched for children who were hiding under beds and in closets and killed them too. There was even a horrible incident in Northern Israel where a mother who tried to shield herself and her son and covered her infant's son's mouth so they wouldn't be found. In the process, she accidentally suffocated him to death.

Yet until that fateful night in March of 1975, I did not consider that it could happen to us.

I'd never sleep through the night again.

Years later, I would come to understand that sleeping through the night felt dangerous. In my traumatized mind, I believed that I had to stay awake and alert in case of another attack.

Suddenly, an invasion of my building was a real possibility. My assumption of safety shattered.

BEFRIENDING THE ENEMY

I t took a full year at Geula school for things to turn around for me. In the first few weeks of Grade Eight during sewing class, I showed a surprising talent for precision sewing that caught the teacher's attention. Gradually, one at a time, the girls who had beaten me the year before came to ask me for help. We talked and laughed until one day, Nira, the scariest one of them all, said, "You're not what I thought. You're okay."

"What do you mean?"

"You know, sons of bitches Ashkenazis who hate us Sephardis and all, think ya'all better than us and all that crap. But you seem cool."

"I don't hate you or any Sephardis," I said and added something I immediately regretted, "I'm just a little afraid since you beat me up last y…"

Nira smiled and gawked at me. My breath got stuck in my trachea. Was she going to turn on me now? My whole body braced for a punch even though a teacher was in the room. Instead, Nira burst out laughing and smack-patted me so hard on the back that I pricked myself on the needle. But that was the last injury she inflicted on me. One by one, as I helped the girls who had treated me like the enemy the previous year and engaged in the conversations they started, the wall between us fell. I even started swearing the way they did and pronounced words with the same vernacular.

As a psychologist dealing with trauma, I now know that befriending the enemy is one way of coping with danger, especially when fight or flight are not possible and freezing is a terrible idea.

It was a huge relief not to be seen anymore as the enemy. I even had moments when I felt it was safe to let my guard down at school and wouldn't need my father to pull strings to get me out early. But my relief would be proven premature.

I made true friends at Geula school, too, friends like Shirley and Carol. On Friday evenings, I often dined with Carol's family. Since she was Moroccan, the food was nothing like the tasteless chicken and potatoes usually served in my home. It was rich and savoury and sometimes packed a bit of heat, too. Other than the sweet paprika that my mother used in a Hungarian goulash she would sometimes make just for her and me, I didn't know of any other spices. Carol's mother cooked with turmeric, cumin, ginger, and nutmeg mixed with cinnamon and paprika—which I recognized—a scrumptious blend. I begged my mother to call Carol's mom to get the recipe, but her response was, "Aba will kill me if I make that."

Carol lived a few houses up from the beach, and twice a week, I'd meet her an hour before school and we'd jog along the beach. After one of our morning runs, she told me about job openings at a small factory in the Kerem neighbourhood and we both started working there the next week. Our small fingers gave us the kind of dexterity needed to fold little boxes fast and that meant making more money than the adults there, more money than we ever dreamed of. There were other teens there, too, so it became a bit of social outing with older boys who flirted with us.

All this time, my mother didn't stop advocating on my behalf at home. With one phone call, my father could have pulled me out of Geula. My mother pushed as hard as she could.

"How can I argue with one side of my mouth that we all have to operate with utmost integrity and with the other side of my mouth use connections and move you to another school?" My father said when I asked him, yet again, to get me out.

So, I just kept folding boxes, which paid for cool Wrangler and Levis jeans and tee shirts, as well as art materials and art books. Painting provided me with an escape. I covered my ugly world with colourful paintings and doodles. When I felt too heavy to face life, I'd sit in front of a sheet of paper and pick the brightest yellows, oranges, red, purples, and greens. I'd paint fast without planning. It was a stream of consciousness process, only rather than put words on a page, I poured colours. Sometimes, I saw a face or an animal in what emerged, and I would highlight it. While I mostly made abstract paintings, I did have one favourite subject to draw–trees. Gnarly ones that looked like humans reaching their branchy arms up, as if begging for help from the heavens, or perhaps wishing to ascend, to be somewhere else. I would paint until the lump in my throat melted. Until my chest muscles let go and I could breathe. The worse things were in my life, the more I painted.

Although in Grade Eight most of my tormentors let me be, it didn't mean I could let my guard down. In fact, the boys started to scare me more. One day, our homeroom teacher assigned me and a boy, who must have been kept behind for three years, to perform an after-class duty. We had to place the chairs on the desks so the janitor could wash the floor. With each chair he lifted, Benny moved several steps closer to me and I sensed danger. In a low voice he said, "Come here Kislev. Let's do a number," and almost cornered me. I knew by that point what he meant by "a number". Without thinking, I threw a chair at him and ran out of the class, his outstretched arm almost grabbing my shirt before I slipped away.

As my parents instructed, I'd done a good job of staying under the radar. Being beaten silly by angry girls was nothing compared to what I imagined the sons of a few of these criminals would do to me, if they'd found out who my father was. I preferred to spend more time in the factory than at school. My feeling so good there might have had something to do with the glue fumes in the air, but that was just a bonus on top of the good pay and the cute boys.

One spring evening that year, as Carol and I were walking home from work at the factory, we stopped for ice cream at the corner of Geula and Allenby streets. Digging with great pleasure into the ice cream, we talked about guys in the factory who seemed closer to us in age. At thirteen, boys were a major preoccupation.

"The boy who always sits at the corner of the table keeps looking at me," I said to Carol.

"Yeah, I noticed," she said.

"Next time maybe I'll smile at him," I blushed. That day, I thought he had winked at me.

"Oh, you don't want to do that," Carol said.

"Why? Does he have a girlfriend?"

"No, that's not it."

"What is it? Do *you* like him?"

"No. He's a Danoch, you know, from your father's articles about organized crime."

"Oh, shit!"

"He's a grade above us so maybe he doesn't know who you are. You'd probably be dead if he did."

And that's when I knew I absolutely had to get out of that school.

Rage at my father consumed me. He could have taken me out of there a long time ago. How could he put his stupid ideals and concerns for his career ahead of his own daughter's safety?

When the school year ended, I announced: "Either you get me transferred out of there or I'm not going to go to any school."

My true salvation finally came when my father activated good old fashioned "protectsias", the pulling of strings to attain favours, and got me out of Geula. He was my hero again. I didn't know who he called and didn't care. Enormously relieved, I started Grade Nine in a new school, a half-hour walk from where we lived, and a world apart.

Irony Alef, a school in the more upscale part of the city and with predominantly Ashkenazi kids, was a culture shock. Most of the students who were brought into the school from a poorer neighbourhood through the Integration Program had dropped out by Grade Nine. I later found out that some of the Ashkenazi kids simply ignored them or bullied them when they struggled academically, or because of the way they talked or dressed. In fact, anyone who was different was bullied, even new immigrants from Russia were laughed at, or kids with unusual names. This school felt cruel, while Geula had felt dangerous. When I spoke at recess with one of the few girls who hadn't dropped out, three girls from the "nice areas" approached me to warn that this was not a good idea and that my social status could suffer. Ignoring them, I formed a friendship with one of the girls who didn't drop out, and after a while, a boy from our class, my love interest that year, joined us. The three of us regularly hung out and cut school to go to the beach.

After falling behind academically at Geula, I wasn't trying too hard to catch up at my new school. My goal was to achieve mediocre success, which was more than I needed, because my plan was to become an artist.

The Past Stays
in the Past

My parents didn't want to talk about their early life experiences, like most parents who survived the Holocaust in Europe or pogroms in Arab countries. My questions were either ignored or treated with anger and laconic responses. Yet, I'd managed to learn a few things about my father during my teens. When my history teacher covered some WWII events, I asked my father to tell me about his experiences at that time.

"Leave the past in the past," was how he shut down my first attempt. All I managed to get from him then was that he was born in Chestohova, Poland, and that there were about forty thousand Jews in this city before the war and less than four thousand after.

One evening when I was fourteen, after we watched the James Bond movie *From Russia with Love* on television, my father said out of the blue, "Apropos Russia, during the war, me and my parents ended up in a labour camp in Siberia."

"*Ma be-emet?* Really? What was that like?"

"I'll give you a book about it. Now go to sleep," he said, shutting me up and out.

"The Russians were worse than the Nazis," my father told me the next week when he gave me the book *Gulag Archipelago* by Alexander Solzhenitsyn. This document exposed to the world the inner system of the gulags. To say it was disturbing would be an understatement. The gulags were basically slave labour camps in the coldest and harshest part of Russia. The word GULAG is an acronym for the Russian phrase, Main Administration of Corrective Labour Camps. Most of these camps were in Siberia and the Far East, where prisoners were forced to work in mines, forestry, or building infrastructure like roads. I skimmed through the book. It was so gruesome I couldn't finish the massive testimony to human cruelty, just like I couldn't watch Holocaust documentaries. After that, I was afraid to ask my father again about his experiences and that suited him just fine.

Years later, possibly after he drank one shot of vodka, or maybe three, we talked about our fair complexions and his blue eyes. He said, "You know, it helped me hide in plain sight. Before the end of the war, I joined a partisan group, but they were not Jewish. It was my blue eyes and the fact my ID, for some reason, had 'von' before my last name that threw them off."

I knew his name at birth was Herman Wexler and that he had later changed it to Ran Kislev. It was very common for people who emigrated to Israel to change their foreign-sounding names to Hebrew ones. But I'd never heard about the 'von' part before that day.

"Oh, why does the 'von' matter?" I asked.

"Jewish last names do not typically have 'von' before them. It suggests nobility or aristocracy," and he chuckled.

His cheerful demeanour suggested he was proud of his partisan days, but when I asked him to tell me what they did, he said, "Well, I better not go there."

I never asked him to say more about that, either.

Avoidance is a known trauma symptom and a coping strategy, extremely common among Holocaust survivors—and understandably so. They don't want to relive the horrors, and many don't want to burden their children with the cruelty they witnessed or suffered and the extent of their losses. Many of them also struggle with survivor's guilt. I think, in my father's case, it was all the above.

Similarly, family members are afraid of their own pain once they hear details of what their loved ones endured—it is called vicarious trauma. As a result, avoidance in family members of trauma survivors is also common. Intuitively, I tamped down my curiosity in my teens and accepted an abstract idea of what it was like for my father during the war.

A Perfect Family

My father had a reputation for pursuing women he was not married to, and it was inevitable that the gossip would reach my mother's ears.

"The gossipmongers are just jealous of our wonderful marriage," my father said, each time my mother confronted him. Sometimes this took place while I was in the next room and I couldn't help but hear my mother threatening acts of violence she would commit, alongside my father's convoluted denials. I also couldn't help but feel dread.

In the spring of 1977, as proof of his devotion, my father cashed in a saving plan set up by his employer, *Haaretz Daily*, for travel expenses, and gave it to my mother.

"This is a true declaration of your father's love and commitment," my mother said to me. She had asked him many times to go on trips abroad, but he was always too busy lambasting politicians and exposing every type of corruption, so he came up with an alternative. My mother thought the real reason he didn't want to travel with her was because he didn't speak English and would depend on her. "He is too proud for that," she said. That the famous Ran Kislev couldn't speak English was a secret my mother and I had to guard. For an Israeli journalist, it was a major disability, and a shameful one. Speaking English suggests the person is worldly and the high-brow *Haaretz*, as an international newspaper, aspired to project worldliness.

There, inside our damp apartment, surrounded by crumbling walls, I allowed my teenage romanticism to blind me to the truth. *He's so selfless*, I shared my mother's fantasy. She used to say our family was the epitome of the American Dream, Israeli style. The night she began her solo trip to Europe, the dream shattered.

I'd like to think that my father reassured my mother that he and I would have no problem caring for three-year-old Mickey in her absence, but I don't recall any such discussion. My mother's limited maternal instincts made it easy for her to leave a three-year-old behind and do as she pleased.

A few minutes after midnight on that 1977 spring evening, even before my mother's plane landed on European soil, the door to our apartment eased shut. I wanted to believe I had imagined the sound of my father leaving. Instead, a routine established itself in the nights that followed throughout the six weeks my mother traipsed around Europe. My father waited until he thought my brother and I were asleep then snuck out of the apartment. Every morning, he returned home at dawn with groceries, claiming he had just left to buy them for breakfast. He didn't know I barely slept—I had become an insomniac and a light sleeper after I had slept through the explosions during the terror attack three years earlier. And I had become so good at hearing noise, I'd be startled repeatedly from sounds outside my room and on the street. So, I heard my father sneak out when he left around midnight, and I woke up when he opened the door, ever so quietly, at dawn. The slight rattle of the front door's handle was all it took to shatter my illusion of a perfect family.

The more I imagined what he was up to, the more I was gripped by adolescent disgust. What woman would want to sleep with him anyway? He was fifty but looked a decade older—bald, his face etched like a wood carving, his teeth yellow from decades of heavy smoking.

At fifteen, I didn't understand that powerful men are attractive to certain women, whatever their looks. I knew my father was well respected for his intellect and knowledge. In social gatherings, he was popular thanks to his fascinating stories. And he was a wonderful dancer at parties, twirling women around and kissing the back of their hands at the end of a dance (to my mother's chagrin). All of this made him charismatic, as I've been told over the years by various acquaintances of my parents.

So, who was he spending the nights with?

Six weeks after we waved goodbye to my mother at the airport, she returned from her adventure with stops in her birth town of Timisoara in Transylvania; in Paris, France; and in Zurich, Switzerland. Within days, her best friend Ella came over. My mother didn't realize I was home, since I had returned early from school while she was shopping at the nearby Carmel Market.

Our kitchen was on the other side of my bedroom wall, and I could hear everything they said to each other.

"I saw Ran with Dalia," Ella said.

"So what? They work together," my mother replied.

"They didn't behave like colleagues."

"You don't know him like I do. He has never loved anyone like he loves me. He tells me that every day." My mother's desperation to negate the truth seeped through the wall. Like her, I also didn't want the truth to be so, even though I had witnessed his deceitful behaviour for more than a month.

"But I've seen him with her in restaurants," Ella said.

"Yes, they obviously discuss work. She's a journalist, too, you know."

My face felt hot.

Dalia worked for *Haaretz* as well, and rumours about their affair had circulated for a long time. I hadn't given it much thought until then and chose to believe it was simply malicious gossip. If what Ella said was true, it made me an accomplice.

"No, Tsippi. You don't understand. I saw him touch her. They were necking like two young and horny lovers," Ella said.

"When was that?"

"It was a couple of weeks ago."

My heart shrivelled with each detail and broke when my mother said, "He's like that. He's touchy-feely with people. I've told him that many times. It's embarrassing in social situations, he always dances too close with other women. I can see why people think he is straying."

"You don't get it. He keeps clothes in her apartment," Ella said in a slightly higher pitch.

Silence.

"How could you know that?" My mother's voice was weak, but I could still make out the words.

"She showed me."

I could barely breathe.

A Dilemma

Ella was the person my mother trusted most in the world. She had always been direct and honest, and my mother loved her for that. Ever since they had worked together at *This World*, they had been inseparable. Ella was the first female photojournalist in the tabloid and was admired by all. She had a keen eye and was very clear about what she saw.

My father needed serious verbal acrobatics to get out of this one.

More than once, I had overheard my mother telling him, "If I ever find out you are cheating on me, I will kill you and myself." So that night it was with trepidation that I listened to my mother confront my father with what Ella had told her. Despite this highly damning new evidence my father resorted to his usual tricks. "It's all lies! Call and ask this Dalia yourself," followed by, "I don't have her number, but I can find it for you." He clinched his routine with, "Make sure you embarrass yourself completely and ask."

The morning after Ella's visit, my mother entered my room and interrupted me swaying to Elton John and Kiki Dee's "Don't Go Breaking My Heart". Following my father's unconvincing acrobatics, she had awoken with the strength and determination to "find out once and for all!" To achieve that, she needed a detective, and the person she had in mind was me.

"Don't put me in the middle of this," I said, my head starting to hurt.

"But you are in the middle. You live here!" She squinted at me and a chill ran down my spine.

"Yes, but this is between the two of you, and you are asking me to take sides."

"Well, if he is having an affair wouldn't you take my side anyway?"

"Why are you doing this? I don't want to do this," I said, tears streaming down my face.

I paused long enough for my mother's vicious imp to emerge from the dark corners of her psyche. She responded the way she always did when I refused to do as she asked. She screamed and wailed at the top of her lungs, not with words but with sounds that a person being tortured makes.

She knew I couldn't handle it. Begrudgingly, I relented.

Just like that, her evil imp retreated, her shoulders fell, and the corners of her mouth relaxed.

My father was a busy man, but I had a good relationship with him, better than the one I had with my mother by that time. He rarely yelled at me even though I was quite rebellious. When I asked him to explain complex historical and political issues, he was always willing. When I begged for a bicycle because "all my friends have one", he bought me the most expensive bike, a pink Raleigh with all the trimmings. The fact we couldn't afford it only seemed like further proof of his love.

Transfixed, I watched as my mother pulled out a small orange notebook from her purse. She ripped out a page and handed it to me. "This is Dalia's address. All I need you to do is look near her apartment building and tell me if you see Aba's car. They say he has lunch with her every day, so be there at one o'clock tomorrow afternoon."

The next day, I rode several buses across town instead of going to school, reviewing the Grade Nine class materials before final exams. On the way to the other woman's apartment, I had plenty of time to think. Dalia lived in the nice part of town, North Tel Aviv, and over the hour it took to get there I reflected on the murder-suicide threats that my mother had made.

"How would you do it?" I once overheard my father asking my mother in a mocking tone while she served him dinner in the kitchen.

"I'd slash your throat first with this knife and then my wrists." I don't think he took her seriously, but I did.

I replayed this memory repeatedly and arrived at only one conclusion: if my mother was confronted with what she thought was proof that my father was having an affair, my three-year-old brother Mickey and I would become orphans.

Throughout the seemingly endless bus journeys, the same image played again and again in my head: the gruesome scene in the kitchen as my mother described it. I pictured the stairways running with blood, I heard Mickey screaming. I imagined the police questioning me while I tried to justify telling my mother that I had seen my father's car near his lover's apartment building. *Why would you tell your mother something like that?* The police officer would inquire.

But if I'd find my father's car near the apartment and chose to lie to my mother, I'd be sealing any cracks left in the fortress of denial she'd built. And worst of all, I'd be helping my father hide his indiscretions. This contradicted my own belief system and the high value I placed on truth. Maybe one day my mother would find out anyway. She could justifiably accuse me of conspiring to hide facts from her. She'd demand to know how I, in good conscience, could have kept her in the dark?

Wasn't it better to offer up the truth, even if it led to the pain of divorce?

Praying that I wouldn't see my father's car and fighting the urge to turn around and leave without looking, I made it to the street where Dalia lived. I glanced around the area for my father's mustard-coloured Triumph. It didn't take me long to spot it. Residents on that street bought mostly white or beige cars to blend in with their mostly white and beige new apartment buildings.

My heart thumped so loud and so fast that I started to feel dizzy. Seeing his car there merely confirmed what I'd already known after hearing him slip out of our apartment night after night throughout the six weeks of my mother's absence. I sprinted out of there, zigzagging between cars to avoid being seen by my father until I reached a bus stop.

Whatever was left of school that day I skipped, although I could have made it to the last class. Instead, I took a bus straight to the beach close to Bialik and walked aimlessly on the boardwalk.

It felt wrong to hold back the truth and just as wrong and scary to tell my mother.

I would have liked to talk to someone and get advice, to lighten the burden. But at that point in my life, there was no one I could confide in. Although I fully trusted my best friends, I could not bring myself to reveal the details of my family drama. I was still trying to pretend I had a normal family.

The decision was mine, and mine alone.

Right until the moment I reached our apartment, I had no idea what I'd tell my mother. But when she opened the door and I saw her red eyes and weak smile, I said, "I didn't see Aba's car," and walked fast past her to my room before she could interrogate me. In my room, I put on my Walkman's spongy headphones and drowned my thoughts with the Bee Gees and Supertramp and began to sketch. I filled several pages with pencil drawings of men hanging on scaffolds and women holding knives. Later, I tore the pages to pieces. Oddly, I felt relief afterwards.

It was impossible to suppress what I had seen, and the truth of it weighed heavily on my conscience for years. Not telling my mother about the mustard-coloured Triumph parked beside Dalia's building would never be a victory of any kind. To this day, my early foray into the world of a private detective remains filed in my mind under "Things mothers should never ask their children to do".

A few months after Ella's visit, little blue pills appeared in our medicine cabinet. I didn't know what they were, but my mother took them daily and slept a lot. I didn't realize yet that they were what kept the angry imp at bay, but when they wore off, the imp would appear and make my life more miserable than it already was. It was 1978 and "Mommy's Little Helper", a.k.a. Valium, was the most-prescribed medication that year, and my mother became addicted to it. She'd cycle sometimes between sleeping almost all day and exploding in anger on me at any sign of disapproval or refusal to do what she wanted when she wanted it, like going for the fifth time in one day to fetch from the grocery store an ingredient she needed for a dish.

Having seen my father's car where it shouldn't have been, having glimpsed his shadow side, I also became deeply disillusioned with the man who claimed to occupy the highest moral ground in Israel. The love I felt for him transformed that day into adolescent contempt. He lived a double life and that lit a fire inside me. Every time he came home late, banging around in the kitchen to show he was dissatisfied with my mother's cleaning, fuses blew inside my brain. Every time red notices of unpaid utility bills arrived in the mail, more fuses blew. Clearly, he spent money elsewhere. But I was not allowed to show anger, certainly not to the full extent I felt it. So, I seethed and I imploded, only occasionally slamming doors. My only safe outlet was art. I was drawn to images of hell, such as the fifteenth-century hellscape depicted in Hieronymus Bosch's *The Last Judgement*.

Helped by raging hormones, my other coping strategy was making out with boys. With no rules other than my father imposing an eleven o'clock curfew, which I violated just to spite him. I engaged in these pseudo-romantic activities not only with boys my age but also adult men, one of them nine years older. Sticking with their practice of minimal supervision and involvement, not once did my parents ask what I was up to. It was easy to escape into the open arms of horny boys and men, mistaking their desire for love.

Anger stayed in my body until my late twenties and left only after a few years of living away from my family, with a vast, cooling ocean between us.

Looking back, I don't recognize the angry person I used to be, but I know she could be a sarcastic bitch. And I know that, before she left her family of origin's home, she occasionally imagined ways of ending her life.

Disillusioned with my father after confirming that he was having an affair, and because I was put in the untenable position with my mother, I became impatient with both of them, especially him. Most of the time, I was able hide it and roll my eyes only internally. It was ultimately between my parents, and I tried to focus on my father's good qualities—his intellect and excitement to share his knowledge and his love of music, art and reading with me. But within a year of confirming that he indeed was having an affair, my father would make his worst transgression, and it would rupture our relationship.

At a relative's wedding, 1977.

On the balcony of 9 Bialik Street, 1977.

Teachers

Quite a few teachers in my high school suffered from an inclination to induce boredom, as well as mental disorders. It was not surprising, as several were Holocaust survivors.

Among them. the one who appeared regularly in my nightmares was my English teacher, the infamous Eva Maior. She was known for psychologically tormenting and humiliating students. Her abuse was so brutal that a few of her victims dropped out of high school altogether.

Maior was scary to look at. She wore intense red lipstick over a thin mean mouth, blue mascara, and thick black eyeliner around her sinking eyes. She looked undead. Her skin, prune-like from too many hours in the pool, made her look much older than her sixty-odd years. She said she needed to swim every morning before coming to school to deal with the bunch of imbeciles we were. To compensate for her short stature, Maior wore a tall and compli-cated up-do and stood on six-inch platform heels. We used to joke that she could commit suicide by jumping from them. The joke turned out to be weirdly prophetic.

Whether it was in relation to ideas or clothes, Maior did not appreciate in-dividual expression and had an issue with my Bohemian fashion sense. I often wore scarves and hats and unusual clothes I bought at vintage shops. My class-mates typically dressed more conventionally or with brand name clothes. She'd pass by me and flick my scarf, muttering, "Pff…Bohemian." I'd laugh.

Maior did not like original answers to her exam questions. Too much of my own thoughts got under her wrinkles. Although I wrote in near-perfect English, she failed me a few times, writing in large red letters over my answers, "Stupid answers. You did not understand the story at all." Another time she wrote, "Re-read notes from my class and maybe you'll learn something."

My mother, who spoke fluent English and had once been a teacher herself, was incensed. The first time this happened, I read my answers to her while she was cooking in the steamy kitchen.

"I'm going to set her straight," she said.

"Please don't. You don't understand how crazy this woman is. She'll eat you alive."

"Don't worry, I know how to stand up to unreasonable people," my mother turned around from the stove to face me, wiping sweat from her forehead. "You underestimate my skills."

"You are underestimating *her*. She is the devil, and she'll make things worse for me. She doesn't like to be challenged," I pleaded.

Despite my objections, the next day my mother marched to my school to confront Maior. When she came back home, she said, "I *have* never met anyone like that." She looked both stunned and defeated. "She hates everyone and everything and is not rational at all."

"I told you. Now she'll hate me more."

I continued to express my original thoughts on exams, refusing to bow down and regurgitate Maior's ideas about the books we read. Besides, I didn't care if my marks were low. I had no desire to do any more schooling beyond high school. My educational experience thus far has been hugely unsatisfying. I still aspired to become an artist.

One morning I had a spat with Maior when she asked a student from a poor neighbourhood to stand in front of the class. She pointed at the girl's slightly stained school uniform and said with a smirk, "Look how disgusting her clothes are." The girl ran out of the class crying.

Incensed, and with a racing heart I said, "What you just did is cruel and shameful. How could you?" By that point in my brief life, I had learned from my father that one has to stand up for what's right and fight injustices, even at one's own peril.

Maior laughed and said, "Pff... If you have a problem with that you can leave too."

I did—and walked straight to the principal's office to complain.

"You can switch to another class and have different teachers," the principal said after I reported what had happened. He removed his thick-rimmed glasses to clean the lenses and looked down at them, the top of his head glistening under the florescent light.

"Why should I be punished and have to leave my friends? She should be fired, she should leave," my voice cracked.

"How is your father, by the way?" He was quite taken by my father's celebrity and occasionally intercepted me during recess to ask about him.

I ignored his question.

"Listen, we can't fire her. The poor woman is a Holocaust survivor."

"And what about us? Her victims."

Most of us didn't understand the implications of what survivors had gone through, yet adults expected us to. Besides, we knew many survivors who didn't behave badly, so to me, it was all just patently unfair. When it came to issues of justice and fairness, I was only applying what I'd learned from my father.

The principal stood up, walked around his desk and behind me, and opened the door. "Say hi to your father for me, would you?"

The following Shabbat morning, my father made us his scrumptious French Toast breakfast from thick day-old challah with poppy seeds, my favourite. I smeared peach jam on top, while my father poured heaps of sugar on four slices.

I told my father what had happened with Maior that week.

"I'm very proud of you for standing up for that student. It was the right thing to do."

"Yes, but why is Maior allowed to keep doing this?" I asked. "She is harming so many students, calls them stupid in front of the class and throws their notebooks across the classroom if she doesn't like what they wrote. Shouldn't she be fired? What does it take to get a teacher fired?"

"Life doesn't always work like this but I'm glad you spoke up."

"Aba please, can't you send a reporter to investigate the school system? You always take on other people's causes, what about mine?" In those days, he held an executive position at *Haaretz* and could assign, or at least suggest, stories to journalists.

"I'm sorry this is happening to you," he said, "but there are other more pressing issues right now in Israel, so I don't think there will be public interest in this."

"Fine," I said, walked to my room and banged the door. Being dismissed twice in one week was unacceptable to adolescent me. It created a layer of resentment that would only be heightened by more disappointments to follow.

Looking back now, I see his point. It was 1978 and the most incredible thing had just happened: Israel and Egypt were in peace talks. A few months earlier, the Egyptian president shocked the world when he accepted Menachem Begin's invitation to visit Israel. Months before that, the right-wing Likud party won the election for the first time in Israel's history. But to a typical self-centered adolescent like me, this meant nothing compared to my personal woes. There were always pressing issues in Israel. People approached my father on a regular basis to look into this or that problem or injustice they suffered, and sometimes he'd investigate it and even wrote articles on some people or issues he was approached about. I had the impression that his door both at home and in his office was always open to strangers seeking his help. Why couldn't he do this one thing for me?

A Cold War

The epitome of injustice was what my math teacher Mr. B. did when I was in Grade Eleven. This was also when my father made his biggest mistake with me. The man who was all about social justice would fail to see the injustice his daughter experienced at school.

Since middle school, I had struggled with numbers and flunked most math tests. In Grade Nine I just barely attained a passing grade. Grade Ten was brutal. In the second month of Grade Eleven, after I bombed the first exam of the year, Mr. B. asked me to stay after class. He was a tall and wide-shouldered with wavy black hair combed back and he always looked angry or spiteful to me.

"Listen Sara, I know you are struggling with this subject. I'll make you a deal."

"Oh…" I was so nervous I could barely utter a sound.

"I noticed your notebook is quite messy."

Duh, I had no clue what was going on and it showed in my notes.

"Here is my offer, if you keep a neat notebook all year, I'll give you a passing grade even if you fail."

My eyes nearly bulged out of their sockets.

"Umm…that's amazing… thank you so much. I'll do it. I'll work hard…" My heart was pounding.

"Right, go now," and he waved me away.

I could not believe my good fortune.

That afternoon, I purchased a new notebook, colourful markers and highlighters. The rest of the year, I kept two notebooks—one that had the chicken-scratch notes I took in class, and another in which I re-wrote my notes, used a ruler to underline certain words that seemed important and used colourful highlighters for emphasis. It was something between a math notebook and an art project.

On the last day of school, Mr. B. asked me to stay after the class again and towering over me with a serious face he said, "Your average is barely fifty percent so I'm placing you in summer school."

"What? But you promised…"

"It doesn't matter what I said, you need to upgrade your math skills or…"

"But but you said…and I…"

He put the palm of his hand in front of my face as if to block my words and walked towards his desk to collect his books, dropping them one by one into his frayed leather bag, ignoring my presence. Tears ran down my face and I quickly gathered my things and ran out of the classroom, briskly passing by a group of friends waiting for me.

When I stomped into our apartment and my mother saw my red eyes, she asked what had happened.

"The bastard math teacher, Mr. B. lied to me," and while sobbing and hyperventilating, I tried to explain what he promised and what I did because of that promise. I took out my two notebooks, waved them as I spoke, then tossed them across the room.

"Calm down. Everything will be okay. He's wrong and I'll go talk to him," she said as she picked up the notebooks and straightened the pages.

When I calmed down and pulled myself together, I mumbled, "Don't. He won't budge, I can tell. It's too late."

"So, what do you want to do?"

"I don't know," and I went to my room to cry into my pillow.

Just after seven in the evening, my father entered the apartment. I figured he'd eat dinner, watch the eight o'clock news with my mother, tell us he had to go back to work, and then leave. Before he left, I intercepted him and told him how Mr. B had betrayed me.

My father, who normally knew what to say to help me feel better or at least do what fathers do best—problem solve and give advice — looked at me for a moment and said the absolute worst thing possible: "Teachers are always right."

"What?! I've been telling you for years that we have so many crazy and unfair teachers and you agreed. Now this is what you're telling me?"

"Well, in Poland…" he began.

"Stop. I'm never talking to you again!" I slammed the door to our apartment and ran down the stairs to the street, bawling.

"It will be okay. Your father will come around, you'll see," my mother said when I came back home two hours later, after I had spent the evening on the boardwalk, in the dark, as waves crashed again and again into the surf break.

My father did not come around and I considered his statement unforgivable. This personal injustice was on top of letting me languish at Geula school for two years.

I'd had enough.

From that day on I moved around the apartment pretending I didn't see him, and he in turn ignored me. I was determined to treat him like air until he'd become the father I wanted and apologize.

"Ask him to pass me the salt," was the most I'd say at the kitchen table if I couldn't avoid meals with him. It was nerve racking for my mother. A week passed and she tried to intervene. She talked to both of us separately and asked me to apologize so we'd have peace restored.

"No way. I have nothing to apologize for. He's the one who should."

She didn't even know the half of it. I couldn't tell her what I knew about his personal ethics. With each passing day, angry thoughts and resentments piled up. How dare he take such a righteous approach with me?

Weeks passed and then a month. My mother was pulling her hair in frustration while my father dug in. I dug deeper. It was war—a cold war. After a while, it became our new status quo.

Again and again, my mother tried pleading, yelling, crying. But my father and I were equally stubborn. Our shadow parts were in full view and clashed in a vicious passive-aggressive battle.

My best friends knew what was happening and they told me I had gone too far. They said I should forgive him because he must be old-fashioned and that's how older people saw things. I disagreed. My father should have known better. He had acknowledged in the past that several of my teachers had loose screws. Maior, and the Math teacher were just two of several bullies during my high school years. For my father to take their side was intolerable. Ran Kislev, the champion of victims of social injustice, failed to defend his own daughter and see the injustice inflicted on her. A wall grew between us, and I didn't care if I'd ever talk to him again.

Running Nowhere

In April 1980, it had been nearly two years since I had spoken a word to my father. I was still angry enough to refuse to make the first gesture towards peace. I felt righteous and indignant. As a parent myself now, I am horrified. I cannot imagine having to live with a child and husband who wouldn't talk to each other for a week, let alone almost two years.

On the morning of April 20, 1980, I trudged to school as usual, forcing myself to finish Grade Twelve. As I walked in the hallway, I noticed a commotion and approached a group of students huddled by a bulletin board. They were shouting and laughing. Some were clapping and others looked for tacks to stick onto the board what looked like a newspaper article. I got closer and saw the headline: "Education in High-School: Matriculation or Ignorance" (in Hebrew, matriculation and ignorance rhyme—Bagrut and Baarut). Below that, in bold letters it read: "Running Nowhere". When I saw the journalist's name, I chuckled. It was Nathan Dunyevitch, a *Haaretz* journalist known for the sharp tongue he unleashed on anything or anyone he disapproved of. He was also a friend of my father. One of the students read a few paragraphs out loud. Dunyevitch ripped into the education system, which he argued did not really educate and did not provide us with the kind of knowledge and skills we needed in life. The matriculation exams did not mean that schools helped students mature, he argued. But the sentence that drew applause from us was that most teachers simply did not know how to teach.

We burst into Pink Floyd's song, screaming that we didn't need education or thought control. The album *The Wall* had come out earlier that school year and it had already become our anthem. When this article, the first in a scathing series, came out, we felt collectively vindicated.

In English class, Maior raged.

"These journalists don't know what they are talking about. They have no idea how hard it is to stand in front of a class of dimwits like you. They don't have a clue. This journalist should be hanged."

She stared at me when she said that.

We could barely contain our giggles.

"You know, teachers may be upset with you," one of my friends said when we walked home together after school later that day.

"Why?"

"Well, your dad is high up in *Haaretz* right?

Indeed, at the time, my father was on the executive of the newspaper and had the clout to recommend topics for the paper to cover. He was already in the process of replacing the editor, Gideon Sammet, who was moving to Washington as the *Haaretz* correspondent. If someone needed to be crucified, the sharpest nail the paper had was Nathan Dunyevitch. I had no doubt that this series of articles was my father's idea.

When he walked through the door later that day, his eyes rested on my face, and he smiled. I knew what it meant, and I smiled back.

Rather than restoring peace at home, I chose a ceasefire. His was not a true apology as far as I was concerned. It was clear he had something to do with the series, and I saw this as an attempt to appease me, but I still wanted to hear him say he was sorry and that he was wrong. Yes, I'd asked him to investigate or send someone else to do so, but it had taken him too long to act.

And just before final exams at the end of high school, my mother ran into Maior at the local market. They exchanged a few polite words. My mother noticed, despite the layers of make-up that Maior's wrinkled face became pale as they talked. She stared at my mother for a moment and finally said, "Wait a minute, you aren't, she isn't…wait, are you Hungarian?"

"Yes. I was born in Transylvania."

"Oh no. I hated Sara all these years because I thought she was Polish like her father."

"What does that have to do with anything?" my mother asked.

"I am so sorry," Maior blurted out and walked away fast. My mother burst out laughing when she finished telling me this. It was a nervous laughter.

"What the hell? This makes no sense," I said.

"Right?! Unbelievable. The woman is crazy as a bat and she looks like one, too."

We laughed, but it wasn't that funny.

During our final high school exams, external staff sat in the classrooms to keep an eye on us. The day we wrote the English exam, the door opened.

I didn't look up to see who entered, but suddenly that person stood next to me and threw a small square of paper on my desk. I turned it over. It was my head in a photo, cut from a larger photograph taken at the school. I looked up. Maior was planted in front of me. She smiled in a crooked kind of way and walked out of the class.

"What the hell?" my friends said when I came out of the classroom and showed them the cut photo. We laughed uncomfortably, not knowing what to make of it.

"D'ya think it's an apology?" One friend asked.

"Don't know."

"She is saying she wants you out of the picture," another friend speculated.

"It's voodoo stuff, throw it away," yet another said.

I didn't throw it away. It felt like a mystery I had to solve—a piece of a bigger puzzle.

A year after graduating, I ran into a classmate who told me Maior had retired and soon after committed suicide.

"What? How?"

"She jumped off the roof of her building."

"No way."

I was both shocked and not shocked.

"I guess she didn't have anyone to torture after she retired so her life wasn't worth living anymore," I said.

At home later that day, I searched for the photo she had thrown on my desk during final exam and dumped it in the garbage. Sadness and a pang of guilt for saying unkind words about her bubbled in me. Was it possible that the person she tortured the most was herself?

I didn't know anything about her personal life other than the fact she had survived the Holocaust although she didn't have a number tattooed on her wrist. It seemed that after she stopped teaching, Maior had nowhere to run to avoid her memories. My anger at her dissipated that day.

Decades later, I'd still have the occasional nightmare involving Maior. In the dream, I fell behind in her class and expected to fail high school as result. Each time I opened my eyes, it took me a while to remember that I did graduate, despite Maior. A type of stress dream, it occurred when I was overwhelmed with academic studies or work.

As trauma goes, a part of my psyche didn't feel safe from Maior's wrath for a long time. My father's delayed reaction in sending the journalist to investigate the educational system was too little too late.

Do the Right Thing

Despite my struggles, I miraculously attained a high-school diploma, albeit with the mediocre grades I had aimed for. Eight weeks later, I donned an army uniform and carried a rifle for the two-year mandatory army service that begins after high school in Israel. Within months, my father disappointed me again.

Basic training was nothing like what I had imagined based on my mother's stories about her army service in the early 1950s. If it had been a painting, I'd say my mother's version was Monet's "Water Lilies" and mine was Munch's "Scream". Physical endurance challenges were beyond my body's capacity on a good day. The three weeks under the August sun, with multiple exercises in the desert, resulted in heat exhaustion and sunburns. The daily drills, in army boots a size too small, left me with grape-size blisters and an urge to run away barefoot. I came very close to marrying my then-boyfriend as a way of ejecting myself from the army.

Originally, I was pre-selected to serve as a psychometric tester. It was one of the most coveted army jobs for women in those days, as most women ended up serving coffee to their male bosses and typing letters all day for two long years.

At the end of basic training our course instructors came to meet us.

"You are the crème de la crème of Israeli society," one instructor told us. "Once you complete the four-month course, you'll be deciding the future of new recruits."

In Israel, what a person does in the army can have life-long implications. It can open doors or close them. I stood a little taller when he said that. Oddly, I scored at the top in psychometric tests. My "kaba" score was the highest possible: fifty-six. Kaba is an acronym in Hebrew for "Quality Group". This score determined whether one would be considered for the best jobs in the army and now it was going to be part of my job to determine the kaba score of incoming soldiers. I didn't know yet how it was calculated or why I scored so high.

It turned out that about fifty percent of the kaba score was based on psychometric test results which measure cognitive skills, aptitude, and personal traits. But the rest had nothing to do with my abilities.

On the first day of training our instructor, only a couple of years older than me, said, "Here you will soon learn how to make life or death decisions regarding your fellow soldiers."

"What do you mean?" I asked, feeling my jaw clench.

"Well, let's say you miss the fact that a soldier is an introvert and assign him to serve in the armoured corps. For someone like that, being stuck inside a tank with three other people could lead to suicide. And it does happen."

Huh?! Shit. That was a lot of responsibility. Barely out of high school, eighteen years old, I wasn't prepared for that. But if they thought I could do it, well, who was I to argue? Besides, after my less-than-spectacular academic performance in high school, I could hold my head high knowing I was deemed super smart by the army.

For the first couple of weeks, I enjoyed the course and attained high marks on the weekly exams. It was fun socializing with the others, who came from everywhere in Israel, although several were a bit stuck-up or too dorky for my taste.

An introduction course to kaba scoring revealed how the army arrived at its decisions. Among other things, the score was determined by the soldiers' ethnic background, their parents' education level, and where they lived. My heart sank. I realized I was being asked to practice discrimination based on ethnic background and socio-economic factors that new recruits had no control over. This meant that the Sephardi/Mizrahi soldiers got a lower score than Ashkenazis. Therefore, a new recruit who had a stellar high school diploma, came from a poor neighbourhood or town, was non-Ashkenazi with parents who didn't finish high school or maybe just didn't go on to university, received a lower kaba score than me, the fair-skinned Ashkenazi with much lower grades. Non-Ashkenazis would have had poorer chances of being accepted into the course I was taking and would likely not have the opportunity to train as a pilot or for any other coveted roles. This was my first encounter with systemic discrimination.

During class, I asked, "How is the parents' birthplace related to what a recruit can or cannot do in the army?"

The blue-eyed, fair-skinned instructor Rina squinted and said, "You don't have to agree, you just need to apply the rules."

I couldn't do it.

When I went home that weekend, I decided to tell my father what was happening, on Saturday morning, while he made French Toast. Shirtless in his tennis shorts, he was dipping the challah slices in eggs and frying them in butter. After a week of inedible army food, the smell was intoxicating. As soon as I finished gulping four thick slices, I asked for his help. I told him what was happening and how uncomfortable I felt participating in this blatant act of discrimination.

"Can you send a journalist to investigate this?" I asked.

By that time, my father was the editor-in-chief of *Haaretz Daily*. I wanted the army to be exposed.

"I can't. It's an internal army matter."

"So, who's going to stop them?"

I knew that soldiers were barred from talking to journalists about their army service, but I told myself they had no right to stop me from talking to my father.

"Let me think about it. But investigating this will not change the course you are on now. Plus, if someone figures out you blew the whistle, you could be charged with treason."

I didn't like my odds.

"But I can't take part in this discrimination. What can I do?"

"Simple. Do the right thing."

"Yes, but what is the right thing here? Quitting won't change the system and at the same time I can't be a part of it."

"Maybe you can change things from the inside? Finish the course and later advocate for equality. No matter what, I know you'll figure it out," my father said.

He sat down and poured heaps of sugar onto a thick slice he had just transferred to his plate.

Figuring out the right thing felt like a riddle that he expected me to solve on my own.

My mother, sitting quietly at the kitchen table reading the weekend paper, turned a page and said, "I like this idea. Finishing this course will be good for your future. It will increase your chances of getting into good programs in university."

University wasn't on my radar at all. My mind was set on becoming a full-time artist after the army. But the idea of changing things from within did appeal to me.

When I returned to base on Sunday morning, I decided to give my parents' plan a try. It seemed like I had no option but to pretend I was okay with the system and only later speak up. In high school, my acts of defiance against teachers had proved futile, and even cost me in the form of lower marks. There was a lesson there and I decided to heed my parents' advice.

But I couldn't stomach it—literally. With each passing day, my nausea and rage intensified. I was thinking about all my Sephardi/Mizrahi friends whose families came from places like Morocco, Egypt, Turkey, and Yemen who were just as capable and smart as the ones whose parents had been born in Poland, Hungary, or Russia.

On the multiple-choice exam that Friday morning, I intentionally marked the wrong answers on half of the questions.

"What happened, Sara?" Rina asked after pulling me aside.

"I don't know. I didn't really understand the material."

"You can ask us to explain things you know."

The following week, I repeated the strategy.

This time two instructors called me in for a chat.

"We figured out what you are doing," the male instructor said with a smirk. "But know this, failing the exam will not get you out, you will have to stay on base over the weekend and study until you pass," Rina said while stroking her long braid.

I fiercely denied that I was intentionally failing. It didn't help. That weekend, they kept me on base while my peers were allowed to go home. Instead, I had to study and rewrite the exam. I was furious.

OUT ON A STRETCHER

There is a saying that you can only get out of the Israeli army on a stretcher. So, I faked a health problem. I asked to see the doctor at the nearby base and told him I had a bladder infection. He scoffed at me. Doctors in the army expect soldiers to fake health problems to get out of certain units, courses or various duties like guarding or kitchen. For my plan to work, I had to make him take me seriously.

"My mother lost one kidney because of an untreated bladder infection. I am scared this will happen to me too," I wasn't lying about the first part.

I was also on the tail end of a previous bladder infection. If I was lucky, the urine test would still be positive. That's how much I wanted to get out of that damned course.

"I guess... Okay," the doctor said, frowning, and ordered several tests.

While awaiting the results I went to the clinic daily, complaining of worsening pain and a burning sensation. My act was so convincing that the army doctor sent me to have a CT scan of my kidneys and bladder. All looked quite normal, although my kidneys appeared to be positioned unusually, pressing on my bladder when I stand up.

But things could turn on a dime with a raging bladder infection, and I played this card fully.

Each time I went to the clinic or a test, I took my sweet time returning to base so that I'd miss as many lessons as possible. On the Friday tests, it wasn't hard to fail. I had mentally checked out.

All three instructors invited me for a chat. In a big and otherwise empty room, they sat behind a long table. Like a prisoner in a parole hearing, I sat in front of the stern-faces of higher-ranking soldiers, my fate hanging in the balance.

I once saw graffiti on an army base that read, *When you urinate on the army it gets wet, when the army urinates on you, you drown.* I hoped this scenario wouldn't materialize for me.

"Sara, we understand you're dealing with a potentially serious health issue," the instructor with the highest rank said, while the other two gave me a sideway glance. He felt more sympathetic, so I kept my gaze on him.

"Yes," I said, and my eyes welled up. They couldn't have known it but these were tears of joy as I inched closer towards freedom.

"The thing is all this missed time is causing you to fall behind. You'll have to decide whether to keep pursuing these medical appointments or stay in the course," the other female instructor said while tapping a pen on the table, something I've always found exceedingly annoying. I couldn't wait to get out of there.

"Umm… I wish I could do both, but I have to look after my health."

Miraculously, the tears of joy rolled down my face at exactly that moment. This was crucial, as I feared they'd put a note in my military file accusing me of using false claims to get out of the course. That would have had serious consequences for me, the equivalent of drowning in their urine.

Things have changed since those days and the discriminatory practice has ended. However, what happened to me after leaving the course made me often wish I'd bitten the bullet and stayed. But the values my father had instilled in me prevented me from complying. I didn't understand why he couldn't challenge the army on its discriminatory practices. If he truly believed in equality and in doing the right thing, he could have found a way to expose them without making it obvious I was his "source."

I knew he was against censorship, so he should have been outraged. He also saw how torn I was. I broke the army's rule of not speaking to journalists to tell him about this injustice. His refusal to investigate was another disappointment.

Aftermaths

From the psychometric discriminatory evaluation course, I bounced back to the general recruitment base where I had an interview for re-assignment purposes. I felt victorious. But where I landed was far worse: for months, I had to fight sexual advances by my commanding officer.

I was furious with my mother when she said, "Can't you just fluff him away?" At age eighteen, I didn't know how to do that, and besides, I said, "Why should he get away with this behaviour?"

Again, I went to my father for help over Saturday breakfast—the time when he was typically the most relaxed. It was embarrassing, but I was desperate enough, and so while he had his back to me frying challah, I said, "I don't know what to do. My commanding officer Katan is trying to get under my skirt and because I refuse, he's been punishing me."

My father turned to look at me and my face turned red hot.

An uncomfortable conversation followed, and by the time I finished explaining what was happening, I was sobbing.

"You know that you have recourse. You can submit a complaint to the Ombudsman for Soldiers, he said."

I didn't know that.

Four of us on the base launched a complaint. This happened a full ten years before the term "sexual harassment" was introduced to the public domain when in the US Anita Hill complained about her previous boss, the judge Clarence Thomas. We simply described our commanding officer's behaviours and the way he punished us when we rejected him.

The investigation took more than a year to conclude. Throughout, Katan was vindictive, sending his corporal after us to find petty violations to charge us with—not wearing a hat outdoors, not buttoning a blouse all the way to the neck and similar nonsense violations. The military police investigators assigned to our case treated us like criminals. But the four of us persevered. During the investigation, I became physically ill, and Katan didn't let me see a doctor on the adjacent base. Soldiers were not allowed to go to civilian clinics.

It was only when I collapsed that a fellow soldier drove me to the army clinic, semi-conscious. Another nightmare ensued—a genuine health crisis. All my lymph nodes ballooned, and I became jaundiced. The mere touch of clothes on my body felt like knives slicing through me. Some nights, I couldn't sleep at all. Blood tests showed my body was fighting something, but the army doctors couldn't figure out what. One doctor told me, "Your blood tests look like that of a cancer patient." Only after four months of repeated hospital stays did they conclude that I had complications from Mononucleosis.

"Had you been allowed to rest for two weeks in the beginning you would have recovered fully," a doctor told me before discharging me from a month-long stay at a convalescence facility for soldiers in the summer of 1981. I never fully recovered from the aftermath, and some years later was diagnosed with Fibromyalgia. Mono is considered a contributor for Fibromyalgia.

At the end of the legal process, Katan was found guilty and received something a tad harsher than a slap on the wrist. I learned from one of the women who joined the complaint that his upcoming rank bump was denied, and a stipulation was entered into his file that if another complaint like ours was made against him, he'd be discharged with no benefits—a serious blow to someone who planned to have a career in the army. We also found out that his wife left him during the investigation.

When I told my parents of the outcome, my father congratulated me for a battle well-fought. While I think I did the right thing by fighting officer Katan just as my father taught me, I paid a high price both in terms of the stress it caused and the long-term impact on my health.

Despite my knowledge of his affair with Dalia, I didn't know at the time that my father was a pathological womanizer, although rumours were already circulating that he "pursued anyone with a skirt." The full extent of his womanizing ways came to light only after a friend of mine who worked at *Haaretz* heard gossip. It was a full decade before she shared it with me and, to make me feel better, added that it looked like it was the culture at the newspaper's offices.

That didn't make me feel better, though. While it was not unusual for the times, it was still inexcusable.

I feel shame when I think about how my father may have used his position of power to obtain sexual favours. I wonder, too, if he saw himself in the officer who harassed his daughter and caused her so much anguish.

A Colossal Mess

After meeting my civil duties and completing the horrible army service, my plan was to work for a couple of years and save enough money to go on a trip and then to art school. But my father found a way to trick me. He noticed my frustration at my low-paying jobs and approached me one day with an offer: "Why don't you pick any program you want in university, and I'll pay for it. They have art programs, no?"

This was an interesting idea. Haifa University had an art program that involved creating art, while Tel Aviv University had only an academic Art History program. After researching my options, I told him, "Well, I am willing to try the program at Haifa University."

"Oh no, no. If you go to Haifa, you'll need an apartment there and we can't afford to pay for that too, only tuition. What about Tel Aviv?" my father asked.

"I'll only learn *about* art, not *do* art there. I'm not interested."

"Well, learning about art will make you a better artist," and he launched into a not-so-brief lecture on the great masters who learned from past masters and so on and so forth.

"But didn't they apprentice with them?" I asked.

"That's the deal. It's a good one," he asserted.

I wasn't convinced, but as time went on and I realized I had nothing to lose, I decided to accept his offer.

Within weeks of starting classes at the University of Tel Aviv, I realized I was actually *very* interested in the history of art and aced all my courses. I also discovered that when I like a subject, I do well in it. My poor performance in high school was very much tied to how boring the teaching methods were and how irrelevant everything felt.

Then, my father reneged on his promise. After paying for one semester, he said he couldn't continue paying. I was furious. I had trusted him and again, the man who claimed to occupy the highest moral ground in the country betrayed me. He did it only after he knew I was hooked, as I would describe to him with zeal what I was learning and how well I did.

Three part-time jobs totalling forty-eight hours a week paid for the rest of my education.

And during my first year, in 1983, I saw Katan sauntering on the university campus in civilian clothes. I took it to mean that he had been unable to control himself and was dishonourably discharged from the army.

In October of 1986, after completing the requirements for a BA in Art History (although I still had courses in Sociology and Anthropology, which I added after the second year), I travelled to Europe with a friend. We wanted to see up close some of the art from our textbooks. When I returned, my parents picked me up from the airport and we arrived home around midnight. My father carried my suitcase and bags up to the apartment door, kissed me on the forehead, said goodbye, and left. I stared at the door and turned to look at my mother, who stood in the living room next to my father's black leather armchair.

"Is he going to work? Is there another war?"

"No. Please, you need to sit down. I need to tell you something." She sat on my father's chair, pulled out a cigarette and asked if I wanted one.

"I don't smoke." I only smoked a few times during my army service for about a year to pass the time during night guard duties, but I didn't make it a habit.

Did she think I'd need one?

Seeing her pressed lips and tears in the corner of my mother's eyes, my heart sank.

"Okay, here it is. Hmm…Right after you left for Europe, your father confessed that he had a long-term affair."

"The coward…" I muttered.

My chest tightened as I watched my mother's quivering mouth and stream of tears.

She was trying to say something, but words wouldn't come out. Was she going to ask me to quit university and support her?

"And he has a three-year-old child."

Her words landed like a knife through my gut. My eyes darted between her and the door. What did she just say? I knew my father had had at least one affair. I remembered all the times people told my mother that her husband was seen with other women. I had flashbacks to the six weeks in 1977 when my mother was away, and he left every night and returned in the mornings with groceries. I remembered his mustard-coloured car near the other woman's home. Unlike my mother, I knew it was true. But could he have been that stupid, that irresponsible?

"Is it Dalia?"

"Yes."

Dammit. I should have said something back then. Oh God, it's my fault…

I tried hard to fight my tears. My mother leaned back. She puffed on her cigarette and looked at the door.

"You know," she suddenly said, "There was a story in the tabloids a couple of years ago saying, "A prominent married journalist from *Haaretz* has been having an affair with another journalist and has a child with her.""

Making shrieking sounds I'd never heard before, my mother sobbed for what seemed like eternity. I sat frozen, unable to offer a hug or words of support. I oscillated between guilt and anger with them both—my father for his betrayal and my mother for choosing denial.

Between sobs she said, "The humiliation!"

"How do you know that story was about Aba?"

After another long sob she said, "Come on. How many married journalists from *Haaretz* had affairs with another journalist and had a child?" Clearly, she had suspected something even before my father confessed, since she recalled this gossip piece.

After wiping her tears on her sleeves, my mother stood up and walked over to the side table to grab a box of tissues. She blew her nose and breathed deeply.

"The only reason they didn't put their names in the tabloid is because of their journalists' code. They don't gossip openly about each other." She was barely able to finish the sentence before she let out a scream so full of pain it pierced through my chest.

The cigarette butt in the ashtray died off and so did my life as I knew it.

"I'll never forgive him," I said. "Son of a bitch."

I'll never forgive myself either.

My mother and I both cried ourselves to sleep that night.

It's Complicated

The next day, I began my final year of Sociology and Anthropology. In addition to working twenty-four hours a week at a television station, I spent another ten hours a week selling car-towing memberships and doing three to four evening shifts relaying messages for a beeper company. I studied between jobs, in the library, on buses, or late at night, and slept on average four to five hours a night. Throughout the day, my only meal was a sandwich made at home. In retrospect, I see how my parents' push over the years to pursue post-secondary education lit a fire under me whenever I was losing steam. My father came every once in a while, to visit and to give my mother money. I asked her to warn me, and I'd be out of the house when he came.

It was at the television station that I met my future husband, Roni. He was a video editor, a year younger, and very handsome. I had refused his advances for a year out of a fear I'd develop the wrong reputation by dating someone at work. Rumours about affairs between married and unmarried directors or producers and their assistants circulated widely and I wasn't going to become fodder for gossip the way my father had been. But in the spring of 1985, I gave in and began dating Roni, on the condition that people at work wouldn't find out. Six months into our relationship, in the fall of 1986 and before I went on the trip to Europe with my friend, Roni told me he'd be moving to Toronto, Canada. He received permanent residency status based on his "needed occupation" as a video editor. I was heartbroken and assumed that we were done. With Roni gone, all I did was work and study and decided not to date for a while. He wrote me beautiful letters and repeatedly invited me to visit him after I finished university.

After my father left and moved in with his lover, my mother disintegrated bit by bit. I'd come home at night and find empty vodka bottles. On more than one occasion she called me at work threatening to kill herself and I'd rush back home, breathless. I'd then have to listen to her bad-mouth my father and recount the ways he'd ruined her life. How could he be so cruel? Outside our home he symbolized the highest moral values, but in his personal life he was a selfish jerk. He had moved on to a new relationship with yet another child he fathered, while remaining married to my mother and abandoning my younger brother. I was an adult by then, but my eleven-year-old brother was trapped with a barely functioning, depressed mother.

I begged her to find a therapist and she claimed that she had. Everything seemed to improve. I no longer saw empty vodka bottles and she stopped calling me at work, threatening suicide. It was a relief.

Then one December morning, before the start of midterm exams, I decided to stay home to study. Mickey was at school and wouldn't be home until four. Besides, it was cold and windy, and I didn't feel like taking the two buses to university only to go to the library to study and lose an hour of precious study time each way. By that time, we moved to Ramat Ha-Sharon, north of Tel Aviv.

"Aren't you going to university or work today?" my mother asked when she found me making tea in the kitchen.

"Not today. I'm going to study for an exam at home,"

"Oh," she said and left the kitchen. I went to my bedroom to study and could tell she called someone. I couldn't decipher what she whispered about on the phone, nor did I care. Five minutes later, she knocked on my door and opened it and in an unusually soft tone said, "Isn't it better to study in the library, though? There are so many distractions at home with the phone ringing and me cooking."

"I'll be fine. I'll put my Walkman on."

She left my room again and banged pots in the kitchen. Was she doing this on purpose? What was wrong with her?

Minutes later, she barged into my room, pushing the glass door so hard it almost shattered. "I need you to get out of the house for a few hours." She fired the words fast.

"What the hell?"

"Well, I don't want you to say anything about this," she said and paused. "Aba is coming here soon."

"So... I don't need to talk to him. I'll stay in my room."

Seeing what his indiscretion had done to my mother, and how upset my younger brother was, made me feel disgust whenever his name was mentioned, and I still didn't want to see him. But that day, I needed to study so I thought it would be okay just to stay in my room while he was visiting.

"No, you don't understand. It's complicated."

"What is?"

"This, us."

"What you mean?"

"Aba and I are having an affair."

"Ahhhhhh!" A shriek escaped from my throat before I could block it. She jumped back, as I'd never done that before. My breath, and the rest of the scream suspended between my lungs and trachea.

"You're not serious," I said when I found words again.

"I told you not to say anything about it!" my mother yelled.

I threw my books and notebooks into my backpack and left the apartment, slamming the door as hard as I could. I hated the drama of it all.

Working or studying that day was out of the question. I sat in the library, trying to stop myself from sobbing.

I hated my parents and my life. My father left three months earlier to live with the other woman and was now having an affair on her with my mother?!

What the fuck is wrong with him? Does he miss the thrill of fearing he'd be caught?

My level of disgust with them both was incalculable. Was my mother so weak she had to take him back after what he put her through?

I desperately wanted to unload the details of this crazy plot but who could I talk to? It was too embarrassing to tell even my closest friends. I had the most fucked up family in Israel, I decided. I couldn't take it anymore. So, I made the decision to accelerate my course work, take overlapping courses in the spring, finish my Sociology degree in half the time, and forget about trying for good grades. Then, I would apply to the Criminology program in the Hebrew University in Jerusalem and maybe also to the MA program in Art History at the Sorbonne. I'd find a way to pay for it on my own and I'd never, ever, live with my parents again.

The alternative was to stay and lose my sanity. Every day, it felt like the pressure in my chest was going to crush my lungs.

It was while sorting out my grad-school plans that I accepted Roni's invitation to visit him in Canada. I didn't talk to my father about it and did not see him before I left. I didn't want to know about his new life with Dalia and about his child with her. I didn't want to hear how he moved on yet again to another family, the way he did when he had an affair on his first wife with my mother.

"You know he is unhappy with Dalia, and she is annoyed with his habits," my mother told me one day.

"Stop it," I told her. "I don't want to hear anything about him."

Was she trying to console herself with the fact he was unhappy, or was she hoping he'd come back to her? I prayed he wouldn't ask to come back and that if he did, she'd tell him to F-off, despite their rendezvous.

On April 16, 1987, a day after completing the requirements for my degrees from Tel-Aviv University, I flew to Toronto. As the cliché goes, the rest is history. Staying with Roni in Canada was both an escape and the beginning of a new life.

I had packed light: one medium-sized suitcase with a few clothes and my warmest winter jacket, which was the equivalent of a windbreaker in Canada. Aside from my wardrobe, I consciously chose to leave in Israel the excess baggage of my childhood and dysfunction of my family. It meant severing my relationship with my father. The present and the future were my focus, and I wasn't going to give him a second thought. The world might have held him in high regard as a fighter for social justice and truth, but that was not the person I knew. I couldn't see beyond his shadow. Any good memories of the past associated with him were buried under the weight of his lies and betrayal and all the ways he disappointed me.

The *Haaretz* journalist and past editor Ran Kislev cast a long shadow, and it was time for me to step out of it. I needed to know who I was besides being "the daughter of." I also needed to protect my sanity.

After I left Israel, my father returned home. He had left like a coward, and he returned like a coward. I was furious with my mother for taking him back.

If he answered the phone when I called, I was curt and cold and asked to talk to my mother. Occasionally, I engaged in a brief conversation with him.

It would take an act of God for me to resume a relationship with him that would be more than civilized.

Unfortunately, that act of God was my mother's diagnosis of Stage IV Breast Cancer in 1989. Devastated, my father took an indefinite leave from *Haaretz* to care for her. He still went to the Sunday-morning executive meetings, but for the most part he stopped writing. He became a devoted husband, a driver, a cook, and a nurse. When my mother reported this to me, I decided it was impractical not to speak to him when I lived abroad. I decided to set aside my feelings about his affair.

"It's between the two of them," my close friends told me repeatedly. I was finally ready to butt out and be nice to him. I had always wanted less drama in my life anyway. Maybe the geographical cure, the physical ocean between us, could help create a bridge across the metaphorical one.

Pseudo-normal

Roni and I first married in a civil ceremony in Canada in January of 1989. Later that year, we succumbed to pressure from his parents to have a traditional Jewish wedding in Israel. We agreed that under the condition they would plan everything and we'd just show up.

In July I called to tell my parents about the planned wedding in late August. Being the opinionated man my father was, he tried to convince me not to go through with the traditional religious wedding.

"Why don't you and Roni avoid the hassle and save thousands of dollars on a wedding and just go on a trip somewhere?" he said over the phone.

"I don't think it will cost us money. The gifts will cover the cost."

"Don't be sure about this," he said in his usual sarcastic way.

"I'm pretty sure Aba. Just give me your and mom's guest list and don't worry about it."

The venue was open-air, on the beach between Tel Aviv and Old Jaffa. It was a very hot and humid evening without the slightest breeze. Yet, the dancing continued into the early morning hours.

I didn't want him or my biological father, Yoav, to walk me down the aisle, but Roni had a solution, "Why don't we have my dad and Ran walk me and your mom and mine walk you?" I hesitated.

"Don't give people a reason to talk," he said, knowing I hated gossip. So I agreed.

I expected the high-and-mighty journalist, Ran Kislev, to frown the whole evening and scoff at the "ethnic" or Mizrahi music, the *kululus* and the Mediterranean-style dancing. But he surprised me by being jovial and prancing all evening. I thought he was a good sport, although he loved parties and dancing and drinking, so perhaps it wasn't that hard for him to do.

My guest list for the wedding consisted of fewer than fifty people. Yet, the total number of guests was six-hundred and fifty. The extra six hundred were a mix of Roni's large family and friends and his father's work colleagues. Even though several guests gave us (the same) cookbooks, as well as other mostly unmemorable presents, the monetary gifts covered all the expenses, including our flight to Israel, our wedding attires, and even an extra two-thousand dollars. Clearly, my father's concerns had been misguided.

The day after the wedding, my parents told me they were glad we went through with the traditional wedding, and that it was best day of their lives. I was delighted, considering the fact my mother had been given just six to twelve months to live.

After one year in Canada, I realized my earning potential was dismal with a BA in Art History and Sociology & Anthropology, so I applied and was accepted to a BA program in Psychology at York University and subsequently continued to complete a master's and a doctorate at the University of Toronto. The girl who had hated school with a passion, and had a less-than-average high-school diploma discovered she excelled when she studied something she was interested in. She was even winning merit scholarships.

This brought my parents much joy and pride.

My mother went into remission twice after diagnosis and treatment. My father finally agreed to travel with her to Europe, and she came to visit me once in Toronto, between recurrences. In total, she lived for four and half years, much longer than her prognosis and long enough to meet her first granddaughter, Sivan.

I was grateful for my father's devotion to my mother during this challenging time which allowed me to focus on my studies and on my infant daughter.

During my mother's final months, my father was in full-blown denial and did not tell me my mother was bedridden and dying. Only thanks to my mother-in-law's intervention I managed to say goodbye to my mother in person. After my mother's passing in March of 1994, my father became severely depressed and told me he feared he couldn't go on and begged me to stay longer. Despite knowing this would set me back in university, I extended my stay from the original two and half weeks to two and a half months. During that time, he took us to the Tel Aviv Country Club and on many day trips, the beach and to local parks. Sivan took her first steps during that time and when she turned a year old in Israel, he threw a delightful birthday party for her. I was both surprised and grateful that he stepped into this role with such enthusiasm and our daily excursions were a reprieve from the grief for my mother's passing.

After returning to Canada, I made the choice to maintain regular contact with my father. Roni had a large family, and both his parents were still alive, so I wanted my children to get to know my side of their family, too, growing up. It was small, just my father Ran, brother Mickey, and my mother's sister and her husband. There was also my biological father Yoav, his two stepchildren, and my half-sister Haley. I kept in touch with my siblings and I love them dearly, but my relationship with Yoav was conflicted due to the kind of things my mother told me about him and their relationship. Over time I saw him less.[4]

As a Saba ("grandpa" in Hebrew), my father did not disappoint. He functioned well in the role, in a pseudo-normal kind of way. Still, my view of him had not improved, and so, as many adult children do, I kept in touch only for the benefit of my daughters. While we didn't have a sweet and harmonious relationship during my teens, and we didn't vibe in my early adulthood, our relationship was only sometimes off-key after my mother's passing.

Following my mother's death, my father and I established a pattern in which we pretended that he was a normal father and that I had a normal family of origin, albeit more interesting than most. On my annual visits to Israel, he played the role of a doting grandfather to my daughters and bought them expensive gifts. His generosity extended to numerous memorable excursions. A visit to the safari in Ramat Gan (yes, Israel has a so-called safari) was but one example of when my daughters got a taste of what it was like to grow up with Ran Kislev as a father. He entertained the girls by pretending to be a monkey and showed them around. Driving through the area where lions dwelt, I offhandedly said, "I hope we can get a good photo of the lions."

Before I could object, my father drove close to where several lions and lionesses napped in the shade. He got out of the car and said, "Let's go!"

"What are you doing?" I yelled. "Come back!"

"Relax, you'll wake them up. They're asleep."

"Not anymore," I said as I watched one lion lift his head to look in our direction. "Come back Aba, it's dangerous," and the old fist in my stomach clenched.

There was a clear warning not to get out of the car in this area. He scoffed at me as he got back in the car. We never got that *National Geographic* shot, although I snapped a quick one from the car.

There was also the time he offered my then-fourteen-year-old daughter Sivan a "great cognac from Poland" straight from the barrel he brought from there.

---

4. I've written about the reasons at length in a memoir focusing on my mother, not yet published.

Occasionally, my father showed interest in my life, too, and I expressed cursory interest in his, more along the lines of "Where are you traveling to next?" and "Which movies did you see recently?" He also introduced me to books by the writer I subsequently considered the best living American author (until he sadly passed in 2024), Paul Auster, when he gave me the books *The Moon Palace* and *Timbuktu.*

Certain subjects were off limits between us. I could not talk to him about my work because he said more than once that "psychology is not a real profession". I could not talk about the way he abandoned his two children from his first marriage and the son he fathered with Dalia, because the one time I did bring it up, he yelled at me to mind my own business. We never discussed actions or lack thereof that impacted our relationship directly, including his outright lies and double life during my childhood, or his refusal to use his connections and pull me out of Geula school while I was mercilessly bullied and beaten. We also didn't go near his racism and prejudice, his irresponsible spending (some obviously on lovers) while not paying bills or how he stopped paying my tuition, his thrill-seeking behaviours and choices that put him and our whole family at risk, to name a few forbidden topics. Still, he was the father who raised me and the only grandparent on my side that my daughters knew at the time.

Just like Israel and Egypt had done in 1977 when they swept memories of past wars and occasional skirmishes under the proverbial rug, I chose pretence for the sake of peace. If truth and reconciliation are needed for complete repair, truth was missing from this unspoken covenant between us.

While I lost respect for him in my youth due to his personal failings, later in life, I recognized that he had had a significant impact on Israeli society and had a good understanding of its history. On one of my solo visits to Israel after my father fully retired in the early 2000s, we were sitting in his living room sipping tea and munching on a variety of sweets and savoury treats he bought earlier that day. He knew I liked cheese-filled pastries, poppy seed cakes, and *rugelachs*, and rather than choose one kind he bought all of them. Excess was always how he handled decisions.

Since he retired in his seventies, I wanted to know how he was keeping busy.

"Oh, you know. I play tennis three times a week, Bridge twice a week, go to the theatre, read. I'm quite busy."

"But are you excited about anything like you were when you wrote?" I asked.

"I am getting used to a quieter, more relaxed lifestyle. It's not so bad," he said and filled my plate with more pastries.

"Why don't you write a book reflecting on your life's work and Israeli so-ciety over the decades?" I asked later as we were putting the dishes away in the kitchen. "A journalist doesn't just observe, he participates in the lives of the people and society he writes about and affects them. Your late-in-life reflections and analysis can be meaningful and have educational and historical value."

"Eh…it's yesterday's news, nobody cares. Didn't I teach you anything?" he said and laughed.

My suggestion was, in part, the result of seeing what happens to my clients who retire and suddenly find themselves with nothing to do, how depressed they become. But maybe it was my laziness, wishing my father would summar-ize his life work for me, given that I had never read a single article he wrote. His work life had always represented a mystery to me. It was a part of his life that caused tension in our lives, invited strange people to inhabit our world, and where illicit affairs began. My unwillingness to read his articles might have been a way of rejecting or avoiding that part of his life.

Six

On a cold, late-November day in 2010, I was savouring a latté in my kitchen in Toronto, when my cell phone buzzed. It was my brother Mickey. In a broken voice he told me our father had a stroke while attending a journalism convention in Eilat, a resort town by the Red Sea on the border between Israel and Egypt.

My father's poor impulse control, which included decades of heavy smoking, frequent alcohol consumption and an unhealthy diet filled with animal fat and mostly devoid of fruits and vegetables, had caught up with him.

I felt a tug at my heart that surprised me when it turned into sadness and fear of loss.

"You might want to come to Israel," my brother said.

On the morning of November 29, I landed in Israel and made my way to the neurological intensive care unit of Ichilov Hospital in Tel Aviv.

"It's not visiting hours. Come back at four," the nurse at the desk of the unit said.

"Can't you make an exception? I just arrived from Canada. I'm his daughter and I want him to see me, just in case, you know..." as tears rolled down my face.

The small-framed nurse gave me a slanted look, and my quivering mouth and tears did the rest.

"Be very quiet, I'm giving you two minutes," and she let me enter the big room occupied by five patients attached to machines, each partially hidden behind a curtain. She pulled back one blue curtain and there, under tubes and wires and an oxygen mask, lay a limp pile of limbs belonging to my father.

All his flaws, as deep as they had seemed to me just hours before, evaporated.

Two minutes beside him were enough to confirm what I already understood from thousands of miles away—I wasn't ready to say goodbye to him. I put my hand on his and whispered, "I'll be back later." He stirred and his eyes fluttered. With his undamaged hand, he lifted the oxygen mask slightly. I pulled the curtain a bit so the nurse in the room wouldn't notice. His lips moved—what was he saying? I drew closer.

"You came…"

"Yes, Aba. I'm here. It's not visiting hours, so I'll go now and come back later."

He nodded and stirred again but soon after slipped back into unconsciousness.

Despite abandoning them when he left their mother so he could be with mine, his older children, Yoram and Irit, came to see him in the hospital, too. In fact, Yoram rode his motorcycle all the way to Eilat when he heard about the stroke and helped facilitate the transfer to the hospital in Tel Aviv.

The staff told us that the stroke affected mostly his left side, and that his first few days in the hospital had been touch-and-go. My father wanted to die rather than spend another moment in a body that couldn't do what he wanted it to. I wondered if he might have prayed to the God he didn't believe in.

"Can you get me a Coke?" he whispered one morning as I stood with Yoram by his bedside. He pulled the oxygen mask off with his good hand and waited for us to respond.

"Aba, the nurses say you shouldn't drink anything as you might accidentally let liquid reach your lungs and you'll get pneumonia. They give you enough fluids by IV."

"No Kooka! I don't care about getting pneumonia. I want Coke. Let me have one small pleasure," and through all the wires and despite his frailness he squinted his blue eyes and scowled.

An invisible hand squeezed my heart.

Yoram and I were unsure how to handle this. We exchanged looks and eventually gave in and secretly brought in a small can of Coke. Yoram motioned me to close the curtain and stand guard while he helped our father have this small and possibly deadly pleasure.

The next day, my father sent me to buy another can.

"Can you lift my head up and bring the straw close to my mouth?" he asked.

In one stroke of misfortune, our roles had reversed.

Acquiescing to his demands over the coming days, I was terrified we may have caused him pneumonia.

On the third day, Yoram and I were caught, scolded, and kicked out of the unit.

A steady stream of friends and relatives came to the hospital, and we'd meet in the visitors' waiting area. My brother Mickey, my step-siblings, and I spent many hours there. Several friends of my father came and those who didn't know me asked who I was. Most knew my mother, so they nodded when I explained. Irit and I waited one afternoon for the nurse to let us in as one of my father's acquaintances who didn't know I existed asked, "So how many children does Ran have?"

Years of playing tennis at the Country Club couldn't undo a poor diet and decades of heavy smoking.

"Six," Irit said.

"You mean five," I said.

"No, actually six."

"Check your math, it's five."

To make my point I counted slowly on one hand and said, "You, Yoram, me, Mickey and Ari, (Dalia's son)."

"Yes, and there is the son he had in Poland from an earlier affair. This one was born between me and Yoram," Irit said holding her two hands with the sixth finger in view. This was a patch in the quilt of my father's life I did not know about.

I laughed, hysterically, bending to hold my belly. When I had calmed down, I said, "Oh my God. Another child? Another secret?"

How come he never mentioned this one?

I suddenly became self-conscious that a friend of our father was watching all of this unfold. I excused myself and took the elevator down to the lobby to process it alone.

When I thought about it more, it made sense. My father was very good at walking away. He did it to Yoram and Irit when he left their mother to be with mine. He did it to my mother and my younger brother when he left for Dalia, and he did it to Dalia's son when he returned to my mother. Leaving and not looking back was his modus operandi.

But now, this deeply flawed father of mine was lying in a broken body, teetering between life and death. I realized I was not ready to lose the man who refused to be reminded that I wasn't his biological daughter. It was no time to judge him.

121

Trapped

Instead of developing a deadly complication that he'd have welcomed, my father would live, trapped in a body he resented, for another two-and-half miserable years.

At first, he chose to believe the rehabilitation staff who told him he'd be able to walk one day and resume a semblance of independence. The damage was mostly to one side of his body and had not affected his cognitive functioning. He pushed himself hard and when that didn't translate to independent mobility, he became despondent.

After his health providers told him he'd never walk again, he asked me during my next visit in 2011, "What's the point of this life?"

"What do you mean?" I asked, pretending I didn't understand what he was referring to.

"I can't travel, can't drive or go anywhere on my own, I am useless. It's my bad luck I survived the stroke and that it damaged my body and not my brain, so I know how bad my situation is."

"But there are so many things you can still enjoy," I said as a good daughter does—one who is also a psychologist. Another time, he surprised me when he asked to put my psychology hat on and help him cope, but then he negated all my ideas with "yes but's", just as my more challenging clients had done over the years. Usually these were people dealing with addictions, and their resistance sounded like, "Yes but, I can't ask my wife not to bring alcohol home", or "Yes but all my friends use cocaine, so I won't have a social life if I stop using." My father's most passionate objection was, "Yes but, if I can't look after Magda, what is the purpose of my existence?"

Magda was his common-law wife following the death of my mother. They had known each other in the old country and had kept in touch over the years. After she had mild strokes, she declined cognitively, and my father looked after her. He seemed to be invested in a caregiving role, and this made me think of the nearly five years from 1989-1994 that he dedicated to becoming my mother's full-time caregiver. Although he drove my mother crazy at times with his controlling behaviour, his intention was good. I had witnessed this directly during my mother's final days, as well.

All his life, he didn't know how to be sick and rarely took a pill, other than the occasional pain medication for a hangover or back pain. He lived in a healthy body most of his life and went from playing tennis in the country club three times a week, playing bridge, going to the theatre, travelling around the world and looking after Magda, to being confined to a wheelchair. He didn't know how to live in a disabled body. If he couldn't function independently and couldn't be useful in the way he recognized as valuable, there was no point to his life. He saw himself as nothing more than a burden. Now, in a cruel twist of fate, after his stroke, my father had completely lost control over his life and his body. Once he realized he'd never walk, he stopped trying.

Seeing me and his granddaughters during our post-stroke visits appeared to please him. My older daughter Sivan speaks Hebrew fluently, so it was easy for them to communicate and my younger daughter Maya, whose Hebrew was more limited made him happy, probably because she looks so much like the woman he referred to as "the love of his life," my mother, in her younger years.

After his stroke, my father and Magda had a full-time caregiver, Jadwiga. She was Christian Polish, a strong, hard-working woman in her fifties.

He had returned to Poland many times in recent years with Magda and his Polish friends. Polish culture and language remained strong in him, embedded in his DNA, and he embraced it again after my mother died.

Jadwiga was easy to communicate with, and a year or so after his stroke, she reported to me that my father was asking to die, that he tried to starve himself but was taken to a hospital. I was both angry and sad to hear it. A part of me wished he could end his suffering in a decent way, assisted by a physician. But that's not a possibility in Israel, where the preservation of life is the highest value.

Another part of me, which surprised me, was not ready to let him go.

The Past Shows Up

A thought that nagged at me since my father's stroke was that I knew so little about his life during the war and in Poland—before he emigrated to Israel. I left the past in the past, as he demanded. During visits and phone calls, we kept things mostly light, talking about movies and books and kvetching about Israeli politics.

Decades after the last time I asked him about his childhood, my younger daughter Maya asked me to tell her about her grandfather's life. She was working on a high-school project exploring family history.

"Tell me about Saba Ran, where was he during the war. What was his life in Poland like?" she asked.

On a sunny and cold winter afternoon in our sun-filled kitchen in Toronto, I was embarrassed to admit how little I knew.

"I mostly know stuff about his journalistic career and his life in Israel. He rarely spoke about his past, so all I know about his life before are a few anecdotes," I said. I told her what my father said about the Jewish community of his hometown, Chestohova, and that he spent time in a gulag in Siberia, and also that he was a partisan.

"What's a gulag?" she asked.

"That's what they called the forced-labour prison camps in Siberia. The Russians sent political prisoners and petty criminals there and they lived in horrible conditions, starving and being beaten. Some people say it was a version of concentration camps and that maybe the Nazis got ideas from them. It's believed that over a million people died there."

"And Saba Ran was there? Wow."

"Yes, for part of the war. But he never said much about that."

"Oh. Maybe we can find more about him online," she said, and before I could say "I doubt it" she Googled her grandfather's name and said, "I found something."

THE PAST SHOWS UP

I assumed she was looking at a few references to my father's articles in various books, like the one mentioned in one of Noam Chomsky's books and by other more obscure authors. While she read quietly and took notes, I decided to look for information about Chestohova. I dove head-first into the rabbit hole as I found intriguing historical information, like the fact that Poland's most renowned monastery, Jasna Gora (Bright Mountain), happens to be in Chestohova. It is the center of Polish Catholicism and the third largest pilgrimage site for Catholics around the world. The church inside it contains what is considered a miraculous icon of the Black Madonna also known as The Queen of Poland.

The earliest documented presence of Jews in my father's birth town dates back to 1620 and 1631. In 1705, a Jewish man called Mosiek loaned money to the Council of the City of His Royal Highness so they could pay a duty imposed on Chestohova by the Swedes. The first Jewish cemetery and synagogue in the town were built in the early 1800s. The town became a major industrial hub in the late 1800s, second only to Lodz. Jews established some of the biggest factories including those making products from metals and factories of toys, textiles and devotional items. Despite episodes of antisemitism, Jews established strong ties with non-Jewish Poles in all areas, especially in industry. There were numerous Jewish newspapers and magazines published locally as well. Many secular Jews belonging to the Haskala movement, or Jewish Enlightenment, inhabited Chestohova and in the late nineteenth century built the so-called New Synagogue. Perhaps my father's family, if they belonged to any synagogue, were members of this one, which was set on fire on Christmas Day of 1939.

While I read about Chestohova, Maya made a remarkable discovery. Unbeknownst to me or my brother Mickey, our father had given an interview for a project on Polish Jews that was posted to a website called the *Virtual Shtetl* or the *Museum of the History of Polish Jews*. An entry for my father under the name "Ran Kislev (Wexler)" contained a treasure trove of information and images. It filled many gaps in my father's origin story.

I learned that Moshe Wexler—my father's father—was born in 1890 in Chestohova. A descendant of a well-off family, he was also the co-owner of a factory that manufactured various bicycle parts, exporting them to England. The financial situation at home was very good, and Moshe's income was five times the average salary at the time. Moshe's brother, Romek Wexler, was the owner of a factory that manufactured toys.

Rivka Wainreich, my father's mother, was born in 1892. She came from a family of rabbis known as the Radomsk Hassidic Dynasty, dating back to 1843. It was the third-largest dynasty of rabbis in Poland after Ger and Alexander.

When Rivka married outside the Orthodox community, her family disowned her. She was obviously a rebel and must have married for love.

Reading this sent Maya and I into a discussion about secular versus religious Jews.

"Maybe that's why your dad hated religion," Maya said, and we laughed about the religious holiday deprivation I'd experienced as a child.

In the Polish *Virtual Shtetl* site interview, my father shared that he studied in a private Jewish elementary school. My brother told me that our father had private Hebrew lessons and the only word he retained was, "sus", horse.

Studying Jewish subjects was forbidden, as was participation in Zionist youth movements. The lessons were conducted in Polish and all the teachers were Jews. However, for my father and his parents this was not an issue, as they were secular.

"I guess it's like in North America. Some Jewish families send their kids to private Jewish schools, either because they think they are better or…", I said.

"Because they wanted them to be around other Jewish kids," my daughter completed the thought. "Good thing you sent me to the local public school, I like that I have friends of different religions."

"It's weird that you know so little about Saba," Maya said as she gathered the material she printed from the *Virtual Shtetl* website.

So many things about my father were confusing, in great part because I didn't have a context for them growing up and in part because I was afraid to ask.

Fragments of information from my mother, combined with tidbits he reluctantly shared, and those I passively gathered over the years by listening to adult conversations, do not add up to a complete narrative.

As a parent I strived to do the opposite—I told my daughters as much as I could about my childhood, my family history as I knew it, the wars I'd lived through, the childhood neglect and abandonment I experienced at a young age. Usually, I lessened the impact by infusing humour and leaving out certain details. Maybe there was some denial in that I didn't want to burden them with trauma stories. What would be the value of telling them that I wandered into a minefield under my parents' watch? They did know, however, about the Savoy Hotel terror attack, the car accident, and that I had a friend who disappeared when I was twelve. And I showed them the many ways I overcame these and how art, friendships, doing meaningful work, therapy, a loving husband, and having children had saved me. When they saw me spend weekends painting in the kitchen, they understood it was more than a hobby. From time to time, I told them about their ancestry, not just the suffering and losses, but also that they come from a line of resilient survivors. Although Saba Ran was a step-grandfather, his resilience had significantly impacted me and therefore trickled down to them as a positive emotional inheritance.

I had been able to name for my daughters the ways my parents' extremely stressful life events, that I knew of, might have explained their dysfunction. I wanted them to feel compassion towards their grandparents rather than judgement. I did enough judging for all of us. My daughters' sad faces increased my empathy for my parents. I told my daughters how my parents grew up during the war, had troubled relationships with their own parents, later with spouses and finally with some of their own children. My daughters needed that context to understand my hang-ups and occasional freak-outs when they were away from me and didn't answer my calls or texts. Severe separation- and loss-anxiety was another part of my emotional inheritance.

When it came to my mother's past, I had more background information because she spoke about her father disappearing from her life when she was two years old, just before the start of WWII, and about the danger they were in. I knew about her difficulties being a war child and being uprooted several times. Eventually, after the war, at age thirteen, she and her mother reunited with her father in America. But the relationship with her father never recovered from the long separation and her experience of abandonment. As for my father, I had only very broad strokes about his early years.

The psychologist in me wanted to understand him so the daughter would be able to forgive his weaknesses and misdeeds. But I wasn't there yet.

Scanning briefly what my father shared in the interview for the Polish website, I saw that it would shed light on his life during the darkest period in his life up to that point—as well as the darkest period in Jewish and maybe human history. I printed the pages and saved them in a "Stuff About Dad" folder.

I put the folder aside for when my mind would be ready to understand, and my heart would be ready to soften.

Death, and a
Birth of an Idea

In 2013, two years after his stroke, my father's health took a nosedive and I was in regular contact with Yoram, Mickey, and the caregiver Jadwiga. Yoram was visiting my father regularly, taking him for fresh air in a wheelchair, and reported to me in brief emails what he observed. I travelled twice to Israel in March of that year—when my mother-in-law was on her deathbed, and again after her passing on March 21st. On these visits I witnessed my father's rapid decline. I knew the end was near for him, too, and we spoke about Do Not Resuscitate and other difficult subjects, like his wish to die at home.

I was thrilled that he called in May to wish me a happy 51st birthday. It was the last time we had a proper conversation, although it was difficult to understand him. Jadwiga sent me photos of him while he talked with me, and I was horrified to see his emaciated state. I told my clients I might be leaving at short notice, and after an urgent call at the end of May, I flew to Israel.

I arrived on June 2. When I walked into his room, he opened his eyes for a moment and with much effort said, "You're here", then drifted into a state in between life and no-more until crossing fully to the other side ten days later.

Ran Kislev, born Herman Wexler, took his last breath on June 13, 2013. Thirteen is a lucky number for Jews and it was for my father who was anxious to part with his physical body. We couldn't bury him within twenty-four hours as is required by Jewish burial laws. This law is informed by Kohelet (Ecclesiastes in English) 12:7: "And the dust returns to the earth as it was, and the spirit returns to God, who gave it." The natural decomposition of the body into the earth facilitates the expeditious return of the soul to its source, to God.

In a final act of rebellion, my father violated this rule, too. But it was not all his own doing. For ten years, all three of us—my father, brother, and me—had neglected to visit my mother, buried in the double plot my father bought before she died. Shamefully, we only discovered on the day he passed that the vacant side of the plot had been overtaken by what had begun as a little bush then grown into a full-size tree. Its roots crawled under neighbouring graves, threatening to expose them. As if I needed more proof that ignoring things doesn't make them go away and in fact can be costly.

At a great cost, we hired a company to grind the roots and chop the enormous tree. Mickey and his wife Shira coordinated the effort and supervised it. The operation lent itself to Magritte-like photos taken by Shira, which she sent me as the job progressed.

"Small bush"? (Photos courtesy of Shira Kislev). The Magritte like scene.

We barely managed to get it done and have the plot ready in time to receive our father on June 16.

The heat was oppressive when we buried him.

Taking refuge in the shadow of a tree, I turned towards the sound of gravel crunching as a car came to a stop near the burial ground. The driver's side door opened, and a figure emerged from a cloud of dust. He walked towards me with purpose—a man in his seventies, deeply tanned, in dark glasses.

"Are you Ran Kislev's daughter?" he said, nearly out of breath.

"Yes, I am."

He shook my hand vigorously. "My name is Jonathan and I'm The Source."

"Hmm?" was all I managed to say as I stared at him.

My brother Mickey joined us and said, "You know what he means, right? Aba's source. The organized crime series—the anonymous source."

I almost lost my balance as I processed this fact. I'd heard references to The Source many times over the years, but his identity had remained a mystery. Now here he was, revealing it to us.

"I'm so sorry for your loss," he said and in the same breath added, "I knew your father very well and admired him. He was one of the last great journalists in Israel. I wish I could stay, but I have to go to another funeral on my wife's side of the family. I'll try to come to the Shiva," and he gave me his card. I tucked it into my purse.

One of my father's children had to identify him before he would be wrapped in shrouds and lowered into the ground. No one was willing to do it. Shira offered to come in with me, and so I did it.

I was also the only one of his children to prepare and read a eulogy, although Mickey gave me his input when I worked on it. I spoke, among other things, about my father's love of the country and the values he instilled in me and how he tricked me to go to university. His long-time secretary spoke and there were several journalists in attendance—the current editor-in-chief and owner of *Haaretz* and many friends, mostly Polish and only those who were still ambulatory.

Although I didn't know yet in 2013 if or what kind of book I'd be writing, I knew I had to interview The Source. It was a unique opportunity to find out about a part of my father's life that was hidden from me, through someone who was directly involved in my father's breakout series. Jonathan was an insider in every sense of the word.

After the funeral, we emailed a few times and zeroed in on June 22, a day before I was to fly back to Canada. I was staying with my father-in-law in Tel-Aviv, and when he was out for a few hours that day, I conducted the interview in his bright living room. The well-dressed man in his seventies showed up on time and I offered him tea and biscuits. Once seated, I brought out a blank notebook.

Our aromatic cups of fresh mint tea were left untouched as we embarked on the most fascinating conversation I've ever had about my father.

"You know, for the whole week before I found out your father died, I felt unease and thought about Ran a lot. I tried looking for him at the Bialik apartment. When I couldn't find him, I called Avi Valentin who told me Ran just passed away."

Avi Valentin was a journalist in *Haaretz*, too, and published follow-up articles about organized crime in Israel.

"Oh, my parents moved out of there in the '80s", I said. "Anyway, had you found him that week, he would've already been in a coma," and I told him about the stroke my father suffered in Eilat at the end of 2010.

We sat quietly for a while and I watched his serious face, waiting for him to continue. I was quite nervous and worried that he'd notice my trembling hands. I have a condition called an Essential Tremor and it gets much worse when I'm anxious.

"Ran was a man of life," Jonathan broke the silence. "Death doesn't become him."

I burst out laughing and so did he. After that I breathed more easily and opened my notebook.

"So true," I said. "At least he lived a long and exciting life. He milked it for all its worth."

"Well, tell me what you want to know," Jonathan said.

Parents at my wedding, 1989.

Pre-wedding party, Iraqi-Jewish style (me in the black t-shirt).

With Roni at the wedding, 1989.

Being a "sport".

On trip to Europe with my mother, post cancer diagnosis, 1992.

Sivan's first birthday.

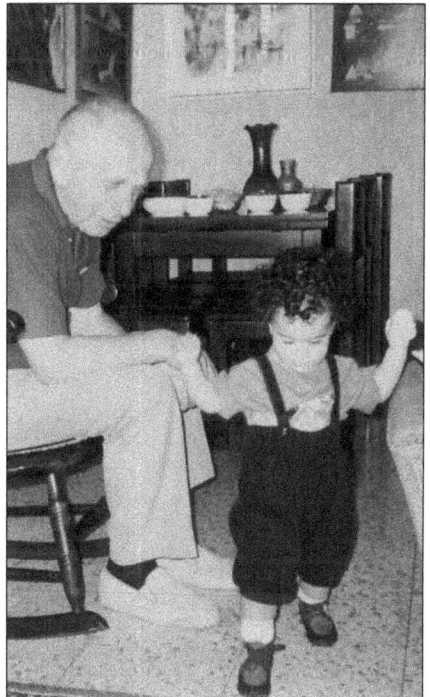

Sivan's first steps at Saba Ran's.

March 1994 Double plot with my mother's tombstone on the right, small bush on the left.

Lions at the Ramat-Gan Safari before escaping their jaws…or yawns.

Politely tolerating flavoured/spicy Iraqi food with my in-laws (Asher and Tikva), with Sivan and Maya.

Part II

The After: Mending the Quilt

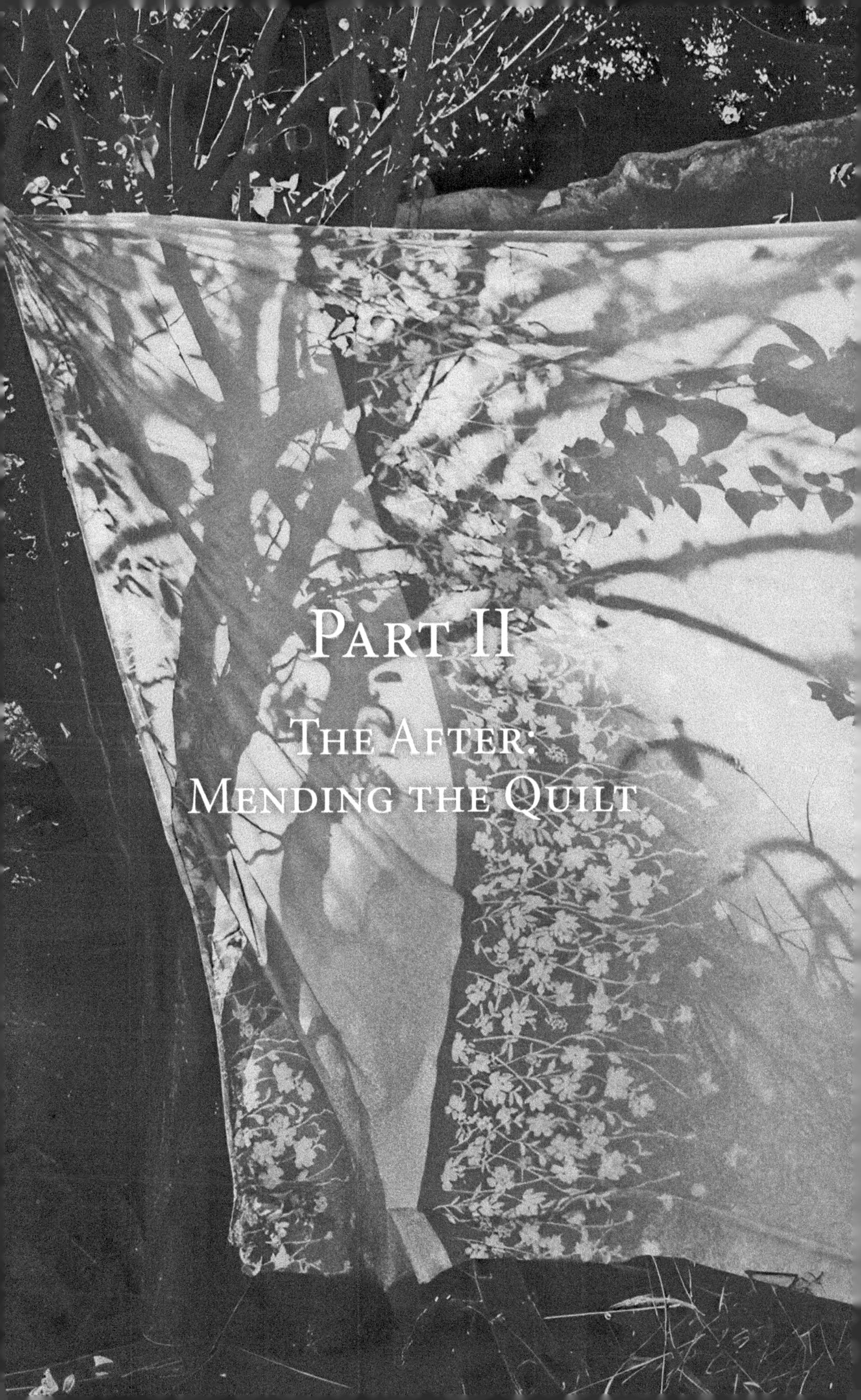

A Vault Opens

My one and only meeting with Jonathan lasted four hours and I filled half a notebook. The biggest thing I learned from the meeting was that I had a lot more to learn. Between my visit to the newspaper archive while my father was in a coma and the conversation with Jonathan, a vault full of confusing memories was opened.

Omar's week-long stay in my room; Vera Gran's visits and her tear-streaked face; the fire at *This World* and my parents' whispers about it—these and other memories emerged. Also rising to the surface were memories of strange phone calls, detectives, and guns, loud arguments between my parents, my father's incessant complaints about religious people, his affairs, my mother's denial, and our poverty. All of these memories lived inside the vault, like an unsorted pile of dirty laundry waiting to be aired.

As my father had declined to write a book after retiring, it was up to me, at age fifty-one, to unearth untold facts and stories. I had to rely on what he and others left behind.

On a mission to acquaint myself with a side of him I didn't know, I embarked on a journey of discovery. In the process, my father gradually came into fuller view.

In the quiet basement archive of *Haaretz*, I sifted through some of the thousands of articles and editorials penned by Ran Kislev, the journalist. A staff member showed me where the material was stored and provided me with a large workspace. I was astounded and overwhelmed by the scope of his work.

Almost forty years of his articles in *Haaretz* were tucked into little worn-out brown envelopes. Only articles written after the year 2000 were digitized by that point. Taking out two small drawers at a time, gently pulling out the yellowing pieces of paper so as not to tear them, I unfolded each until my fingers blackened from the ink.

Occasionally, I gasped as an article triggered an unexpected flashback and fragments of memories surfaced. In a painstakingly slow process, I began to sew patches and fill holes in the vast quilt of my father's life.

The experience was disorienting at times, yet ultimately revealed missing patches of *my* life's quilt, not just his.

Would I eventually perceive my father in a more favourable light? Would I have to re-write the narrative of my childhood? I had no idea where my search would lead.

The first article to spark a memory was one with a photo of a familiar Arab man in a keffiyeh. Could this be the nice man who stayed in my room for a week when I was five years old and gave me his keffiyeh?

I tried to suppress laughter, not to disturb the staff and visitors working in the archive quietly. My heart was pounding as I walked through a time tunnel. What could my father have written about the week Omar stayed with us? My senses flooded with the smell of the strong coffee Omar made every morning, the vision of how at night he folded the red-and-white keffiyeh he later gave me, and the melodic sound of his voice as he prayed from his book before going to sleep on my sofa.

I leaned back and began reading a most bizarre and new-to-me version of those events.

Omar's Story

T he article about Omar was published in 1969. In the article, my father reflected on the visit that had taken place two years earlier.

It was July of 1967, a month after the Six Day War and days after the re-unification of Jerusalem, my father explained. At the end of a long day of driving around the different parts of Jerusalem, an hour or so before military curfew started, he found himself in an unfamiliar area, at the intersection leading to Bethlehem, right at the entrance to the village of Silwan. It was so like my father to ignore rules and risks and get carried away.

Finally, he stopped to ask a young man for directions back to Tel Aviv. This man's name was Omar Ahmed Adulah. He was twenty-one years old, "dark, smiling, open and friendly." From the day Jerusalem was unified, Omar became an Israeli citizen, together with the rest of his village of Silwan.

My father wrote that the next morning, he drove Omar to Tel Aviv. Fragments of conversations about Omar came back to me. I recalled my father telling me that he had got lost in Jerusalem and Omar brought him to dine at his home. Omar's parents then invited him to stay overnight, as it was getting late. I don't think Omar came the next day to Tel Aviv with him. My guess is that he needed more time to build trust in an Israeli Jew he didn't know. I also recalled my father telling me they kept in touch by telephone and that he returned to visit Omar's family over the next few weeks, with my mother. It was quite a while after their initial meeting that they made the plan for Omar's week-long visit to us.

But the article got really interesting for me when my father claimed that he and Omar spent only one day together.

Taken at face value, according to the article, what they accomplished was quite a feat. My father described an astounding urban expedition in which he played the whirlwind tour guide for Omar. He wrote, "The Tel Aviv City Hall amazed him (Omar). Going up the express elevator of the Shalom Tower was a fascinating adventure to him. A visit to the Gordon swimming pool embarrassed him."

The Shalom (Peace) Tower was the tallest building in the Middle East at that time and housed government offices and a mall. With thirty-four floors and a special cream hue façade brought from Italy, it became a defining feature of Tel Aviv's skyline at the time. A little-known fact is that a subway station was built under the tower, but rails were never laid. The builders and designers were clearly visionaries. As I write these words, Israel still doesn't have a subway, but does have a "light train," running mostly above ground.

The Shalom Tower was a popular tourist attraction, and it makes sense that my father would take his young friend there. But all the places my father claims in the article that he took Omar to are a fair distance from each other. Beyond that, my father wrote that they also took him to a swimming pool and a night-club at night and finally to our apartment, where he and Omar spoke into the wee hours of the night.

Considering that they also would have needed to eat and change clothes several times, it was not humanly possible to do all the above in one day. The article condenses a multi-day itinerary into one implausible day.

My parents once explained to me that Tel Aviv was very different from where Omar grew up and they hoped to expand his horizons by showing him a different world. But a swimming pool and a nightclub? A keffiyeh-wearing Arab obviously came from a traditional and non-secular background. I cringed when I read about their visit to the Gordon swimming pool: "He was afraid to look at the women in bikinis. While the young Israelis, when they realized he was a 'real Arab', became excited and took him under their wing."

What did my father mean by "when they realized he was a real Arab?" His keffiyeh would have given it away. I wondered if Omar removed his traditional head covering during the days. He must have, especially with the high level of hostility between the two cultures at the time.

My father wrote that Omar "was particularly nervous when a dark-skinned young woman volunteered to teach him to swim." What were they thinking? The poor guy. My father next claimed that Omar said, "If you have a daughter, don't let her come here… The young women here are not good." Huh? Omar knew my father had at least one daughter, me—he stayed in my room. I began to think that my father chose to hide the fact he brought Omar to meet the family and let him stay over for a whole week, sleeping in his five-year-old daughter's room.

My mother went with them to the nightclub and pool (she loved clubs and pools), but my father made it out to be a two-bro expedition in the big city—possibly to protect Omar's reputation in his community, whatever would be left of that reputation after this article was published.

Next my father wrote, "He suffered another shock when we took him to Mandy Discotheque. To the regulars, Omar was a sensation. Yanuka, an ex-paratrooper officer, tried to recruit him for an interview for his radio program. Many men exchanged addresses with Omar. Even the owner, Mandy Rice-Davies-Shauli felt obliged to look after him personally. But when Mandy invited Omar to dance, he forcefully resisted."

Oh my God, Aba.

"Mandy is a beautiful woman, but I have a girlfriend, and she would have been very angry if she knew I so much as talked to another woman," Omar told him. Well, as of April 1969, the date the article was published, Omar's girlfriend and everyone in his village would have known.

Since the Profumo scandal in Britain in 1963, Mandy Rice-Davies had become a celebrity. She was a showgirl and model and was a friend of Christine Keeler; both were involved in intimate relationships with powerful men. Profumo, the War Minister, had an affair with Keeler and when it was exposed, he was forced to resign. But Omar may not have known any of this, or maybe my parents shared the saucy details.

They left the club at two in the morning (according to my father's article). Omar was in a great mood and told my father, "People in Israel live well. They all look happy."

My father added that after the visit to the club, "We sat on the balcony and talked for hours."

Omar, my father wrote, came from a highly respected family—his father was a Mukhtar, a chosen head of a village or neighbourhood, in the village of Silwan. Omar planned to go to America and study Aeronautic Engineering, but after the Six Day War of 1967, he cancelled the plan.

Researching the village of Silwan, I learned that today it is a neighbourhood in East Jerusalem, but in biblical times it was called Shiloach. It has a spring that's sacred to both Jews and Muslims.

Omar spoke about his studies and he and my father discussed politics, too. Regarding his community, Omar said, "There were many who wanted war but they didn't know war. Now they know." He explained that his father used to like Nasser, the Egyptian president, and saw him as the greatest leader since the prophet Muhammed. "Now he is silent when people are talking about Nasser. He is a great leader. But he has many words in his mouth and very little truth behind them."

Our guest did not want to live in Israel or Jordan. "May there be a Palestinian State. It can be small but it needs to be independent. Most importantly, may there be peace," he told my father.

After this supposed whirlwind twenty-four-hour visit, my father dropped Omar at the taxi station. As they parted ways, Omar told him, "Our people are afraid of Israelis, think of you as cruel, inhumane, now I know it is not so. I know you are good people, people exactly like us, but you just live a bit differently. And we can live together in peace. I'll share that with everyone. Believe me—I'll be like a radio."

I remember the high my parents were on after Omar's visit. They felt they had made a real impact on him, a positive impression, and that they had gained a friend "on the other side". They must have thought he was going to be an ambassador of peace.

My father saw reasons for optimism where most didn't.

SEARCHING FOR OMAR

I couldn't help but wonder why my father had shortened Omar's visit from one week to one day. The next part of the article shed light on his creative choices. In it, he provided background information about the young man. He explained that two years after Omar's visit, he felt nostalgic and decided to look him up. My father drove to Omar's family store in Jerusalem. He wondered if, after the passage of time, Omar would still be as friendly and open to their friendship. A lot had happened since Omar's visit, including many terror attacks in bus stations and supermarkets, and explosions in houses in Jerusalem and even in Silwan.

A young man at the family store's counter told my father, "Omar is not at home or in Jerusalem. He's simply gone...." Only after my father mentioned Omar's visit to Tel Aviv and who he was did the young man open up and tell him that Omar was in prison and his father had only been allowed to see him once.

Speaking about Omar, the man said, "He is a quiet guy who worked from morning until night at the store. He is not guilty of anything. Your police arrested many guys his age from the village and they only do that to prove they are doing something." He was probably referring to trying to catch whoever was responsible for terror attacks. The young man explained that Omar's girlfriend had left him and returned to Bagdad. Omar returned to his plan to go to America to study, but a week before he was supposed to leave, the police arrested him.

Omar's father arrived at the store and asked my father to go with him to the jail. He thought that he had a better chance of seeing his son if an Israeli journalist accompanied him. My father called the Jerusalem police and was told that Omar was arrested according to normal procedures and that his arrest had been extended three times by fifteen days each time and would likely be extended again until his trial.

"What is the charge?" my father asked.

"Security offence," was the answer.

My insides shriveled.

I imagine that my parents were shocked and hurt. Maybe they believed they could make the whole village of Silwan change their opinion of Jews. In the article about Omar's visit, my father seemed to feel good about having changed one mind, at least. Finding out that Omar had been arrested indicated they had failed even with the latter. Maybe that is why my father decided to publish an article about this visit two years after it took place. Otherwise, I am sure, for my father, this visit was nobody's business.

Could showing Omar how good life was in Tel Aviv have intensified the young man's sense of injustice about what his village and other Arab communities experienced after the Six Day War and led him to crime? Or was he falsely accused?

In my father's article, the "day" that was actually a week when my parents hosted Omar reads more like a circus show with Omar as the main attraction. Knowing my father, I am sure his intention was honourable. He believed that peace was possible, so he needed to fight for the rights of Arab citizens and highlight injustices against them. He believed that once wrongs were acknowledged and righted, it would be possible to have peace. Truth before reconciliation was my father's approach.

With Omar, as with other Arabs he'd met, my father saw an opportunity to reach out to the other side, to create a bridge. He believed that good could triumph over evil, that kindness and love could dismantle deep historical hate.

I wonder if, when he found out Omar was arrested on security charges, he did feel fear. Fear that the week-long adventure in Tel-Aviv could have been misinterpreted as collaboration with the enemy. What if Omar was radicalized and would be accused of planning a terror attack inside Tel Aviv? What if he'd mentioned his visit with us as his reconnaissance? Had my father entertained these ideas? Based on what I know about that time in Israel's history, it's quite possible he decided to write the article as a preemptive move. In case Omar shared with investigators how an Israeli journalist brought him into Tel-Aviv and showed him around for a week, my father had already admitted to inviting him as a gesture of peace and friendship.

Another possibility is that, by writing about Omar, my father was trying to help him. I think my father ultimately believed in Omar's innocence.

Throughout his career, my father and the newspapers he worked for championed the rights of Arab Israelis and Palestinians. To him, violation of the rights of any person or group needed to be exposed, no matter the consequences. That could have fuelled his scathing comments and articles about how the religious parties in Israel were infringing on the rights of secular and non-Jewish people. Justice was an absolute concept to him, not relative. Whatever Israeli Arabs or Palestinians were guilty of, whatever peace offerings were rejected by Palestinians or neighbouring countries, it did not excuse any abuse of rights. This stance made my father many enemies.

The platform his journalistic career provided allowed my father to publish many exposés on Arab-Israeli issues and the Palestinian conflict. In one series published in the 1980s, he exposed illegal land-grabs from Arab communities inside Israel, perpetrated by Israeli businessmen. The series on that subject became teaching material in higher-education institutions and made him new enemies, some of whom called our home to let him know how they felt about him and what they would do to him, or his family, if he kept up his writing. None of that rattled him, but it did rattle my mother and arguments erupted again after these calls.

My father was one of the last journalists in Israel to be welcomed in Arab towns and villages before hostilities became too dangerous for any Israeli.

But what was he and my mother thinking, bringing a twenty-one-year-old man into my bedroom?

What's In a Name

After my father's Shiva and after interviewing Jonathan, I packed my notebook and all the photocopied material inside giant envelopes the archive staff gave me and flew back to Canada. My research filled half a suitcase.

Back in Toronto, over the coming months and years, I continued researching digital archives of the tabloid *This World*, looking for anything my father had worked on. On future visits to Israel, I returned to the archives of *Haaretz* a few more times and bought books that had relevant material about the history of journalism in Israel and similar topics.

I never thought to ask my father how his career unfolded. If a person's life can be compared to a giant quilt, I always assumed I was looking at a complete one. But I was proven wrong when I discovered several patterned blocks of fabric that I didn't even realize were missing.

On one of my return visits to the *Haaretz* archive, I found an interview that filled in large hole in the section of the quilt that represented my father's professional past.

In 1981, when he was the editor-in-chief of *Haaretz*, my father spoke with journalists for a publication called *Ottot* (Signs). They asked him about his beginnings, and my father explained that when he arrived in Israel in the late 1950s, the Journalism Association of Israel arranged an "Ulpan"—Hebrew lessons for new immigrants—which, in his case, was geared to journalists who emigrated from Poland. This was followed by offers of internships in newspapers. He landed at the prestigious *Haaretz Daily*, but after three or four months of struggles with the language, gave up and left. The *Haaretz* archive had very short pieces he wrote under pseudonyms in 1958 during his failed stint there.

Some of my father's Polish colleagues started a Polish-language weekly newspaper they called *Od Nova*, loosely translated to *Starting Over*, and he joined them. Working there was a wonderful transition period for him. He became the fourth and last founder of that newspaper, which was also a publication of the left-wing political party, Mapam in the Polish language[5]. He wrote there under the name Weis rather than Herman Wexler.

"It was like a continuation of my work in Poland," he explained. "I wasn't a new foreign immigrant in a Hebrew newspaper, but I was part of a group that spoke the same language, in the wider sense of the word, and went through the same process of adjusting to a new country."

Although Mapam funded the newspaper, the staff had some freedom, which my father happily took advantage of. Several people felt he went too far, and the party was unhappy with the fact that he criticized the government for certain failures. In an article titled "Beit Ha-Shemesh" (House of the Sun), he criticized the way the government failed to inspire hope in new immigrants in the under-developed town of Beit Shemesh. He had personal experience, as he had taken his Hebrew lessons there. To appease the party, another journalist and co-founder published a fake angry letter-to-the editor under a pseudonym, criticizing my father. Another time, he was criticized for an article that suggested he was not Zionist enough. It was about "yordim", the word used for people who leave Israel. The general attitude towards them in Israel was very negative, yet my father was more sympathetic.

Knowing my father, he would have been pleased with the controversy his articles created. It signalled to him that people were paying attention.

In 1959, Herman Wexler, a.k.a. Weis, left *Od Nova*. A colleague there recommended him to the tabloid *This World*, whose editor provided him with a translator named Yoela Har-Shefi and a copyeditor named Uri Aloni. My father thus became a freelance reporter, writing mostly about crime. That's where he honed his Hebrew. "But I learned something else there," he added in the interview. "It's very important to get to know the country and its unique problems."

There was no shortage of problems for him to become familiar with.

Prominent journalists who started at *This World* referred to it as excellent schooling in the field. "It was more than a newspaper, it was an institution," was how my father and many others described it.

The tabloid's editor, Uri Avnery, followed the principle: "Without Fear, Without Prejudice". Aside from publishing many controversial articles, Avnery did foolhardy things like secretly crossing the border into Lebanon in the summer of 1982 to meet with Yasser Arafat, the leader of the Palestinian Liberation

---

5. From "Shattering Altars to Zionism", by Elzbeita Kosovska, In *Connections* no. 43, Summer, 2012.

Organization (PLO). He was the first Israeli to meet with a Palestinian leader. The anti-establishment stance of the paper and its owner's courage to do and say what he thought was right appealed to my father's value system.

It was at this tabloid that he changed his name permanently to Ran Kislev.

Kislev is the third Hebrew month in the Jewish calendar and Ran means singing or expressing oneself happily. His copy editor, Uri Aloni, suggested the name after playing with the Hebrew letters of Herman Wexler. Avnery himself had been Helmut Ostermann at birth (born in Germany) and couldn't stand foreign-sounding names. He wanted only Hebrew-sounding names writing for the paper in order to suggest the writers were born in Israel. This was deceptive, considering both he and my father were born in Europe. The name Wexler was far more consistent with my father's background and his inadequate Hebrew. Most of the time, Avnery didn't let his journalists attach their names to what they wrote, anyway.

This World was an amalgam of scandalous gossip, scoops, and photos of half-naked women, as well as serious subjects like crime and politics. Most, if not all the political articles, were written by Avnery himself.

In my research, I came across a great source of material about the newspaper and about Avnery in a book by Nitza Erel titled *Without Fear and Prejudice.*

The paper was an anti-establishment platform and Avnery used it to promote a very specific political agenda—a far-left agenda on the fringe of Israeli society at the time. He criticized Israeli governments for the way they dealt with the Palestinian issue and believed in the "Two States for Two People" solution, which was not popular.

On the tenth anniversary of the paper in 1960, Avnery said, "I believe that a real newspaper has to take on the role that past prophets took, of preachers at the gate, manifesting the national conscience, whipping the tyrants and defending the helpless.[6]" My father was already freelancing for the paper by that point.

Inspired by a biblical phrase from the Book of Jeremiah, Avnery saw newspaper editors as "quarrelling people". Journalists were supposed to stand against the false prophets who are mouthpieces for the rulers. They had to use tricks and mischief to draw the masses in. This explains the number of semi-nude photos, scandalous stories, and gossip columns he published. That's how

---

6. Erel Nitza, *Without Fear and Prejudice.* 2006, Magness Press.

Avnery tricked readers who wanted the tantalizing content to read his anti-establishment material and thus influence their minds.

Standing up to the rulers was what my father did throughout his career, an eager avenger on the front line. Headlines and words were his weapons.

Bullseye

Before *This World* came on the scene, Israeli newspapers avoided dealing with issues like national security, immigration, foreign affairs, and military procurement. The absence of such discussions resulted in a unity of views, which was seen as a value in and of itself.

In 1965, the tabloid stopped being a fringe anti-establishment platform. That year, Avnery was elected to parliament as leader of the party called This World – A New Force. At that point, the newspaper became an instrument of that party's agenda.

Avnery wrote most of the articles in the newspaper, including several he didn't put his name on, and he was involved in the shaping of all columns. Nitza Erel wrote that, because of his influence on his journalists, the newspaper "spoke in one voice, Uri Avnery's voice."

Both my parents worked for Avnery, at times overlapping. My mother started there in 1967, when I was still in kindergarten and my father wrote as a freelancer for various papers, including *This World*, *Bullseye* and even for the weekend section of *Haaretz*. Growing up, I'd heard discussions about several articles my parents wrote for the tabloid and as a result I can identify a few of them even though their names were not attached.

In 1966, when covering court cases for *This World*, my father met Shmuel Mor, the editor of the other salacious tabloid, *Bullseye* (Bool in Hebrew). He met him when Mor was arrested along with his assistant Maksim Gilan, for publishing an article involving a matter of state security without letting the military censor approve it first. According to Yigal Laviv, a journalist at another newspaper[7], Israel was involved in the murder of Mahadi Ben-Barka, who was a leader in the left-wing opposition to the King of Morocco. The Mossad gave the Moroccan security services a lead that allowed them to locate him in Geneva. Ben-Barka was tricked into travelling to France, where he was murdered. This made the French President, Charles De Gaulle, quite upset with Israel.

---

7. Online article by Yigal Laviv dated May 30, 2019 https://yigallaviv.com/2019/05/30/10065/

Shmuel Mor found out about this, and the cover page of the December 1966 issue read: "Israelis in the Ben Barka Affair?" Immediately after that, the Israeli police and security forces raided the newspaper office and confiscated all the issues that had not yet been sold. Mor and his assistant Gilan were charged with violating Israel's security, and with high-level espionage.

To avoid extra publicity and further international crisis, Mor was told to keep his arrest a secret and was allowed to continue editing the tabloid from jail. His wife Ora approached my father and asked him to help. In the meantime, Laviv, who travelled to Paris, leaked details to *The New York Times* and the story broke internationally. A petition circulated demanding Israel release Shmuel Mor and his assistant from jail. Among the names on the petition were Bertrand Russell and Jean Paul Sartre. The prime minister of Israel, Levi Eshkol, wished to avoid further scandal and a secret trial took place. A deal was struck, and Mor and his assistant received a one-year sentence but were released after four-and-a-half months.

My father stayed at *Bullseye* for a while after Mor's release, mostly covering crimes. While *This World* usually had photos of scantily clad women on the back cover, *Bullseye* often had photos of fully naked men and women with merely a black strip covering their private areas. Finding some of the issues stashed in my parents' wardrobe during those years, I stared at scenes with naked men and women doing things I didn't understand. It was the sixties, after all—the early years of the sexual revolution.

In 1969, the owner and editor-in-chief of *Haaretz Daily* Gershom Schocken, reached out through his secretary, to my father and offered him a job.

From conversations I'd overheard as a child, I picked up a certain degree of embarrassment in my father, associated with having worked at *Bullseye* once and for *This World*. At times, I heard him engage in self-ridicule. Ultimately, that turned to pride he expressed in having risen up from the scandalous, pornographic tabloids all the way up to the high-brow, intellectual *Haaretz*, where his career really took off.

Trends

I n Canada, whenever I had time and the right mindset, I would take articles out of the giant envelopes and peruse them. Eventually, I sorted the photo-copied material by subject. "Politics" would have been the biggest category had I copied more of them, but instead "Crime" was the largest pile, and I organized it chronologically and began the task of translating them. I wanted to get into my father's head and figure out how he had reached the conclusion that there was already organized crime in Israel by 1971.

While I followed the breadcrumbs left in the *Haaretz* archive, and looked at articles in the tabloids, I had other sources of information, too. Jonathan, "The Source", offered a unique perspective, and I found interviews my father gave, mentions in other articles and books, and interviews he gave for documentaries. I contacted people who knew him, too. Some didn't respond to my messages, but others did. And there were fragments, as well as complete memories, of my own.

I wondered how this poor investigative journalist, a new Polish immigrant whose Hebrew left a lot to be desired, had managed to achieve the monumental task of stringing the highly detailed, earth-and-myth shattering series into a coherent and convincing narrative. So, I looked for the earliest crime pieces my father wrote and worked my way from there.

Sifting through his early articles on crimes in Israel, it is evident that by the late 1960s and early '70s, something was brewing in Israel's collective shadow that my father could not yet fully articulate, but which he actively tried to make sense of. After years of visiting the courts almost daily and speaking to people on both sides of the law, he detected changing trends. Soon, he put the puzzle pieces together and it led to the series that shook the country.

Among the trends my father observed early on was what appeared to be the formation of an organized syndicate of diamond thefts.

On December 12, 1969, *Haaretz* published the first of Ran Kislev's series on this topic. He reported on a wave of diamond heists in Tel Aviv and began by painting a scene that would be repeated several times that year in the city. It went like this: the owner of a diamond-polishing shop arrived early in the morning and was followed by two masked men who held both a pistol and an Uzi. Within three minutes, they left with the loot. The robberies became more brazen and didn't stop until the police discovered a polishing shop that ordered the diamonds and shut it down. Unloading the diamonds afterwards was impossible, so the gang ceased its activities—that is, until they found a new buyer, a rich diamond merchant in Hong Kong and one of the richest people in the Far East.

When my father proposed that there was an organized network of diamond-theft crime syndicate operating in Israel, the police disagreed. They saw it more as individual gang activities.

On December 19, in his last article in the series, my father described problems in the way diamonds were stored at the diamond bourse (trading building) in the city of Ramat Gan, located in the greater Tel Aviv area. He was given access to all the rooms in the building accompanied by Mr. Stern, a retired policeman in charge of security. My father had permission to describe in detail the structure and the security issues in the bourse.

The article ended with, "What is deterring the thieves from robbing the diamond bourse? According to Mr. Stern, they are deterred by the dozens of guards at the entrance. But according to another source, on the other side of the law, it's not the guards who create an impediment but the elevators. The four elevators in the building are horrendous; you have to wait a long time for an elevator and when it arrives you don't know if it's going up or down. How can anyone plan a heist under these conditions? – asked 'the source.'"

I was becoming familiar with my father's penchant for punchy first and last lines.

In January of 1970, my father highlighted other changes in crime trends in Israel.

An article titled "A Rising Wave of Violence" was about a surge in violent crimes and the increase in use of weapons against civilians and police. He listed twelve events from November 29, 1969 to January 20, 1970. The list included robberies, murders of children including Hanna Horovitz, and a murder of a twenty-year-old man by the man's friend because he called him a "homo". (He didn't mention that my mother was the first to figure out who killed little Hanna when she went to investigate the case as a freelancer, a source of great pride for her).

My father wrote, "The list is scary. Within only seven weeks there were five murders and four attempted murders using guns, and seven cases of armed robberies using machine guns and pistols."

He felt that the list of crimes was worrisome, but again, high-ranking police officers disagreed. It appears they only looked at the fact that in 1969 there were fewer criminal charges than the previous year. My father offered an alternative interpretation. He looked at the type of crimes and noted that although the number of robberies remained steady, the methods had changed drastically. In 1967, robbers used guns in two robberies; in 1968, seventeen times; and in 1969, twenty-nine times. He argued that the use of guns against police in robberies was much bolder. He doubted these events were unrelated occurrences.

DRUGS AND TATTOOS

No one would have predicted in my childhood that I'd end up working mainly with people dealing with various health issues, addictions, and traumas. During elementary school, when I weighed barely as much a mid-size dog, all I wanted was to hold fluffy cats and pet cute puppies. I thought that's what veterinarians do all day and declared that was my dream job. Seeing one slightly injured dog was all it took to erase that dream.

Later, I declared I'd be an artist, to my parents' chagrin. Through art, I expressed what I couldn't articulate in words and art saved me from the confusion, stress, and wounds that growing up in my particular family and country left in me.

Thanks to my father's sneaky gambit, I pursued higher education, and through my choice of a career as a Health Psychologist, I would learn that addiction was how many people get through a challenging life. While some end their lives prematurely due to intolerable pain, others might numb, medicate, or escape anguish with the help of substances, sex, gambling, thrills, food and even work.

At the end of January 1970, when I was seven, *Haaretz* published my father's series titled: "The Trend of Mood-Altering Drugs". In it, my father's focus was on hashish, a popular mood-altering substance in the Middle East derived from the flowering buds of cannabis. While he made astute observations on trends, I think my father missed a big one related to trauma.

Part one of the series opened with: "Mood was at a peak in the room. The conversation switched from topic to topic without getting too deep, and every once in a while, those present burst out laughing—even if the joke told wasn't that funny. Everyone felt good and carefree."

My father described the rolling of joints in a room with psychedelic looking posters and music coming out of a stereo. He pointed out that this took place not in a Hash den, but in a fancy apartment in Tel Aviv and the participants were all law-abiding citizens of different occupations. Those present didn't come specifically for the hashish, they were just socializing, and hashish was a minor element.

"This was three weeks ago, my first meeting with hashish," he wrote, conveniently massaging the facts.

I know he was fibbing because I remember more than my parents hoped I would.

On more than one occasion, my parents—who couldn't afford babysitters or chose to keep any spare change for other things—brought me with them to places where the air smelled funny. The pint-sized me often dozed off while they hung out with Tel Aviv bohemians or interviewed them. I remember odd-looking cigarettes being passed around the room and my parents puffing on them before I drifted to dreamland. My earliest recollection of such visits is from 1968, when I was six. So, the encounter my father described in 1970 was not his first. Visiting with the golden-haired singer Miri Aloni and her life partner at the time, the bohemian character and actor Jessie Nachyasi, is but one earlier example. I remember the dark dungeon-like hideout we descended to and how whatever was in the air put me to sleep quickly. After such visits, I'd open my eyes the next morning, groggy and not quite myself. Years later, my mother told me that it was a nightclub called Perspective and admitted that the smell was hashish and that they all smoked it. Memories of my parents talking about Jessie and the trouble he was in, probably drug-related, surfaced. I remembered calls in the middle of the night from him or his lawyer Tzvi Lidsky, and more than once my father accompanied them to the police station when Jessie decided to turn himself in.

In the exposé on drugs in Israel, my father explained that a survey done right after the Six Day War in June of 1967 showed a significant increase in drug use starting in June-July of that year. Four possible reasons were identified: the wave of volunteers from other countries coming to Israel brought this social trend, connections between Israelis and Arabs in the West Bank, the decrease in the price of drugs, and the ease of obtaining them.

A widespread belief at the time was that drug use was only the domain of the criminal underworld, especially prostitutes and their pimps. But, as my father pointed out, perhaps they hadn't surveyed the right people until then. He reported that the age of drug users was dropping and the ratio of users who were not criminals was going up. Previous estimates were based only on police data, but the new survey looked at the issue more broadly.

The amount of drugs caught by police in Israel was skyrocketing. In 1967—only one hundred and sixty-nine kilograms of hashish were nabbed, while a year later, three-thousand eight hundred and sixty-five kilos were seized—a twenty-fold increase. Similarly, there was a huge surge in Opium seizures from eleven kilos in 1967 to one-thousand one hundred and sixty-five the following year. This, my father believed, reflected an upsurge in smuggling.

The result was a drastic rise in police arrests in the late 1960s, and my father summarized the article with a warning, saying, in bold letters, that the situation was very serious.

Over the years, I had seen my father's two crude blue tattoos—a squiggle on his left arm and a heart on his thigh—a strange thing for a serious man. He sat me down one day when I was fifteen years old for a chat after we watched the news about boy who was killed while attempting a dangerous feat.

"Apropos being young and stupid," my father said, "you see these tattoos? I did it to myself when I was your age."

"What? How?"

"A sharp knife and ink…"

"That's so dumb," I said, falling straight into his trap.

"Here is the thing. I took Opium twice in my life and each time I tattooed myself."

"Oy," I said covering my mouth. I didn't know what else to say. My father, the man in suits and ties who worked for the most prestigious newspaper in the country, took drugs in his teens and not just any drug: Opium. And he tattooed himself while high. Yikes.

"Oy indeed," my father said, squinting at me. "You see, now I can't get rid of them and let me tell you, being in my position with these ridiculous tattoos, well, it's embarrassing." He laughed, and before concluding his little talk added, "Good thing I'm expected to wear suits all year."

In those days you'd rarely see a person with a tattoo in Israel (other than those done by the Nazis in concentration camps), and it's prohibited according to Jewish law. Although my father took great pleasure in violating Jewish laws, he felt foolish in front of his esteemed peers, and it didn't fit the respectable persona he worked hard to create and maintain.

After that revelation and a glimpse into a hidden corner of my father's shadow, I spent days pondering all the idiotic things I could do under the influence of drugs. All my father had to do was wait and let the seed of total abstinence from all illicit substances take hold in my psyche.

It was a smashing success. I avoided drugs in my youth completely, other than once accidentally ingesting a chuck of hashish in my boyfriend's kibbutz, mistaking it for dense bread. It resulted in a very bad trip which I luckily returned from. And it cemented my aversion to drugs.

Escape to Addiction

"The Trip Not Everyone Comes Back From" was the title of the last installment in my father's series on drugs in Israel, published on February 13, 1970. He was still going on about hashish but also tackled potentially more harmful substances that were becoming readily available in Israel. He started the piece with an incident that took place five years earlier.

In 1965, he was shadowing police officers in the Jaffa division and joined them as they intervened in a neighbours' dispute and investigated suspects. After midnight, while in the station, a man was brought in—not to be charged or arrested, he was just allowed to sit near the intake clerk while no one bothered with him. My father wrote, "He was completely indifferent and oblivious to his surroundings. He was short, skinny, and wore loose and wrinkled khaki pants and a torn shirt. His face looked frozen, his mouth agape and from his eyes, the colour of water, tears rolled down. The sergeant in charge explained, 'This is a constant issue for us—he is a narcotic drug addict.'" My father learned that the man went to a certain agency asking for morphine. He didn't cause problems, just nagged them. When they couldn't get rid of him, they called the police, who took him in for a few hours, then let him go.

At one point, the sergeant searched the man's pockets for identification and an address so they could take him home. A photo fell from the man's wallet—a photo that the sergeant recognized from the Sinai War of 1956. A group of young men in khaki uniforms carrying guns, smiled at the camera, their camp in the background.

"'Guys! That's me in the photo!' The sergeant yelled suddenly. 'That's our unit at Beit Dagon. How the hell did my photo end up with this dude? This is Shaul the commander, this is Avrasha from the Red Army and this is Motke…Guys, this is that guy,' the sergeant yelled with excitement, 'Motke, do you remember me? Do you remember Shmulik? We were together in Kis Faluja, remember?' The dishevelled ex-soldier raised his head with a spark of recognition in his eyes, but it only lasted a short moment. His face became expressionless again. 'Take him out of here,' the sergeant ordered and left in a hurry."

From this sad scene, my father catapulted to reporting on the issue of pro-liferating drugs in Israel.

I sighed.

As I read his words, decades after he'd written them, my gut twisted a little. Did he completely miss the tragic and devastating impact that wars have on soldiers? Was he so clueless that he couldn't make the connection? Or did he want readers to make the connection themselves? The ex-solider in the police station was probably self-medicating to block the horrors of war.

I wonder if my father's lack of sensitivity to the predicament of the drug-using ex-soldier was, in part, because he coped with his own past traumas so differently, making him a typical high-functioning addict. A workaholic, a pleasure and thrill-seeker, a serial cheater, and a smoker who polished off four packs of cigarettes a day. These were his socially acceptable ways of escaping certain emotions and shutting down painful memories.

The sergeant who had recognized his former comrade was at first confused, then shocked, and later dismissive. Sort of like how society treated and still treats ex-soldiers and first responders living with operational stress injuries. Too many end up addicted and living on the fringes of society, abandoned. This is the real "trip" they do not come back from.

Failing to see a link between adverse life events and addiction means that interventions for addicts are often inadequate, addressing only the addiction or only trauma-related symptoms in a revolving-door phenomena. When I worked on my doctorate thesis at Bellwood Health Services, a residential ad-diction rehab facility in Toronto, I read the files of all two hundred and twenty-eight clients I recruited for the research, front to back. Every one of them re-ported significant childhood and later-in-life trauma during group therapy. Yet not a single question on the intake and assessment forms examined that. The approach at the time was that what clients needed was "simply" to become so-ber, attend twelve-step programs and aftercare groups that would allow them to maintain their sobriety. In short, stop drinking or using drugs, go to meetings, and you'll be fine. A few years later, when I was hired to replace my retiring supervisor, I had a chance to modify the approach. It was an opportunity to change the system from the inside.

Within months of coming on board, I was asked to develop a concurrent PTSD-Addiction program for soldiers and once it kicked off, I served as the clinical director. This had been, by far, the highest honour of my professional life—to be given the opportunity to help the men and women who served their country in missions that left them with deep wounds, mostly invisible. They returned to a society that did not recognize their sacrifices, and they were not given sufficient mental health support or other resources to help them reintegrate into civilian life successfully. Escaping into addiction is sometimes the only way these soldiers and first-responders know as a mean to keep going after witnessing the ugly side of humanity.

In a way, by poring over his early work, I shadowed my father as he led me on the trail of violent crimes. It was on that trail, much of it spent in courthouses, that he made important connections. That is where he likely met Jonathan, The Source.

A Trip in Time

"Did you know my father outside of your professional relationship?" was the first question I posed to Jonathan.

Having practiced psychology for more than three decades, I automatically started with a topic that was likely to put him at ease. It may have also helped me ease slowly into the heavier stuff I knew was to come.

"I used to see your parents at parties with people like the journalist Ahra'le Bachar, the Lidskys, businesspeople, members of the Israeli arts community. There were many beautiful women there and lots of alcohol."

"Yeah. They went out every weekend, sometimes during the week, too. They and the Lidskys were party animals. In parties at our place on Bialik, they'd get so drunk and rowdy. They drank vodka, brandy, and whiskey like it was orange juice."

He laughed and nodded. I didn't tell him how once when I was eleven, I came out of my room and disconnected the record player and told everyone to go home because I couldn't sleep, nor that my parents had called me a party-pooper ever since. I also didn't tell him that I suspected there were orgies and LSD (though probably not at our apartment).

"I remember your mother, an amazing woman, so charming, beautiful, personable. The relationship between Ran and her was beautiful."

This was certainly the impression they projected. And maybe early in the '70s they did have such a relationship. But my father had other "beautiful" relationships, too.

Then Jonathan talked about the men in these circles, comparing their sexual escapades. I wasn't comfortable pursuing this subject and steered it elsewhere.

"My parents loved to hang out with artists and poets, in restaurants, clubs and coffee shops, at Abie Nathan's California and at café Kassit and I remember Haskel and Moshe Ish-Kassit really well."

"Some of them, like Moshe Ish-Kassit, were on the periphery of the criminal underworld," Jonathan said.

I didn't ask in what way. I had many pleasant memories of Moshe Ish-Kassit, from when my parents brought me to café Kassit at ages five, six and seven. Usually, after he ran his fingers through my curls, Moshe would place in front of me a gigantic ice cream covered in mountains of whipped cream and chocolate syrup. The enormous man would say, "You're too skinny and need to finish all of this or I will make your parents pay for it," and laugh. He had the friendliest smile, and I was always excited to see him. Why taint fond memories with images of criminality?

After reminiscing about the bohemian cafés of Tel Aviv in the '60s and '70s and the unique characters we saw there, Jonathan spoke about his own role in the organized crime series. He launched into the subject without my prompting. My hands tingled with excitement as he opened a crack into how the journalist Ran Kislev operated.

"I met Ran in early 1970. We used to meet in coffee shops, and I told him what I knew."

As he spoke, I imagined my father sitting in a café across from the young Jonathan who surely wore a sporty jacket and Ray-Ban sunglasses. He was probably looking around nervously to make sure he wasn't recognized, while my father jotted notes furiously in his orange notebook.

"Ran and Ahra'le Bachar came to me, went over the material I showed them. Ran began to publish articles and every time it developed into something else. Ran knew how to listen and he listened well to the environment. He received excellent schooling at *This World*."

For a few minutes, we talked about this anti-establishment tabloid.

"It was also an anti-police newspaper," Jonathan said.

"Yeah, very opinionated but with salacious photos," I said, and we chuckled.

"I would meet with Ran, give him info and at the same time Ran did his own investigations. I told him things he wouldn't have been able to find out on his own."

"Why did you decide to come forward to a journalist?" I asked.

"There was denial at the highest ranks. Yehuda Faraj denied on television that there was organized crime and persuaded the general Super Intendent Kopel, who was an honest man, that there was no organized crime."

"Yes, even the first inquiry committees denied this reality," I said, as if I knew more than a few crumbs about the subject at the time.

"You know, Ran had intuition and Avi Valentin had material. Valentin didn't know the criminals the way Ran did."

Spending years in and around the courthouse, my father befriended lawyers and gained the trust of both criminals and police. He was very good at making people open up to him. He knew how to disarm them and get information that served his goals.

Talking to this stranger, Jonathan, about my father's work felt like having a fly-on-the-wall perspective I could not get from anyone else. I was very grateful for that. After the meeting, I told myself I would need to read all the articles to put all the pieces together one day—just not yet.

LAW AND DIS-ORDER

D id my father have the tiniest inkling as to how drastically his series on organized crime would change our lives, the trajectory of his career, and the country's future? Did his hands tremble on that April morning in 1971 when he opened the newspaper and saw the fruits of his labour screaming from the page? I wish I'd asked him.

Allowing his six-year-old daughter to wander into a mine field was a stupid mistake, but publishing the series on organized crime deliberately exposed us to a field full of live landmines. Taking on top government and municipal officials, the police force, the local underworld and even international underworld players was next-level risky behaviour. Risky not just for Ran Kislev the journalist, but also for his family. It also meant going against the public opinion of a large segment of Israeli society that refused to accept his claims as valid. The notion that the young country they had fought for, that so many had died for, that the soil of a country built on the ashes of the Holocaust had already sprouted a complex crime syndicate, was unfathomable to many.

I "sat" on the organized crime articles for a long time, unable to look beyond the headlines. I was derailed by two different cancers—thyroid cancer in 2014, and a year and half later, stage-three breast cancer. I continued to work, but chemotherapy, surgery, and radiation took their toll and my ability to focus on anything else was diminished.

In 2018, I was ready to pick up where I'd left off. I rented a cabin with two friends in the countryside of Quebec, about an hour-and-a-half northwest of Montreal. It was located near a small town called Magog, which I found funny because there is a Magog in *The Bible* that refers to the farthest place in the north, harsh and barbaric (today's Russia, some argue). Compared to Toronto, the much colder weather in Quebec felt harsh, yet it was beautiful and the fireplace inside made it cozy. Cold weather always increases my chances of staying indoors and getting words onto a page.

It was early October, and because we were seven hours northeast of Toronto, most of the tree leaves had already fallen to the ground. On the first morning, we shared a scrumptious breakfast of omelets with mushrooms and fresh fruit, then each of us found a comfy corner of the cabin in which to write. Before starting, I stepped outside to take in the beauty of the land. The world outside was covered in carpets of gold-coloured leaves. The sound of crunching leaves is one of my favourite sounds in nature, so I took a short walk around the nearby pond and, after taking a hundred photos, returned to tackle the monumental task I had set for myself for that week—the organized crime series. Back inside, I spread all the articles on the large dining room table with lots of natural light flooding from the large windows.

Wrapped in a warm scarf, a hot tea mug in hand, I read the first paragraph in the first article of the series that changed our lives, and smiled. My father began by naming a defence mechanism he was all too proficient at, denial. He wrote, "The most denied issue in the country is the existence of organized crime in Israel," he wrote. "In recent months, high-ranking officials—including the Minister of Police Affairs and the General Superintendent of Police in Israel denied its existence endless times and at every opportunity… The intensity of denial naturally creates suspicion…".

Denial by the government and police that Israel already had organized crime only emboldened my father.

The first article read like a convoluted episode of *Law and Order*. In fact, the whole series reads more like *Law and Dis-Order*.

A good storyteller, my father opened with a murder plot. About a year before, he explained, one of the highest-ranking members of the criminal underworld was murdered in what some described as "a very professional way." A suspect was apprehended almost immediately and there seemed to have been war-like tension within the underworld. Certain facts began to leak from this closed world and bits of information reached my father's ears. In the months before publication, he had conducted dozens of interviews with high-ranking police officers, retired heads of police, lawyers, businessmen, custom officers, politicians, and people who were on the fringes of society, as well as full-fledged members of the criminal underworld. Most of the individuals he approached asked to be left alone; they were afraid to talk. Several vehemently denied all his theories, but a few did agree to talk.

"The final picture that emerged scared even me," he wrote. "Not because of the 'good advice' I received, through various channels, to stop inquiring, but because of the picture itself. Most stunning is that despite obvious dissimilarities in background and conditions, the final picture reminded me of the famous American Mafia."

Organized crime in the idealistic and young country of Israel? That was a bombshell, and it made the highbrow *Haaretz* suddenly a very popular newspaper. The idea that the twenty-one-year-old country already had an underworld with a sophisticated structure resembling the Italian-American mafia stunned the nation and formed the first cracks in the rose-coloured lenses that Israelis saw themselves through. At the time, the prevailing romanticized belief was that all Israelis were patriotic idealists, incapable of criminality.

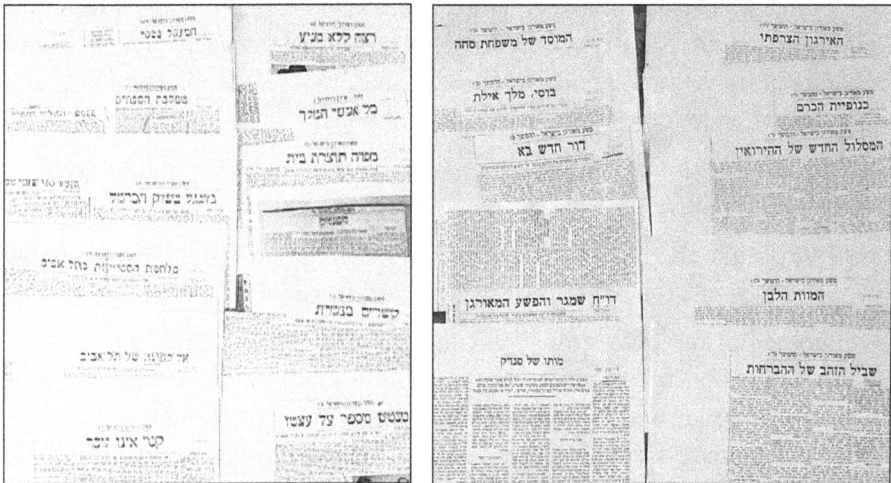

Ran Kislev's first and second series on organized crime in Israel, *Haaretz Daily*, 1971 and 1972.

My father referred to the model of a network of crime families in the US as described in *The Godfather*. He argued that in Israel, too, the criminal organization relied on connections between families, or as they are called in Israel, Hamulas, borrowed from the Arabic word for a clan or extended family.

The focus in the rest of the article was on a particular case wi th several shady characters involved in a murder of one Ezra Shem-Tov Mizrahi, to be referred to from now on as Shem-Tov, and his bodyguard Aaron Elmalech. The plot included a beautiful young blonde from Spain called Olga who may have been in a relationship with one Sammy Abu. Two versions of events were put forward. The official story was that Abu brought her to Israel for the purpose of turning her to prostitution. The story the police went with was that Shem-Tov helped the young woman escape the grasp of Sammy Abu and sent her back to Spain. This, in turn, infuriated Abu. There was a physical fight followed by a "Sulcha" —a reconciliation gathering. But ultimately, Abu murdered Shem-Tov and his bodyguard. Several army soldiers who happened to be in the area heard the gunshots and saw Abu running from the scene. They followed him into the side streets of downtown Tel Aviv and found him hiding inside an old fridge.

Information provided by Interpol later revealed that Sammy Abu was linked to organized gangs in Europe. There was a rumour he was involved in a gang battle in Spain where several dozen people were killed. However, holes in the police's official version were too big to ignore. The police claimed that the motive for the murder was that Shem-Tov had bought a plane ticket for Olga to return to Spain. However, Tzvi Lidsky, Abu's lawyer, showed my father proof that the money for the ticket actually came from Sammy Abu and was given to Olga by his friends. In addition, Abu held her passport and obviously had to return it to her when she flew back to Spain. There were other holes in the official story, which Abu's lawyer pointed out in his summation. Despite all that, Abu received a life sentence, and the judge stated that the motive remained unknown.

The last line in this article is: "According to criminologists: there's no murder without a motive."

It looks like the real murderer was still at large, and my father certainly made the case that the police investigation was incomplete, at best.

Looking at my notes from the conversation with Jonathan, who was an insider in the police, confirmed what my father saw. I hadn't yet read the articles when Jonathan and I spoke and didn't know how much and how often my father and *Haaretz* criticized the police for their incompetence and corruption.

"Bad specimen" was how Jonathan referred to certain members of the police force in those days, these high-ranking army personnel who came to the police from an army career.

"Reports made by ex-military intelligence officers were garbage," he said. "They came to the police and did annual reports and didn't pay attention to who did time (in prison) with whom and failed to see the connections that were formed there."

One of the photos accompanying the text of the first article was of Shem-Tov at his son's Brith with his friend Mordechai Tzarfati, also known as Mentesh. He'd become a key figure in future articles and in our lives.

And the "good advice" my father had referred to earlier came in the form of numerous direct and indirect threats that he, or more accurately, we, received.

The phone in our apartment rang non-stop after the first article was published and for the most part, the callers weren't congratulating my father for a job well done.

ALL THE KING'S MEN

T he spring of 1971 was glorious. Wildflowers were in full bloom. Since I cut school on a regular basis, I spent many hours alone, joyously. If you were looking for me, you'd find me following cats or chasing butterflies and birds. If you couldn't see me, I might have been lying on the ground watching clouds change shapes. At times, I could be found perched on the widest arm of a Sycamore tree enjoying a bird's-eye view of the carpet of poppies and daisies.

When the sun lowered, I'd watch impatiently from a distance as my friends walked back from school so we could play imaginary games. But they had to go home after school, eat lunch, and nap. Only after four o'clock were they allowed to come out and play. Sitting outside our apartment block one day, on top of a big empty wooden box someone left outside, I repeated a nursery rhyme I had read at a friend's home.

Humpty Dumpty sat on a wall, Humpty Dumpty had a great fall, I made myself fall and recite the rest, *All the king's horses and all the king's men, couldn't put Humpty together again.*

The first friends who came out and saw me doing that asked what I was up to and eventually joined me in the game. No one was hurt and there were lots of giggles. In the innocence of youth, we failed to grasp the true meaning of nursery rhymes like that one.

I smiled when I read the second instalment in the organized crime series, which was published on April 18 with the title, "All The King's Men". The article provided the context and rationale for the murders of Shem-Tov and Aaron Elmalech described in the first article.

Shem-Tov was born to a large family from the Caucasus, the geographical area between Eastern and Western Europe. His family had been well-off before immigrating to Israel, but like many of those who escaped Antisemitic attacks, they arrived with nothing. They settled in a poor area in southern Tel Aviv— the Shapira neighbourhood. However, Shem-Tov rose from poverty to driving expensive cars and spending big money in nightclubs and gambling holes. He became known as the King of the Shapira neighbourhood. He was on top of the world when standing next to his gold Pontiac, my father wrote. A black-and-white photo of him by his car illustrated the point.

In the early 1950s, the police observed that robberies in Tel Aviv looked more organized, and they believed Shem-Tov was the brain behind them. Members of his gang were caught, yet he managed to avoid charges. The police could never find direct evidence linking Shem-Tov to the crimes.

Maybe there was another reason why Shem-Tov wasn't charged, my father mused—it was around that time that Shem-Tov entered politics. Specifically, he became involved with Mapai. In the 1950s, Mapai was a center-left Zionist-Socialist party, formed in the 1930s by members of the second wave of immigration from Eastern Europe (or Ashkenazis), who escaped pogroms. The party later morphed into the dominant party in Israeli politics—the Labour Party. It held on to power continuously until 1977.

Back in the 1950s, Mapai was struggling to organize in the southern parts of Tel Aviv. In those neighbourhoods, the poorest in Tel Aviv, a right-wing Nationalist and Revisionist party was far more popular. This earlier version of the Likud was started by Menachem Begin in 1948, and from the outset it was seen as sympathizing with the underdog. At the time, the underdogs were the Sephardi/Mizrahi population. They were at a serious disadvantage as they typically arrived in Israel after the Ashkenazis, who already occupied positions of power. The Sephardis/Mizrahis typically didn't have opportunities to pursue higher education. In most of the countries they came from they were only allowed to work in certain trades or as merchants. They also didn't speak the eastern European languages, including the Jewish mashup of these called Yiddish spoken by those who arrived before them. All of this resulted in a marked socio-economic gap between the two immigrant ethnic groups and in the creation of neighbourhoods separated along ethnic and socio-economic lines (as I witnessed in Geula school). In their attempts to gain ground in certain neighbourhoods, the challenge Mapai encountered was how to avoid the disruptions of their meetings in southern Tel Aviv.

"The key role in Mapai's battle in the southern neighbourhoods of the city was in the hands of one man, Mordechai Tzarfati, 'The King of the Thessalonikis', who was known better as Mentesh," my father wrote.

Shem-Tov's friends said that he was in fact a 'Mentesh soldier.' He himself had many of his own "soldiers", which gave him power. He organized his men to become "ushers" in the Mapai meetings and placed them in other roles. With the help of Shem-Tov's soldiers, these meetings could take place with less interference. As a result, an important meeting, which included David Ben Gurion, who became Israel's first (and later third) prime minister, took place without a hitch.

In America, historically, it was not unusual for politicians at all levels to recruit the mafia to help organize voters or intimidate some to vote "the right way." My father's investigation was uncovering similar trends in Israel.

Shem-Tov, my father explained, "didn't rise up high because the one who did was Mentesh". He lacked the personal connections Mentesh had formed during the British Mandate period before the formation of Israel. Instead, Shem-Tov remained a simple soldier and received compensation from Mentesh. He was granted permission to set up a vegetable stand in the Carmel Market in Tel Aviv. While it may not sound exciting, it was a lucrative business since it involved large sums of (undeclared) cash thanks to a high volume of cash-paying customers. Shem-Tov didn't actually stand to sell the produce himself but contracted it out to others who brought in large sums of money daily, with little effort. Later, the benefits he received from Mentesh expanded into a partnership at a store in the Wholesaler Market of Tel Aviv and, over time, more stores were added.

When my father asked other storeowners in the Wholesaler Market about Shem-Tov, they refused to talk, but it was clear he was ruling the market in a protection racket. The muscle gangs operating in the market wouldn't bother him—he was the strongest among them. Rumour had it that Mentesh loaned Shem-Tov money in the beginning of the (produce) season and collected in return part of the profits at the end of the season. Mentesh denied giving these loans and claimed he just acted as guarantor for bank loans.

In addition to the market stands and stores, Shem-Tov owned illegal gambling clubs and was a silent partner in other gambling joints. No new club could open without his approval. For those running the clubs, knowing he was involved with them allowed them to sleep at night. The prevailing opinion was that clubs under the patronage of Shem-Tov were protected from sudden police raids and other problems. If he was involved, complaints from neighbours drowned in a sea of bureaucracy.

Aside from presenting alternative motives for Shem-Tov's murder, my father also laid the foundation for his argument that criminal actors and gangs operating in the Tel Aviv area had had political and municipal ties and possibly even connections with the police - necessary ingredients for the successful operation of an organized crime alliance.

In the last two months of Shem-Tov's life, his status became more tenuous. He was losing huge amounts of money in card games and needed to fill the dwindling pot in his stores, as he took out the cash for gambling. People close to him said he was urgently seeking a loan for twenty thousand liras[8], a substantial sum in those days. He turned to Mentesh, who refused to help and was furious with Shem-Tov and made open threats towards him. However, Mentesh denied there was strife between them. He also denied that Shem-Tov had approached him regarding the loan.

After Shem-Tov's murder in April 1970, Mentesh remained involved with his stores and was assigned a Power of Attorney for Shem-Tov's house. He also looked after Shem-Tov's widow and children. As a last show of respect, or perhaps of a guilty conscience, Mentesh bought Shem-Tov a burial plot at a coveted cemetery. From Jerusalem he brought a special stone, erecting one of the fanciest gravestones in the cemetery.

The known conflict between Mentesh and Shem-Tov made for a second motive that the police should have investigated.

Shortly after the first articles came out, the strange phone calls to our home began. In time, I learned that the calls stopped the day the police started phone surveillance. The police informed my father at ten o'clock in the morning one day that they were beginning to wiretap our phone, and the last call came at twenty-to-ten that same morning. My father suspected an inside job and to him this was critical proof of the existence of organized crime in Israel.

---

8. Lira was the currency in Israel then, before it was changed to Shekels in 1980 and to New Shekel in 1986.

Murders and Olga
the Spanish Blonde

The articles finally gave me context for another name I'd heard growing up. A name I feared. For a while, Shem-Tov was a business partner of Shimshon Danoch. The name Danoch struck either respect or terror in many, and in time, it drove fear into me, too.

Shimshon Danoch was a younger brother of Kochva Danoch, who was tried and sentenced for murder during the British Mandate days. Another Danoch brother was Yisrael, who worked as a superintendent in the Tel Aviv municipality—the very municipality that buried complaints about gambling clubs. The gambling club the Danoch brothers co-owned did very well until Shem-Tov opened another club nearby and "a black cat passed between them," as my father wrote. Most of the gamblers followed him and Danoch's club teetered on the brink of bankruptcy.

Shem-Tov remained strong—the number of his "soldiers" in the Shapira neighbourhood grew and he had permanent bodyguards.

My father outlined the elements in play on the night that Shem-Tov and his bodyguard, Aharon Elmalech, were murdered which suggested a possible third motive. It played out like an American Mafia movie.

The night of the murder, Shem-Tov was at his new club when an individual contacted his bodyguard, Aharon Elmalech and demanded Shem-Tov come to a meeting. Elmalech located Shem-Tov, got him out of the club, and walked with him to his car. On the other side of the street one of Shem-Tov's other bodyguards, Yoskay, sat in a car with a friend. Yoskay told police that he sat with his back to the direction Shem-Tov was and didn't see him … some bodyguard!

Yoskay said he heard the shots and saw the murderer running away from the scene. No one chased him and it seemed that if not for the IDF soldiers who happened to be there, Sammy Abu would not have been caught. Elmalech was shot in the stomach and lived for another week. He was conscious for most of it and claimed he couldn't identify the murderer from a photo lineup. The police didn't press him, as they felt they had the full story—a story involving Olga, the Spanish blonde.

However, one of Elmalech's acquaintances told the police he heard Elmalech say to Shimshon Danoch on the phone, "Why did he shoot like crazy? That's not what we talked about!" There was no trace of this message, and no one seemed to have asked Elmalech if he indeed had said such a crucial thing.

My father didn't reveal how he obtained this information, but I wonder if Abu's lawyer Tzvi Lidsky, who by that time was a close friend, shared the details with him.

Yisrael Danoch happened to be around the murder scene and came with the IDF soldiers who chased and found Sammy Abu. Danoch claimed that Sammy Abu and his friends planned to kill Shem-Tov and he also told the police about Olga.

In a later statement, Danoch added that he saw two French guys whose faces he recognized on the street corner after the shots were fired. He said these were friends of Sammy Abu. They were arrested as possible accomplices for the murder and released without bail five years later!

It's not surprising that Abu's lawyer and my father doubted the police's official version. When looking at the broader picture of who was involved with Shem-Tov's murder, the possibility there were other motives looked increasingly plausible.

The dispute over gambling clubs, therefore, made for a third possible motive. The plot kept getting thicker as my father dug deeper into the underworld.

Such a strange coincidence, too, that Danoch was near the double-murder scene and went to the police station to give a statement. And what were the odds that one of the IDF soldiers near the murder scene, who chased and caught Sammy Abu, was Danoch's son?

My father's third installment about organized crime in Israel was published on April 19, 1971. The first line read, "As a side product of Shem-Tov's murder, the existence of a French Mafia in Israel was revealed." In the early stages of the investigation, when the police sought to extend the suspects' arrests, they raised the possibility that it was a gang war. They hinted that members of organized crime gangs in Europe had been trying to infiltrate Israel. Representatives arrived to "feel the market." These Europeans met with local resistance and my father argued that the murder of Shem-Tov and Elmalech were the first shots in the attack of the French Mafia on the Israeli market. A fourth conceivable motive.

Altogether, my father's investigation yielded four possible motives:

1.   A dispute over Olga the Spanish blonde, which Abu's lawyer debunked.
2.   Mentesh's frustration over Shem-Tov's debts.
3.   Danoch and the competing gambling club.
4.   An attempt of the (Jewish) French mafia to take over the Israeli crime world.

In an article my father wrote in 1991 after Mentesh's death, he mentioned a fifth possible motive. A source from within the crime world told a version involving stolen diamonds. According to that source, following a diamond heist, Shem-Tov was asked to hold on to the large loot. At a later point he claimed that the diamonds were stolen from his home. This, the source said, led to a contract on his life.

So many possible motives, yet Sammy Abu, the least likely killer, was languishing in prison, serving a life-sentence for the murders.

I can see how this probable injustice created an itch in my father's psyche, an itch to repair the world. An itch he passed on to me.

In the April 19 article, my father explained that around the time of the murders, several wealthy families arrived in Israel. Among them were two families from North Africa who lived for several years in different European countries. According to police sources, the wealth of these families was made through "non-kosher deals." It was said that these families were in the center of organized crime gangs in Europe, especially the "Protection Racket Network," an organization involved in the "protection" of night clubs, bars and other businesses.

"Unlike in other cases, the Tel Aviv police demonstrated praise-worthy speed and decisive action in preventing crimes and nipping the network in the bud," my father wrote.

About a month and a half after the murders, the police went after French and North African families. They showed up with search warrants at the Marrakesh restaurant owned by Eli Abutbul and at the houses of three brothers who may have been part of the French mafia. The search was very efficient, and the police knew exactly where and what to look for. They found counterfeit dollars, guns and ammunition.

The story about the French Mafia quickly spread and there was excitement in the courts about it. Eli Abutbul remained under arrest although the only charge against him was illegal gun possession. The police and the prosecution refused to release him on bail despite medical documents showing he suffered from heart disease. A prolonged incarceration cost him his life. After Abutbul's death, the police withdrew from the French Mafia version and turned their attention to the North African gangs.

For such a young and small country, there were already so many different gangs and mafia groups.

Implied in the article is a possible police collusion with certain criminal elements, helping them fend off foreign interference. My father described the typical way the police stopped "protection gangs" from taking over various restaurants and clubs in Tel Aviv. All the while, Danoch's "security company" was pretty much left alone, even though it was clearly a protection racket.

"To give the affair a more dramatic flair, a new story was born," my father wrote and went after the Danoch family with greater zeal. He described how Shimshon Danoch, a gambling club owner and the brother of Yisrael and Kochva who owned the "security company", complained to the police that certain people were trying to murder him. Shimshon Danoch claimed that three masked men with guns approached a taxi driver near a night-club in Tel-Aviv and demanded from him, at gunpoint, that he tell them where they could find Danoch. Not knowing it was him, they didn't hide their intention to murder him. Following this peculiar encounter, Danoch provided clues that led the police to the French Mafia.

It was after Danoch's revelations and the embarrassing death of Eli Abutbul while in custody that the police began to examine the version of the story that suggested potential infiltration attempts by the French Mafia. They investigated the possibility that these families, who might have indeed amassed their wealth through illegal means, moved to Israel to invest and take a breather. However, high-ranking police officers denied the version held by lower-ranking officers regarding the presence of an international organized crime ring and asserted, "We are strong enough to block any such attempts."

My father explained, "the American Mafia tends to kill the competition in a sure yet quiet way: by leaking information about them to the police."

Taken as a whole, it certainly looks like there was far more at stake than Olga the Spanish blonde.

The way my father unfolded the story reflected his love of a good murder mystery. He devoured all of Agatha Christie's books. On rare nights when he was at home, after my parents watched a movie and the evening news on television, they'd read in bed. My mother usually read psychology or philosophy books, while my father often read murder mysteries or fantasy books like Tolkien's *The Hobbit* and *Lord of the Rings*.

In the classic whodunit *Murder on the Orient Express* (by far my father's favourite), the real murderer goes free. Initially, Inspector Poirot's suspicion falls on twelve passengers. While one of them clearly has committed the murder, as each has a motive, Poirot cannot prove who it was. Instead, an imaginary murderer is created and so Poirot reports that the murderer escaped from the train. As my father demonstrated, in the case of Shem-Tov's murder, the police could not, or maybe would not, deal with all the possible motives and the fictional murderer created was Sammy Abu. Only this convicted "murderer" was flesh-and-blood.

As I was discovering, my father and *Haaretz* had a long history of criticizing the police for incompetence and, in specific cases, corruption or worse. The story of a botched murder investigation is but one example.

THE MAFIA MEN

I wonder if my father would have thought it a stretch to compare him to Mario Puzo. But I can't help myself.

Before coming up with the storyline for *The Godfather*, Puzo worked for pulp magazines like *Mae*, *True Action*, and *Swank*, under a pseudonym. These were fiction magazines printed on cheap paper, as opposed to the more expensive "glossies." My father also wrote for a while under different pseudonyms, and he worked for several years in the two sensationalist tabloids *Bullseye* and *This World*, where his real name was rarely attached to his articles. For both men, the experience in these magazines created connections with members of the crime world, which served as inspiration.

Most of the vignettes that comprise *The Godfather* were based on real events involving Italian gangs in New York, where Puzo lived. Several were based on rumours and some on what was reported in the media. Puzo's genius was to fictionalize them and create a compelling storyline.

My father's brilliance was in examining all the criminal events in Israel and turning the fiction the police created into non-fiction. He noted parallels to *The Godfather* and that set him on a particular course.

"Your father has a unique ability to take details and synthesize them into the big picture, in a way others usually can't," my mother told me in my teens.

His ability to take seemingly unrelated parts and see the whole served him well. His articles were vignettes that told the story of the Israeli mafia in its infancy.

Yet all the while, he failed to see both the details and the big picture of my challenges during childhood.

As I perused his articles in chronological order, I saw what my mother meant. Looking at various pieces he had penned about crime in Israel, I got a glimpse into his psyche and internal processing style, which ultimately led him to conclude there was organized crime in Israel.

"What Is Organized Crime?" was a subheading in his April 19 article titled, Home-Made Mafia. My father argued that a naive Israeli citizen might have thought of organized crime through a Hollywood lens, but this was misleading. The best insight about the mafia in real life was given through Joseph Valachi's testimony to the US Senate committee. Valachi was a low-ranking member of the Genovese Family of the New York mob who became an informant. From his testimony given in 1963, the authorities learned more about organized crime in America than from anyone else. He confirmed the existence of such a network, and according to an American Justice Department official, Valachi "showed us the face of the enemy[9]."

My father referred directly to *The Godfather* (in Israel it was titled, *Don Corleone—The Mafia Man)*. This book, he said, offered a glimpse into how organized crime operates.

The American Mafia can be traced back to the Italian immigration at the end of the nineteenth century and the beginning of the twentieth century and was born in the impoverished areas of New York. It later spread to other parts of the US. The mob's biggest activities were in the largest cities. In Israel, it meant their focus was on Tel Aviv, as that was where opportunities lay.

In comparing organized crime in Israel to the Mafia in the US, my father noted the role of various immigrant groups and described the role of Jews associated with the French Mafia who may have tried to claim a stake in Israel's organized crime network.

The gang families in Israel were also members of the visible minority Sephardi and Mizrahi ethnic groups that immigrated after the Eastern European Jews and were poorer and more disadvantaged. Their business activities—such as gambling clubs, prostitution, protection rackets and drug dealing took place in some of the poorest neighbourhoods in Tel Aviv.

My father described how the Italian Mafia was structured: "The families were weakly linked to each other. At the helm stands the strongest family. The mafia's power is measured not only by the number of its 'soldiers,' but by its connection with higher-ups—politicians, police officers, and organizers in professional institutions. The strongest family provides the others with protection and receives favours in return."

Each family had its own "Don" who was a wealthy and well-connected person responsible for different areas. People turned to him for help with illegal or even legal matters through his connections and he, in turn, gained the support of those he helped, thus increasing his power.

---

9. Jones, L. Thomas, *"The Dying of the Light: The Joseph Valachi Story." Online article from crimelibrary.org* searched on June 27, 2020.

The head of the protection business, which the Tel Aviv police worked hard to free from "French Mafia" interference, was Yisrael Danoch. He was from the poorer Sephardi/Mizrahi neighbourhood called Kerem Ha-Teimanim (Vineyard of the Yemenites) in southern Tel Aviv, where Geula school was located. Danoch, a Yemenite Jew, was a muscular man and a superintendent in the Tel Aviv municipality. In the past, with his brother Kochva, Yisrael and their "security company", they used force to keep order in the night clubs and discotheques. The company no longer existed when the article was published but the protection business was still booming. This is how it worked—for those in the nighttime entertainment business who didn't get the Danochs' protection, fights and disruptions happened every night. The customers would go elsewhere, and the club owner would face bankruptcy. There was also a chance that the club would get burned down. With protection, things went smoothly. Any fights were squashed efficiently without police involvement.

"Danoch once explained to me," my father wrote, "'I don't even need to place guards, it's enough that they know that this or that place is under my protection, the restaurant and club owners know very well, because my name is guaranteed to work.'"

Another popular endeavour of the underworld, illegal gambling, was controlled by Shem-Tov of the Olga the Spanish Blonde story. These were not publicly known clubs. Some were licensed, others weren't. They operated in old apartments with two or three rooms. The kitchen became a cafeteria, and each room had one or two big round tables that sat ten to twelve people each. One of the tables was dedicated to dice games. Large sums of money passed through these tables—tens of thousands of liras each night. The money came from various criminal activities, such as thefts, heists, and prostitution. Whether or not someone won big, the house always took ten percent from each win. These clubs were owned by multiple partners—about ten of them. One of the partners was always the primary. The clubs were well guarded and anyone who knocked on the door went through strict security checks. A guard kept watch at a distance, to warn if the police were approaching. But police hardly ever came, and the explanation was always the same: not enough manpower and no complaints.

Perhaps more important and telling is the fact the police used the clubs as a source of information. In the past, the Shem-Tov family controlled the business. He had the right ties and used to send fruit baskets as gifts to various municipality clerks. Once Shem-Tov was murdered, the family's power decreased and the Danoch family's power increased.

My father linked Danoch to Mentesh. He explained that Shimshon Danoch dined with Mentesh once a week. To quote Mentesh, "They all come to my home, and they all eat at my place: porters, criminals, ministers, police officers and judges."

From April 1971, when my father's series was published, Danoch and Mentesh became household names in many homes in Israel, including mine. I remember overhearing conversations between my parents about a dicey situation at my father's work. Although my parents did their best to shield me from that aspect of our lives, I managed to pick up on the fact that someone, maybe Danoch, had gone to my father's office, yelled or maybe threatened him, and the police got involved. It was only after my father's death that I pieced together the full story, filling another hole in the quilt.

Psychology and Logic

The Danochs, my father argued, dealt with debts in addition to their protection rackets and gambling ventures. Some debts you wouldn't want to pursue through the courts, so you'd turn to Shimshon Danoch or his people, who were happy to get the job done in return for fifty percent of the amount owed. During one of my father's conversations with him, Shimshon Danoch denied that his approach was based on violence. He elaborated, "I work with psychology—I come to a person and explain things, use logic and people listen to me." As my father explained, other people called Danoch's method by another name: blackmail. The police, while aware of all this, stayed silent and took no action.

My father experienced the "psychology" and "logic" firsthand when Shimshon Danoch paid him a visit at *Haaretz* on the day the third article came out. Danoch was most displeased with my father for linking him to the murder of Shem-Tov and other criminal activities and he let it be known. Reading these accounts[10] shed light on what I had overheard as a child but couldn't comprehend at that time.

Later, during his trial, Danoch denied that he had threatened my father with murder. All he did was warn my father that if he'd continue to write about him, he'd punish him severely since "life is a jungle and only the strong ones survive." The judge acquitted Danoch because the Shem-Tov murder trial was still in the courts. Therefore, he ruled it was illegal for the newspaper to write about the possibility that Danoch was linked. Despite the acquittal, the judge did not appreciate the aggressive nature of Danoch's visit to my father's office and demanded a Surety Bond as a guarantee he would not engage in violence for one year.

The *Haaretz* newspaper appealed the decision, claiming that the court had erred in that Danoch's intention was to scare a journalist from mentioning his name and that my father was allowed to do so. A new trial began. More details about the "conversation" with my father were brought forward.

---

10. Information regarding this incident and the trials that followed was taken from short articles in *Haaretz* published without the journalist's name, dated May 12, 1972, June 13, 1972 and July 18 and 20, 1972.

Apparently, Danoch "pleaded" with the cheeky journalist Ran Kislev, saying that mentioning his name in the articles was making his life difficult and if my father kept doing it, he'd make *his* life difficult, too. He said, "I told him that to preserve my honour, I can beat him right then and there so I'll get punished for something I did instead of something I didn't do. I told him he lives in a jungle and that he is just shooting at innocent beings." Then he added, "If you hurt me, I'll hurt you."

Danoch's logic and psychological prowess was evident in his testimony. He claimed that he never threatened to use a knife or a bullet; that it was a lie and that all of Ran Kislev's articles were lies and that all journalists lie.

The second time around, Danoch was found guilty. A witness—another *Haaretz* journalist testified, "I remember Danoch saying that life is jungle and I eliminate whoever tries to eliminate me." Danoch was also heard saying, "I don't want you to write about me. Listen, I'm not afraid of anything and I am willing to go to prison, as long as I come out a real man." That witness also saw Danoch throw a thick wad of bills on my father's desk, saying he was willing to pay him to write about other things and accused him of discrimination on ethnic grounds.

I can imagine the scene. My father, sitting at his desk hard at work, click-clacking with two fingers on his typewriter, when Danoch walks in. Snapped out of his reverie by Danoch's monologue, the deep grooves on my father's forehead grow deeper, his blue eyes open wide in astonishment. He reaches for a cigarette or picks up the one already burning in his ashtray, while the large muscular brute makes his not-so-veiled threats. If his heart rate increases at all, it is due to excitement.

I am sure he found it amusing. Herman Wexler, a.k.a. Ran Kislev, had survived far greater threats to his well-being in his youth. Perhaps he didn't even take Danoch's threats seriously.

Indeed, it wasn't my father who complained to the police about Danoch's visit.

From a *Haaretz* article dated May 12, 1972, I learned that the confrontation arose during an investigation into another incident at *Haaretz*. Police chief-commander Eli Lavi testified in court that my father recommended to *not* pursue the case against Danoch. He thought Danoch's words were just bravado.

Memory fragments of intense conversations between my parents suggest that my mother did take it seriously and was scared and worried. I remember my father trying to calm her down.

"Nothing will happen. They're not that stupid that they'd try to actually hurt a journalist."

"But you know that journalists get killed by the Mafia, like that journalist in Italy who was recently killed."

"Come on Chip, you're being ridiculous. Stop with the hysterics."

Variations of this conversation took place several times over the next few years, as my father followed up the first series with another one in 1972, then another exposé two years later that he co-wrote with his colleague Avi Valentin. He had no desire to stop spreading the word. Instead, he happily accepted invitations to lecture around the country, including in many kibbutzim and took us along. We travelled the length and width of Israel with him and were treated like royalty. My favourite part was being allowed to sleep in the kibbutzim's Children's House and getting into mischief with the other kids.

My father often spoke on radio and television, too, though he preferred to avoid television so his face wouldn't be so well recognized. It didn't help. I remember people stopping him on the street to congratulate him for a job well done, praise his courage, or occasionally, to curse at him. Until I was about twelve years old, none of it seemed unusual to me. I assumed all fathers received that kind of attention in public.

The judge during the *Haaretz* appeal was critical of certain facts being brought to the courts' attention so late. This time Danoch was found guilty of threatening my father's life and was fined and received a twelve-month sentence with three years of probation. Danoch appealed the results of the appeal. In July of 1974, the judge ruled against him, again, explaining that Danoch had the right to ask my father to stop writing about him or even sue him, but not to threaten his life.

Looking up the Danoch family history, I am struck by my father's nonchalant attitude about the people he aggravated with his articles.

According to the French-Jewish journalist and author Jacques Derogy,[11] who researched and wrote extensively about Israel's history and its mafia, the Danoch family arrived in Palestine from Sanaa in Yemen in the early 1900s. The patriarch Yehia was a butcher and passed the trade on to his children. The family set up an illegal slaughterhouse and a butcher shop in the southern part of Tel-Aviv. Yehoshua Danoch, Yehia's son, had four sons of his own and several daughters. Three of his sons achieved notoriety: Kochva, Yisrael and Shimshon.

---

11. *Israel Connection, la Mafia en Israel*, 1980, Jacques Derogy (out of print).

Yehoshua was also the one who gave the name to the neighbourhood they lived in: Kerem Ha-Teimanim. His eldest son Kochva was trained in the slaughter of animals. One Friday evening, Kochva tried to enter a *mikve* (bathhouse) in his neighbourhood to purify himself before the beginning of the Shabbat. He arrived at closing time and was turned away. This led to a violent exchange between Kochva and the mikve owner. The son of the bath owner intervened by stabbing Kochva in the leg and back.

Various pieces on the Danoch threat against my father, *Haaretz Daily*, 1971-1972.

A reconciliation agreement between the families was achieved later and one of the conditions for avoiding retaliation was that the son of the bath owner would not walk on the street where the Danoch butcher shop was located. But the son violated that rule and Kochva stabbed him to death. Since this took place under British law in pre-state Palestine, Kochva was tried under that law and sentenced to death. But his sentence was later commuted to life in prison. Twelve years after the proclamation of Israel, he was released. In the meantime, the father, Yehoshua, along with his son Shimshon, were also involved in the murder of a person who tried to blackmail the father by threatening to report his illegal slaughterhouse and butcher shop business. They invited the young man to the butcher shop and suddenly the power went out on the street. It was out for less than a minute, but when it came back on, the man's lifeless body was lying on the sidewalk. Yehoshua was sentenced to death, but less than a year later he was acquitted by the Supreme Court due to lack of evidence.

After Yehoshua's death, his son Shimshon left the family business and opened poker clubs. The other son, Yisrael, built a protection-racketeering enterprise, masked as a security company for Tel-Aviv's adult-entertainment venues. There was also the debt-collection business. Initially, violence was used to collect debts; however, after a while, just hearing the name Danoch was sufficient, and debts were paid. Several people have been harmed and a number of them filed complaints against Yisrael Danoch. As Derogy explained, "But in court, they became mute and lost their memory. One of them was even chastised for giving a false testimony! As for the police, Yisrael Danoch has many friends there: 'Thanks to me,' he says, 'there are no problems. The police even send me clients!'"

Derogy wrote, "Yisrael Danoch was the type of guy born into poverty, educated in the cult of force and raised in violence, to the point of making it an integral part of his life."

And so were his brothers.

The Danoch family was not to be trifled with.

And yet my father did.

It must have been soon after Shimshon Danoch's visit to *Haaretz* that I made a cool discovery in my parents' bedroom.

Like the feral cats I followed around the neighbourhood, I loved jumping to high places and hiding. Being mostly alone at home after dark, I occasionally climbed and hid on top of my parents' wardrobe, and laying on top of it I would trace bumps in the ceiling. I got up there by using the shelves of the wardrobe as steps. Trying to find new ways of entertaining myself, I also used the shelves as a springboard to jump onto my parents' bed. But mostly, I'd just lay on my back on top of the wardrobe, eyes closed, imagining exciting adventures.

A couple of weeks before my ninth birthday, as I scaled the shelves and stepped too hard on the top shelf, it came momentarily out of place, and I heard a strange sound. Once on top of the wardrobe, I lowered my head down into the wardrobe shelf and pulled out my mother's sweaters one by one, dropping them on the floor, until something black and shiny revealed itself. Were my parents hiding a cool toy from me? On the far end of the top shelf appeared a black pistol, like the ones I'd seen on episodes of *I Spy* and *Mission Impossible*. My heart beat faster. There was also a metal case with shiny gold things stuck inside. It seemed to belong with the pistol. Cool, bullets! A gray carton with lots more bullets was stashed deeper inside. When I managed to fish it out, I realized the bullets fit perfectly into the little holes of the thingy that turned around inside the pistol. I rolled each of them in the palms of my hands, looked at their details and put them one by one into the holes. I'd never known that bullets were so beautiful until I saw them up close. Once I filled all the holes, I was ready to shoot evil people. Bang-bang. I pointed the pistol at the wall across the room and pulled the trigger.

I didn't know about the safety switch. Fortunately.

Within a short time, a second pistol appeared in my parents' wardrobe, along with a cool looking holster.

From the spring of 1971, every time a journalist, a prosecutor or a judge was attacked or killed anywhere in the world, my mother brought up the subject. It was pointless—my father did not give in to threats.

"Don't worry, I can defend myself and us if needed," he told my mother.

"Not if they shoot you in the back," she said, "or blow up your car."

Was it courage or stupidity on my father's part? Was he reckless or did he believe he could protect us with his little pistols?

When people told me over the years that they felt my father was brave to pursue this and other risky subjects, I felt pride. But as a parent it is inconceivable to me to put yourself and your family in such danger. That part of me gets angry when I think back to those days and my father's nonchalant attitude.

His psychology and logic are a mystery.

A Meeting with the King

There was so much I didn't see or know about my parents' world growing up. Hearing them repeat a name didn't mean I knew who they were speaking of. Mentesh was one of those names and I just had a sense that my father didn't like this person. And of course, I had no idea that there were people who disagreed with my father's opinion of Mentesh.

As I've discovered since, several were quite vocal and took to defending Mentesh in the same newspaper where my father worked.

While there were also those who, like my father, believed Mentesh was the Godfather of organized crime in Israel, others saw him as a philanthropic and well-connected businessman and the actual godfather of many children—a real mensch.

So, who was Mentesh?

Dubbed "The King of the Thessalonikis", (he was from that city), Mentesh had friends in all the right places, from high-ranking officers in the army and police, to judges, politicians, religious figures, government ministers, and powerful municipal employees in Tel Aviv. His ties to politicians dated back to the early days of Israel and even pre-state, when he worked at the Jaffa docks. Later, he became a leader of a large group of muscular porters, some of whom he recruited to help keep the order and prevent disruptions during meetings of the Socialist (Labour) party that rose to power and stayed at Israel's helm for decades.

Somehow, Mentesh found out that my father was planning to write about him and requested meetings. My father acquiesced, of course.

First, Mentesh suggested they meet at the upscale Café Skala in downtown Tel Aviv, but he didn't show up at the agreed upon time. Instead, one of the café owners, Munia Shapira, approached my father and told him that Mentesh was waiting for him at a nearby store, also owned by Shapira. He led my father there. It was a clothing store but there were no salesclerks or customers inside.

Mentesh sat behind the counter, close to the display window. My father noted that he looked pale, his hands trembled a little, and drops of sweat gathered above his lips. Odd, considering that this man, whose chiseled face resembled that of a ruthless Caesar, struck fear in others with the lift of one eyebrow.

After letting them in, Shapira locked the store and went to bring cognac and coffee.

"I want to lay open my heart and my whole life for you," Mentesh said and asked to arrange another long meeting at his home.

My father agreed. Could he have been more reckless?

At one point during the conversation in the store, my father turned his head and noticed in the corner of his eye that Mentesh made a hand signal to an individual standing outside the display window.

"I leaned over to see who was outside, but the window was blocked from me. 'What happened? Something happened?' Mentesh asked nervously."

My father ended the meeting abruptly and left.

Near the coffee shop, my father saw two men with a certain body type and faces that didn't seem to belong to the landscape of Café Skala, which typically attracted classy or Bohemian characters. Maybe a scar on one man's cheek and a nose that had been broken twice on the other guy's face?

Next my father observed, "They didn't look at me. I entered my car, which was parked nearby and observed the developments. After a minute or two Munia Shapira came out of the store, turned to the two men, exchanged a few words with them and they left the area."

Why did Mentesh and Munia Shapira invite these goons? Were they planning to use their "psychology" on my father? Or maybe they initially planned to beat common sense into him, but Mentesh changed his mind.

Three more times, my father obliged Mentesh and met him at his home. Why did he agree to that, rather than meeting at a public place again?

To the first meeting at his home, Mentesh invited Munia Shapira as well. He refused to let my father record the conversations, so my father brought a witness to transcribe what was being said—he covered his bases well.

Mentesh pulled out favourable articles that were written about him, including articles by other journalists in *Haaretz*. "You can write a book about me," he told my father, and only reluctantly shifted the conversations to the topics my father wanted to address. It was important to him that my father describe him in a positive light, as he wanted to preserve his honour for the sake of his children.

Could this explain why he was nervous when they first met?

"When I heard that you were going to write about me I approached Ezer (Ezer Weitzman—a cabinet minister and future president of Israel) and asked him to help me. I told him that they are working on me, that they say Mentesh—mafia. I waited two weeks, I came to him again, and then Ezer said: 'Nothing can be done. They are looking. They will write.'"

After mentioning Ezer Weitzman, Mentesh went on to tell my father about his connection with General Moshe Dayan, who was the Minister of Defence at the time, and Shimeon Peres, who was then the Minister of Transportation (and future prime minister and president). This was serious name dropping, possibly to intimidate my father.

It didn't work.

CONNECTIONS AT THE TOP

On Mentesh's turf, in his apartment in Ramat-Gan, a town near Tel-Aviv, my father went straight for the jugular. Ignoring any veiled or obvious threats, he told Mentesh it had been argued that he knew a lot more about Shem-Tov's murder but chose not to help the investigation.

"Why should I help the investigation? That's what the police are for," Mentesh said, probably with a smirk as it was likely the police were in his pocket and surely my father thought that, too.

Undeterred, my father steered the conversation towards Olga the Spanish blonde, whom the police argued was the reason for the murder. Mentesh denied knowing her and said that several of Shem-Tov's family members who thought he had millions of liras went to the police and pointed a finger at him. This probably had something to do with the fact that Shem-Tov named Mentesh in his will.

"It pains me that he died." Mentesh said. The ones who were suffering, he said, were himself, Shem Tov's three children, and his wife. Mentesh was expected to help with Shem-Tov's daughter's wedding and the son's Bar-Mitzva and Shem-Tov had left him debts.

That wasn't where my father wanted the conversation to go, so he redirected.

"In court, it turned out that the issue around the woman wasn't the motive," he said to Mentesh and pointed out that, while a person was charged with the murder, they had no motive.

"Do you know the people in Shem-Tov's circle?" my father asked.

"I didn't know and didn't inquire."

"Do you know who gave the police the story about the woman?"

"No? Was it me?" Mentesh asked.

"Not you, Yisrael Danoch," my father replied. I can imagine him suppressing a laugh.

"They came to me at four in the morning and said Shem-Tov was dead. I fainted."

With quite a bit of dramatic flair, Mentesh was making the case he had no reason to order the murder of Shem-Tov.

Skilled in investigative journalism, my father asked plainly, "Who benefited from Shem-Tov's death?"

I wonder if the police had asked that question, too.

Mentesh argued that no one benefitted from the murder but that someone suffered, suggesting again he was a victim. He was prickly when it came to the way he was portrayed in the media. Ignoring this sensitivity, my father kept looking deeper into his business dealings and that of his people. He closely examined issues that Mentesh had with the mayors of Tel Aviv. During the reign of the previous mayor, Mentesh was very helpful. For example, he was called to help put an end to the strike of the city's street cleaners and garbage collectors. But when Mayor Rabinovitch came to power, things became complicated.

Two big rows between Mentesh and Rabinovitch took place. The first one involved Shem-Tov's brother, who opened a disco-club in Tel Aviv. The municipality demanded thousands of liras for parking permits, so Mentesh went with the brother to the new mayor and asked him to allow his friend to set up a monthly payment plan. Rabinovitch refused and an ugly fight erupted, including swearing and a threat by Mentesh that he'd ruin Rabinovitch's career. Later, several party members (i.e. the Labour party of which Rabinovitch was a member) and city employees approached the mayor, and the matter was taken care of to Mentesh's satisfaction—whatever that meant.

The second dispute occurred after the fire in Ariana, a night club Mentesh was closely linked to. The city refused to issue a permit to rebuild and demanded the payment of a large tax debt first. This time, the discussion between Mentesh and Rabinovitch turned uglier.

According to my father, "Mentesh grabbed Rabinovitch by the throat and threatened him. The mayor of Tel Aviv didn't react, but the permit was issued."

After that incident, the wife of the previous mayor spoke to Mentesh and arranged a *sulcha*, a reconciliation.

"Since then, the two live in peace, but without love," my father wrote.

On April 20, 1971, my father's article titled "Mentesh (Mordechai Tzarfati), The Servant of Mapai and Raffi"[12] was published. Now my father was going af-

---

12. An earlier left-wing political party, later merged with Mapai and the Labour Union parties to form the Labour Party.

ter the dominant political party, too, and linking them to the person he believed was at the top of organized crime in Israel.

The next two instalments were all about Mentesh and his links to police and several political figures.

Throughout that autumn week in a log cabin in the countryside of Quebec, I read my father's accounts with bated breath. Was there anyone my father didn't try to antagonize?

Occasionally, I needed to stop reading and go for a brisk walk in the crisp air. For the first time in my life, I was aware of how much danger my father had put us in. It was one of the many ways that I was re-writing the narrative of my childhood.

The article published on April 21 was titled, "Connections at the Top—the Police, a Special Chapter in the History of Mentesh's Empire". The next one, published April 23, was titled, "Mentesh About Himself—Connections with Ministers Namir, Rabinovitch, Officers and Members of the Party."

The picture that emerges in these articles about Mentesh is both chilling and complex.

My father referred to Mentesh's many connections and "philanthropic activities". People who worked for Mentesh said that he could arrange anything, including having police records "go away". However, Mentesh claimed he had not done anything illegal and showed my father proof of the many cases where he helped people with their legal matters. These were letters to the Minister of Police or Attorney General that were signed by different people. Most of these achieved their goals—usually closing a police record on various charges. From car theft, breaking and entering, and possession of stolen goods, causing damage to property, Mentesh could take care of any "problem", including successful requests to convert jail time into community service. There was even a request to provide a letter indicating the person had no criminal record so he could live in Germany. While Mentesh argued that these documents proved everything he did was kosher, my father saw it differently.

So, what did all this mean? Was Mentesh a Don Corleone type, a philanthropist, or something else entirely?

Protectsias or Protection

A possible way to understand what Mentesh was doing was to consider the fact that Israel was built on a culture of favours, or *protectsias*. My father explained it me this way: "Those who arrived first in British-Mandate Palestine and then to the newly created Israel helped their families, friends, and acquaintances who immigrated later. They, in turn, owed them."

As a result, those who were close to Mentesh saw him as a very powerful man who could get almost anything done. His strongest connection appeared to be with the Minister of Police, Bechor Shitrit, whom he described as a close family friend. They were seen together often. Police officers who spoke to my father joked that Mentesh was the one who picked the district chief of police, Yaacov Kanner.

Mentesh had his hands in many different endeavours. One story my father told involved watermelons. In 1965, two watermelon growers rented a piece of land from a farmer, an owner who lived in Paris. That year, the yield was exceptionally good. The farm owner asked the growers to pay him the exorbitant amount of twenty thousand liras as compensation for the unexpected high yield. The growers refused. The farm owner was a friend of Bechor Shitrit, the Minister of Police Affairs, and asked for his help. Shitrit called Mentesh, who in turn, sent his strongmen "to reason" with the stubborn watermelon growers. They saw the light (or darkness) and paid the landowner the additional payment he demanded.

Growing up, I remember my father telling me, "All politicians are corrupt and if they are not, they become corrupt in time." The deeper I dug into his articles, the more I saw why and how he came to that conclusion.

In addition to his great friendship with Shitrit, Mentesh was close to the police chief superintendent at the time, Mr. Wolfson, who headed the prosecution office of the Tel Aviv district.

"Mentesh does not deny that most of his smaller requests he gets taken care of through this officer," my father wrote, and added that the two were often seen together at a bar in Tel Aviv.

There were also restaurants and steak houses in Tel Aviv that received licenses despite major issues and violations. Neighbours' complaints about problems like excessive noise into the wee hours of the night, illegal dumping of garbage in yards, and ensuing rat problems, were silenced. These businesses were either partially owned by Mentesh or by his business associates, including another character my father named in the series as a big shot in the underworld, Betzalel Mizrahi.

While Mentesh presented himself as a harmless, well-connected, fatherly, philanthropic figure who was a victim of bad press, to me, it all reads like scenes from mob movies where politicians and police personnel are in cahoots with mobsters. In the case of Israel, connections extended in those days to high-ranking military men and religious figures, all powerful in their own ways.

None of this was a secret, in great part due to the fact Mentesh enjoyed having his picture taken with generals and politicians. My father wrote, "Most of the important people—Moshe Dayan, Shimon Peres, high ranking police officers, army generals, judges and more—he didn't use directly. It was enough for him to be seen with them—to increase his power among the lower ranking clerks in various institutions who had the power to get things done."

Photos of Mentesh with different powerful figures peppered some of my father's articles. It included, of course, the Minister of Police Affairs, Bechor Shitrit, and the one-eyed General, Moshe Dayan[13].

Mentesh was involved in soccer, too. He had a monopoly on the business of security in soccer games going back to the late 1950s at the recommendation of the chief of police Amos Ben-Gurion (the son of the first and third Israeli prime minister David Ben-Gurion).

This was possible because Mentesh had a small army of strong men whom he reassigned from other roles to be ushers at soccer games when needs changed. Over time, he attained control over the veteran ushers, who had to agree to accept his authority if they wanted to keep their jobs.

In one case, one of the soccer clubs had problems with its ushers, some of whom were members of the underworld. It reached a point where the ushers

---

13. Dayan lost his left eye in 1941 when he fought with the British against the Nazis in the Syria-Lebanon Campaign (https://www.ifcj.org/news/stand-for-israel-blog/moshe-dayan-s-eye-patch).

dictated who played in a game. Mentesh was called to help and brought a few extra guys to put a stop to the problem.

My father dedicated another article to the war between steakhouses and the protection racket in the Carmel Market in Tel Aviv. Again, Mentesh was portrayed as an important player, although he denied any wrongdoing and said he was simply trying to help mediate. My father interviewed Yaacov Kanner, the head of the inspection department in the Tel Aviv municipality who used to be the Tel Aviv Chief of Police. My father challenged him on different cases where Mentesh intervened to help obtain various licenses for criminals. Kanner denied anything untoward happened or said he didn't remember.

In the seventh article, titled "Kanner Doesn't Remember", my father asked Kanner about the time Mentesh was arrested in relation to an investigation regarding the smuggling of hashish through the Jaffa port. The next day, Mentesh was no longer among the detainees, and it was argued that Kanner arranged for his release. Kanner claimed it happened a long time ago and he couldn't remember. My father also brought up a story he heard that Mentesh was involved in an attempt to kidnap a prostitute from Haifa who fell in love with a taxi driver and wanted to stop working for her pimps. Mentesh's fingerprints were found at the scene but a police officer from Tel Aviv was sent and asked, in the name of the Chief of Police, to close the file and get rid of the fingerprints. Kanner said he heard that story but added that he heard a million stories and didn't take any of them seriously.

In that article, my father quoted Kanner, who said that the late Minister of Police Affairs, Bechor Shitrit, didn't make a move without Mentesh.

I wonder how the average Israeli in those days felt when they read the articles. Were they upset that the police, which they were supposed to trust, was under the thumb of a questionable character like Mentesh?

As I would soon learn, views on this were split and a debate raged.

MENTESH—
CROOK OR MENSCH?

Not everyone agreed with the way my father saw Mentesh. Even before the full series was published, a public debate erupted.

So, who was Mentesh—a crook or a good guy, a mensch?

During the publication of the organized crime series, a businessman by the name of Baruch Rosen wrote a rebuttal to my father's article on Mentesh titled, "Mentesh the Way I Know Him" and it was published on May 11, 1971, in *Haaretz*. He felt that my father's depiction of Mentesh was wrong and described an event my father wrote about in which a man, referred to as "a rich old man", one of the biggest importers of sugar and flour, was told he had to pay a merchant tax determined by the pre-state activists. The old man refused and threatened to report this to the British Mandate authorities.

After attempts to coerce him by plastering posters around town demanding payment failed, one of the pre-state Jewish activists suggested that men should be sent to the stubborn merchant's apartment for further convincing. Mentesh sent his men into the old man's apartment, and they threatened to shoot him if he didn't pay. Mr. Rosen felt that if Mentesh was admonished for that, he should also be admonished, as he was involved in such activities too, along with activists who later became respected members of the community. I remembered from history class the pre-state tax imposed to help support the cause of fighting the British with the goal of achieving independence. These were seen as necessary, so it was a grey area at best. But there is nothing grey about a threat to shoot someone who refuses to pay.

My father's point was exactly what Rosen argued: powerful people recruited Mentesh's services and he, in turn, used his connections to attain favours for those close to him, including members of the criminal underworld. That's precisely how these things work, by doing favours for political actors and threatening those who didn't like the methods. This in turn allowed Mentesh to, among other things, make his drug-smuggling charges disappear, cut through bureaucracy and eliminate obstacles to getting business licenses. It also made it possible for him to help criminals disappear police records, jail terms, shorten their time in prison, and so on. Some saw this activity as helping to reintegrate those who went astray back into society. But I am not sure any of them ever made it onto the path of good citizenry.

Rosen shared with readers stories that he felt showed another side of Mentesh. For example, he was involved in getting supplies to Jerusalem during the events of 1948.

As the United Nations was moving towards the declaration of Israel's independence, the Jordanian army attacked and took control of the west bank of the Jordan River including Jericho, Bethlehem, Hebron and east Jerusalem, where the old city was. Several Jewish religious sites were turned into chicken coops or animal stalls. The Jewish quarter was destroyed and the cemetery on the Mount of Olives, where Jews had been burying their dead for thousands of years, was ransacked. Thousands of tombstones were smashed and used as building material. The Western Wall became a slum, and Jews were not allowed to visit it or other holy sites. The Jews who lived in the city were under siege and depended on the arrival of trucks that delivered food and supplies. Deliveries took days, as Arab forces laid mines, set traps, and ambushed the trucks on the road to Jerusalem. Things got worse when air raids began. During that time, Mentesh was involved in getting supplies packaged to be shipped to Jerusalem. Baruch Rosen wrote that the Mentesh porters who were recruited to drive supplies to Jerusalem were freaked out by the air raids and stopped working. So, he had a pep talk with them. He convinced them to keep working despite their fears, doing the difficult job without a break or food, thus getting essentials like milk powder to the children of Jerusalem.

Another impressive story Rosen shared about Mentesh was regarding his intervention on behalf of Greek women who were Holocaust survivors whom the Nazis had sterilized. Mentesh heard about an expert who might be able to help. He contacted him and arranged for dozens of the women to be treated, and he gathered the money to pay for it. Mentesh became the godfather of the children born to these women.

"What's the story with Mentesh?" I asked Jonathan, The Source, back in 2013.

He answered me first by referring to the Bar Mitzvah party for Moshe Dayan's son that Mentesh arranged for free. He said that an investigation began, and Dayan complained.

"Yeah, amazing how Dayan got away with so much stuff," I said thinking of the rumours about him stealing antiquities from archaeological sites in the Sinai dessert and his many extra-marital affairs.

"But I think Ran was wrong about Mentesh." Jonathan said.

"What do you mean?"

At that point, I hadn't yet read the articles and letters to the editors, so his comment shocked me.

"Mentesh was a well-respected *Macher*, a fixer. Neighbourhood people came to him for help. If someone was harassed in jail, Mentesh went straight to the superintendent. He was the chair of the Thessalonikis and had political power. He was close to the Labour Party and convinced the Tikva neighbourhood, which was a Likud stronghold, to vote Labour. Peres was a Histadrut[14] member, and Mentesh got to Peres through his personal driver. The only one who didn't get involved directly was David Ben Gurion."

This was an interesting angle. I hadn't known this yet about the Labour Party and Mentesh. I remembered my father telling me that Shimeon Peres was corrupt; he couldn't stand him—another secret I kept for him.

While Jonathan shared his perspective on Mentesh, I felt growing tension in my neck as I considered the possibility that my father may have falsely and so publicly named Mentesh as a criminal mastermind. I remembered hearing that Mentesh claimed my father destroyed his life.

If my father was wrong about Mentesh, he'd caused him great harm. I can see now why there was such a noisy debate about the series and the people my father named.

---

14. The largest workers' union in Israel.

The First Inquiry Committee

"The Circle Closes" was the title of the final article of my father's series on organized crime, which came out on June 4, 1971. In it, he laid out several examples of what could have been seen as police incompetence at best or police collusion at worst. He described limited interventions in the illegal gambling clubs, in relation to prostitution, illegal construction in the Carmel Market, and more. My father described a couple of police measures that had taken place and seemed more for show than substance. He wrote, "It is possible that there is still a chance to eliminate the organization. If such surgery won't happen quickly, we might be too late. In the meantime, there are no indications that the authorities intend to perform this operation…".

The article concluded: "Maybe the authorities will get a push to act against organized crime from the place where I started the series at: the mother of Shem Tov Mizrahi who was murdered and asked the government bodies to re-open the investigation into her son's murder."

When searching the phrase "organized crime in Israel", I came across an academic paper by the criminologist Avi Davidovich. The 1993 paper was titled, Organized Crime in Israel and Around the World. Theories and Reality.

Davidovich reviewed the responses to my father's articles. In response to the accusations in the series, the police embarked on a mission to save their reputation. First, they engaged in self-defence. On June 15, 1971, Moshe Hillel, the Minister of Police, claimed in an interview that they operated with limited resources. A few months later, the same minister contradicted himself when he addressed accusations against several officers and claimed Israel had a good police force that could deal with any public entity or government body. In December of that year, however, he said one shouldn't put the blame solely on the police. It was a complicated system, he argued, that involved education and socioeconomic factors.

Right from the start, high-ranking members of the police, politicians, and even army generals claimed that Mentesh was a good guy and what my father saw was nothing but fiction. Possibly as a result of public pressure, the Minister of Legal Affairs directed the Attorney General, Meir Shamgar, to examine the claims made in my father's articles. This was to be the first formal inquiry on the subject.

Haaretz, my father, and many in Israel were anxious to learn the results.

Davidovich noted that Shamgar said that he found no evidence for the existence of organized crime in Israel and disagreed with my father's repeated claim that certain crimes happened with police knowledge and silent approval.

Shamgar didn't mince words, and in his summary he wrote: "These accusations against the police are baseless and repeating them in the different articles [in the series] and especially in the thirteenth article, does not add weight to them…Therefore it is regrettable that these accusations against the police even saw the light of day."

I was nine when the report came out and I had no idea what it said, but I do remember how upset my parents were, as I overheard late-night conversations between them. I recall my father mentioning the name Shamgar, as well as, "ignorance", "denial", "waste of taxpayers' money", and "organized crime." There were only a few times I remember my father pacing in our living room as he did at that time.

Memories of phone calls of people laughing on the other end of the line resurfaced. It must have happened after this report came out. Were the calls from members of the police or criminals? Were they gloating?

In his report, Shamgar examined several issues addressed in the articles. He looked at whether the model of organized crime my father described in Israel matched the American model as described in *The Godfather*, probably because my father mentioned similarities. Looking at my father's descriptions of Mentesh's connections to the police, army, and government, and as godfather to many children, Shamgar understood this to mean my father saw him as equivalent to Don Corleone and made it clear he saw things differently.

Shamgar was highly respected, and the position of Attorney General was considered high and mighty. So, it was tricky to challenge him in the manner that my father and *Haaretz* were accustomed to. However, *Haaretz* published my father's bold response on September 27, 1971.

Channelling his frustration with Shamgar's report into a rebuttal, my father pointed out several weaknesses in his analysis. In the report, Shamgar answered the larger question posed to him by concluding that Israel had no organized crime, after comparing it to the American and Sicilian mafias. My father's response to that was, "No one argued that organized crime in Israel exists in a form identical to that of the Cosa Nostra." He noted certain similarities and argued that poorer and disadvantaged immigrants in both countries were the ones who created the organized networks of crime.

Reading this now, frustration bubbles up my throat. What my father was up against reminds me of the comparison I read once between how we treat traumatic experiences and garbage. In both cases, we try to ship what we reject as far away as possible, thinking it won't come back to haunt us. But it does. Suppressed memories and painful truths we deny find a way back through symptoms; similarly, the toxins in garbage contaminate the soil we grow food in, the water we drink, and the air we breathe. Denial and suppression do not turn truth into fib, nor do they make a problem disappear.

The main point my father made was warning at the end of the series that there was still an opportunity "to perform surgery" and to prevent the problem from getting worse. It was a reflection of his wish to create a better Israel.

About the claim that there was no sign that Israel had organized crime because it didn't look like the Italian or American, my father wrote, "There is also a significant difference. The economic power of the organization in our small country is far from the immense power of the Mafia. Another difference: although it already exists for several years, the Israeli organization is still in its early stages." My father explained that there was still time to eliminate the mafia, but he warned that in a year or two it would be too late.

Interestingly, despite refuting my father's claim that Israel had organized crime, Shamgar recommended passing laws that would limit the activities of organized crime. This included fast-tracking the law related to security companies. The goal was to prevent them from hiding their protectionist activities under the guise of a security company (the Danoch brother's security company was an example) and implementing licensing of gambling clubs. Shamgar wrote that Mentesh was just a harmless lobbyist, but asked public authorities to avoid such lobbyists and wrote that "they would benefit from avoiding and staying away from connections that distort unjustifiably their image

My father ended his rebuttal of Shamgar's report by praising him for making these recommendations despite the many weaknesses and faulty conclusions. While he appeared to keep his composure publicly, at home, I heard him swear a lot (in Polish) after this report came out. *Idiota* and *kurde* (damn), were his favourites.

I can't help but think of what the first mayor of Tel-Aviv, Meir Dizengoff, once said: "We will be a normal country when we have our prisons and people to put in them." Well, according to my father, Israel did better than expected on that front. At the young age of twenty-two, it already had every type of crime, including an organized network of criminals with ties to politicians, high-ranking army personnel, and police. The country's shadow was in full view and my father claimed that denying reality would only enable the proliferation of criminal elements to uncontrollable levels. In time, it would become clear that he was right.

Denial and suppression are not a long-term solution and are not without consequence.

What a Wonder

Mentesh's menacing shadow hung over our home, looming at least as large as that of the Danoch brothers. His name was mentioned with such regularity, it was as if he rented a room down the hall from me, a room I wasn't allowed to enter but could hear scary sounds emanate from.

In the years since, Mentesh was for me the archetypal Godfather figure of Israel's organized crime. To see him more clearly, I looked beyond my father's articles. There is a fair bit of information about him online, as well as in Derogy's book.

Long before my father wrote about this all-powerful figure, Mentesh was a Greek teenager who tried to enter British Mandate Palestine with a group of Greek Jews from Thessaloniki. They were turned back.

Derogy wrote, "the genesis of the Israeli Mafia is closely linked to the birth of the state. In these heroic times, Mentesh, also known as Mordechaï Tzarfati, reigned over the land. If anyone needed to solve a problem, collect a debt, resolve a conflict or unleash a warning, Mentesh was the answer. Mentesh was known as the first 'Godfather' of Israel." Derogy described him as "the man who, for all the circles of Israel and especially for the Mafia, incarnates the 'Godfather of Godfathers': The one who inspires respect, at times affection, but more often fear, in those around him."

But how did Mentesh reach his mythical status?

He first arrived on the shores of British-Mandate Palestine in the summer of 1933 at age sixteen. In those days, he went by the name Mordechaï Shimshi. Along with a group of Greek Jews from Thessaloniki, he made his way on a shaky boat with other illegal immigrants who had escaped the surveillance of the Royal Navy ships that blockaded the coast and landed in the port of Jaffa. As soon as they set foot on shore, British soldiers seized the refugees and sent them back.

A year later, with a certificate in the name of a certain Mordechaï Tzarfati, the young Shimshi followed the same route, and this time was allowed in. He settled in Palestine without difficulty and assumed his borrowed name—it is the name that appears on his Israeli identity card. It was a wise move to leave Thessaloniki which, before WWII, had close to sixty thousand Jews. Fifty thousand of them perished in concentration camps once the Nazis occupied Greece. It was the only city in the diaspora that had a Jewish majority before the war. It was called, "la madre de Israel (the mother of Israel)" or "The Jerusalem of the Balkans."

Once in Palestine, Mentesh found a rundown room in Jaffa close to the sea, which reminded him of Thessaloniki. Work at the time was scarce, and the available jobs were firmly held by Arabs.

Derogy wrote, "It was in Jaffa where the leaders of the Jewish union, the Histadrut led by David Ben Gurion, faced the greatest difficulties in integrating their Jewish friends into the labour market, to realize the Zionist ideal of "Hebrew Labour".

Mentesh was eighteen years old, but unlike his Greek friends, he could not claim to be an athlete. Along with forty other unemployed men, he posed as a dockworker in the port of Jaffa. The encounter with the Arabs was far from cordial. Their leader seized a wooden orange crate, brought it to his mouth, and began a wild dance with the crate held only by his teeth. After a few minutes of this dance, to the cheers of his protégés, the Arab worker put down the crate and gave the Jews an unexpected challenge: "If one of you is able to do the same thing, it will mean that you will be able to work at the port!" The Thessalonikis and the representatives of the Jewish union looked at each other. None of them felt they could repeat the feat of the Arab. Without warning, Mentesh, the youngest and smallest of the lot, moved confidently towards the crate left on the ground, lifted it and grabbed it by the teeth. He began to dance a Greek dance, while his stunned friends cheered him on, singing *Eize Pele, Eize Pele* (what a wonder, what a wonder).

It is indeed the stuff of legends, although apparently it is true.

As I learned more facts about Mentesh, he came to life and slowly turned from a one-dimensional name to an almost three-dimensional character in my mind. I found myself vacillating between seeing him as a criminal overlord through my father's critical eyes, and as a mythical figure through the eyes of those who admired him. Was I betraying my father by considering another perspective? But, reviewing all the evidence is, after all, what the daughter of a journalist should be doing.

In an article after Mentesh's funeral in 1991 which he titled, "The Death of a Godfather", my father wrote that after the showdown on the dock, the Thessaloniki Jews stayed in the port as dockworkers with equal rights. Mentesh was a charismatic leader who was able to get things organized. When the first ship arrived at the new port of Jaffa with cement, he organized porters to unload it, which is how he made his first connections with the Hagannah (Defence), the secret Jewish army which later became the IDF (Israeli Defence Forces).

From that day, the port of Jaffa was open to Jews and Mentesh became the supervisor of the Thessaloniki dockers. The creation of the Jewish port of Tel Aviv was the first in two thousand years and Mentesh became its leader. The goods sometimes included weapons. Derogy wrote, "From boats to ships (he eventually bought a fleet of them), from boats to warehouses in different parts of Palestine (he soon had his own trucks there, too), the cargo-handling monopoly was his."

Seeing Mentesh's resources, the head of the Jewish Agency[15], Levy Eshkol, entrusted Mentesh with the task of safeguarding hidden weapons for the Hagannah, coal for the immigrant ships, and wheat and other food items that were crucial to the Palestinian Jewish community at war with the British occupier.

"In this style, involving a mix of Zionism and crime, the cooperation between the Jewish Agency, Levy Eshkol also tasked him with breaking into the British's emergency storage to get oil for the refugee ships," my father wrote. Their cooperation included bringing Jewish refugees from Greece and finding them accommodation in Tel-Aviv. Mentesh's men broke into laundry rooms in buildings at night, let refugees in and "calmed" the angry homeowners down, probably using some combination of "psychology" and "logic".

To carry out his missions, Mentesh was freed from all military obligations and was exempt from the taxes and other duties that were expected of everyone else. He was obviously seen as an asset, a valuable warrior, one serving the political agenda through both conventional and unconventional means—and he was handsomely rewarded. Granted tax breaks and literal get-out-of-jail cards, endorsements and privileges provided by the highest authorities, he had every reason to think himself a righteous soldier for the Jewish cause. I understand the confusion he and others experienced.

But the larger context for understanding Mentesh lies in the history of the Jewish state and how Israel came to be, which my father did not address in his writing.

Following growing antisemitic attacks in France, Russia, and other Eastern-European countries in the late 1800s, Jews realized that they needed a na-

---

15. An organization that played a central role in the creation of Israel. Pre-state, it facilitated the smuggling of Jewish refugees from Europe to British-Mandate Palestine when the British set very low quotas.

tional home where they could live freely, without worrying about persecution. Zion was one of the names for the land Jews were expelled from two thousand years earlier, thus, Zionism was born. Theodor Hertzl founded the political movement of Zionism and, in a pamphlet he published in 1896, called for the creation of a Jewish State in the biblical homeland. The first Zionists arrived at their indigenous homeland during the reign of the Ottoman Empire that ruled the area from the 16th century to 1917. Jews who escaped pogroms in the late 1800s were able to establish themselves in the area under the protection of foreign consulates.

In 1922, the League of Nations gave Great Britain the mandate to govern a newly created territory they named Palestine. In recognition of Jews' historical connection with the land, Britain was asked to facilitate establishing a Jewish national home.

Following pogroms in Eastern European countries in the early 1900s and the growing Nazi threat and hostilities, more Jews made their way to Palestine. Initially, the British were in favour of the establishment of a Jewish national home there. But a surge in immigration led to increased pressure in Britain by local Arab leaders to limit the number of Jews entering. Consequently, from the 1930s on, the British authority provided fewer immigration certificates than there was a demand for.

Mentesh's destiny was tied to these events, and the trajectory of his life made much more sense to me as I learned about the broader context.

DOWN THE MIDDLE

The major change in policy by the British happened in 1939 when restrictions and criminalization of Jewish immigration to Palestine went into effect. This was happening while Hitler and his allies were systematically murdering Jews throughout Europe. Attempting to appease the Arab population, Great Britain produced the *White Paper* restricting Jewish immigration to Palestine to seventy-five thousand people over five years. They also limited the purchase of land by Jews. Desperate to escape the intensifying antisemitism in Europe, Jews turned to illegal immigration, finding different and often creative ways to enter and establish themselves in Palestine. One of their channels would be through the young Mentesh.

In total, between 1939 and 1948, over one-hundred-eighteen thousand Jews reached Palestine.

Even after WWII, and after all the horrors of the Holocaust were widely known, Great Britain continued to turn away thousands of Jewish refugees and jail them in detention camps in Cyprus. At the same time, the urgency of harbouring Jewish refugees intensified. Breaking the British law was a necessity without which tens of thousands more Jews would have perished in the Holocaust. This is where the value of people like Mentesh lay. He could circumvent British law and bring in Jews seeking safety in their ancient homeland, helping them to find jobs and places to live. Stealing weapons from the British, getting supplies to Jews in Jerusalem who were under siege, and similar activities all won Mentesh a great deal of respect and gratitude.

It's hard to argue with that.

In 1971, there were still quite a few Israelis who remembered Mentesh's role and who, like Baruch Rosen, wished to express their support. They did so by writing letters to the editor. In letters published in *Haaretz* after the articles about Mentesh came out, the opinion of readers about him seems to be split down the middle.

Was my father's view of him unbalanced?

BLURRED LINES

Decades later, reading letters to the editor in response to my father's articles feels like overhearing conversations between people in cafés debating the controversial news of the day. It's like listening to the chatter of people, their emotional responses to matters they may or may not know much about. Some were louder than others. I imagine my father in his office at *Haaretz*, a colleague or secretary reading the letters aloud to him before they were published. Leaning back in his chair, a cigarette hanging from his mouth, he surely furrowed his brow at some and laughed at others.

A letter signed by real-estate builders named The Brothers Gindi may have produced both a frown and a laugh. They felt that what my father wrote about Mentesh was unfair and slanderous and they stated that Mentesh had involved them in charity work.

Similarly, one member of the Israeli parliament, Menachem Cohen, provided what amounted to a letter of reference for Mentesh, naming his philanthropic activities. After listing these, he asked why those activities had not been publicized in the newspaper. Answering his own question, he asserted that Mentesh was simply a modest man who hadn't looked for recognition, motivated only by his wish to help.

If not for him, Cohen claimed, great harm would have been caused. He argued that Mentesh helped the police through his influence over criminals and he argued that my father exposed the informal aspect of police work, not its shortcomings. He argued that Mentesh helped politicians reach the suburbs and if Israeli society was organized differently, Mentesh would not have emerged.

Another reader wrote that Israel didn't have organized crime as my father described it, rather, it had "an organized society", in which Mentesh played a functional role as a liaison between the police, politicians and residents of suburbs.

When my father read these letters, did he have an urge to respond? To defend his position? I know it was important for him to be "right". He might also have thought of the debate that erupted from the point of view of selling newspapers. His series was quite a scoop and his boss, the owner of *Haaretz*, was very pleased with the jump in sales that year.

Other letters indicated that several readers saw Mentesh through the same lens my father looked through.

Yitzchak Ziv-Av, chair of the farmers' association, responded to Rosen's op-ed. He argued that Mentesh's past good deeds did not excuse his bad behaviour nor his involvement with criminals and illegal activities. He also stated that in the case of the American Mafia, a big group of supporters was arranging large gatherings and public prayers in churches to make them look good.

Yet another reader, M. Halpern, felt that the picture that emerged from my father's article about Mentesh was that the emperor had no clothes even if he was wrapped in charity work. He commended *Haaretz* and my father and argued that Ran Kislev should receive a citizenship award for exposing the scandal without fear, and felt his article was the top article of the year. In fact, my father was awarded Journalist of the Year in 1971 for the organized crime series, which also hit international news outlets.

David Ganor praised *Haaretz* and my father for exposing a serious negative phenomenon in Israeli society. He argued that if the situation as my father described was allowed to continue, the foundation of society would be undermined. He wrote that *The Godfather* demonstrated clearly where Israeli society was heading if they failed to address the issue. Ganor added that he had dealt with many of the things Ran Kislev wrote about, and that the descriptions were accurate, clarifying he did not know my father and was not trying to defend him. He simply experienced pain as a member of society and as a resident of Tel Aviv.

Menachem Eisenzwieg, also from Tel Aviv, asked why esteemed members of society my father named—including Moshe Dayan, the past mayor of Tel Aviv, Rabinovitch and his deputy, and the past Tel Aviv chief of police, Kanner—did not publish a response to the accusations. He asked if their silence was an admission of guilt.

Finally, two more readers supported Mentesh. Betty Rubiner described Mentesh's involvement with the needy, including disabled people, widows, injured soldiers, orphans, the elderly, and others. Moshe Fuchs, the owner of a banquet hall, wrote that he was stunned to see Mentesh's name under a headline that didn't fit his personality. He knew him as a selfless philanthropic man.

This sample from letters to the editor published by *Haaretz* following the article about Mentesh offers a narrow window into the debate that my father's articles triggered in Israel—not just about Mentesh, but also about the larger matter of whether or not the young country already had an organized crime syndicate.

For me, having Jonathan's view of Mentesh and the letters to the editor only complicated the enigma rather than clarify what Mentesh was about. He blurred lines around right and wrong during the early days of Israel, done in part from the necessity created by Britain's rules regarding immigration at the most crucial moment in Jewish history.

After reading the letters, I paused and wondered: where was I when all of this was taking place? While my father shone light on the darkest corners of Israel's shadow, his young daughter, me, continued her carefree existence in a corner of paradise—the flower fields and orchards of Maoz-Aviv.

It was just me and the birds, butterflies, stray cats, and herds of sheep and cows from the neighbouring Bedouin settlement of Sheikh Munies. And as always, once my friends returned home from school, finished their homework, and napped, they joined me.

One of my favourite activities with friends was to help each other climb the tallest trees. Being the lightest and most adventurous, I'd usually climb the highest and sway in the branches, dangerously close to snapping the one I hung on to. When the sun disappeared behind our apartment block and mothers called their children home, we helped each other climb down. But in 1971, my parents were rarely at home in the evenings, so I was in no rush to go home. On an evening in the spring of 1971, I declined my friend's outstretched arm and said I'd be staying up on the tree a little longer. The tree was just beside the path between the main street and our apartment block.

When I had enough of looking at the world from above, I climbed down to the lowest branch, but it was still too high above ground for me to get myself down. I had overestimated my ability and was too scared to jump from such height onto the cement path. I don't know where the detectives who usually followed me were, but they sure didn't come to my rescue that evening. From six or seven o'clock, when my last friend left, I was stranded. My only hope was that I would see my parents when they arrived home. Hours passed and other adults walked from their parked cars to our building. One by one, lights in the apartments turned off. I could see just the flickering blue light of televisions until they disappeared, too.

Silence fell and the wind picked up.

Rain drops tapped—first gently, then harder—on my head and I began to cry. Right at that moment, I heard the familiar voices of my parents as they came down the path, struggling to open their one broken umbrella.

"Aba! Ima!" I called when they approached the tree.

My father stopped in his tracks and looked around.

"Kooka? Is that you? Where are you?"

"Here, on the tree," I said quietly, embarrassed about my predicament.

"What, where?"

"Look up Aba…"

"Oy vey! Are you stuck there?"

"Take it and run home Chip," my father told my mother, and I saw her sprint with the umbrella half opened.

"Yes, I can't come down on my own."

"Here, jump into my arms," he stood under the branch with his arms open. I jumped and landed perfectly in them, and I sobbed into his chest all the way to our apartment while he tried to comfort me.

"We can't both continue to work such long hours," I heard him tell my mother after he tucked me in that night. But it would be more than a year before my mother stopped freelancing for *This World* on a regular basis.

Nightmares about being trapped in high places, too scared to jump, continued for decades after that night. But the story of Sara stuck in a tree and my father hearing her calling him from above his head became part of our family lore. The fact that it was an outcome of parental neglect would not occur to me until I became a mother myself.

The Biggest Mechdal

While a debate raged for two years on the question of organized crime in Israel following my father's two series on the subject, the issue virtually disappeared from the media between 1973 and 1975. There were more serious matters to worry about, and my father shifted his focus to politics as he became *Haaretz's* parliamentary correspondent. He bought better suits and ties and looked sharp in them. My mother seemed happier, too, as they were rubbing shoulders not just with celebrities, but also with the top political figures in the country.

One of the events that occupied the media's attention in those days was the disastrous Yom Kippur War. On October 6, 1973, the morning of the holiest Jewish holiday, a day of atonement when observant Jews feel closest to God and ask his forgiveness for their sins in the previous year, the Arab League, led by Egypt, launched a surprise attack.

For kids, this day of fasting and prayers is the one day of the year when they can walk and bike on roads anywhere. Israeli Jews do not drive on that day and there is no public transportation. Early that morning, I was already outside with friends walking on the main roads and taking turns riding a friend's bicycle. At two in the afternoon, we were rattled by wailing war sirens and scampered to a nearby shelter. It was the first siren in a war that lasted nineteen days. Since our apartment building on Bialik Street didn't have a shelter, my parents sent me to stay with my aunt and uncle in the Bavli neighbourhood. Between sirens, I played on the grass with friends, oblivious to the horror of war.

The word *Mechdal*, which is a legal term used to describe a failure (a colossal one, in this case) to do something, was introduced to the public sphere in the context of the Yom Kippur War. The government, with Golda Meir at the helm, was widely criticized for failing to heed warnings and my father was one of the loudest critics. The result of the Mechdal was a massive loss of lives and a collective trauma associated with the failure of the army and politicians to protect. The point of creating the state of Israel was so that Jews could defend themselves from attacks, on their ancestral land. After the Holocaust, nations of the world came to the same conclusion and gave their stamp of approval. The scathing findings of the subsequent inquiry committee published in April of 1974, resulted in Meir's resignation.

Other issues that occupied the media—and my father—included several mass terror attacks in the early seventies and the War of Attrition with Syria between March and May of 1974. There was also the financial crisis of 1974-75 that led to a period of austerity.

Only in 1976, after the security threats had decreased, did a member of parliament (and future prime minister), Ehud Olmert, revive the discussion about organized crime. The media ate it up.

Olmert became the youthful crusader who championed the cause of acknowledging and addressing the issue properly. During that time, my father was often interviewed in other newspapers and on radio shows, though for the most part he still avoided television interviews.

I was still in Geula school at the time, doing my best to stay under the radar in Grade Eight. But my father's name was mentioned so often in the media, I expected my life to be drastically shortened at any moment. I felt that the hidden noose was lowering into full view. At the end of that year, after realizing a workmate of mine was the son of one of the Danoch brothers, I announced that under no circumstances would I return to Geula school.

I reached again for Davidovich's paper about organized crime in Israel. The first time I read his paper, I didn't notice an important observation. What I discovered the second time would shake me for days.

According to Davidovich and others, it was the combination of the Yom Kippur debacle and the refusal to accept the reality of organized crime that led to the toppling of the left-wing Labour government in the 1977 election.

The Labour Party had been in power since the formation of Israel and in the previous elections of 1973, the right-wing party Likud began to gain momentum. The Likud pointed to the persistent denial of organized crime and the fact that Mentesh was associated with Mapai and several MPs as well as the denial of the Minister of Police affairs, a Mapai member, as evidence of their corruption. The strategy worked. As of May 1977, the Likud became the dominant party in Israel and the one to beat.

Before reading Davidovich's paper, I had never heard the argument that my father's articles had a significant role in toppling the government. It meant that my father inadvertently contributed to the rise of the right-wing government.

I wonder if my father felt any regret; he was left leaning politically. But could anyone predict how these things would unfold, and is that a reason to shy away from difficult subjects? My guess is my father would have said it wasn't.

Other than a brief unity government, the Likud has remained in power since, with Benjamin Netanyahu (Bibi) at the helm for almost four decades.

In a twist of fate in 2019, the wealthy British family who bought the whole building we had lived at on Nine Bialik Street, threw a 70th birthday bash for Bibi there. Mercifully, my father didn't live long enough to see the photos of the gaggle of right-wing politicians, businesspeople, and celebrities invade the space he once called home.

Back to its original glory. Bialik 9 after restoration by the wealthy British family who bought it.

As far as my mother was concerned, there was a bigger Mechdal associated with the Yom Kippur war. During the war, my father travelled close to the battlefield near the border with Egypt, at the Suez Canal, to cover the action. Israel was taking massive casualties and bloody battles were taking place everywhere. He did not inform my mother he was going to put himself in harm's way. At the end of the war when he returned home, while having dinner together in our little kitchen, he told us he had had a little adventure, an almost misadventure. But when we heard the whole thing, my mother and I saw it differently.

"If I believed in guardian angels…" he started and before he could finish my mother said, "What happened?" The colour draining from her cheeks.

"Oh Chip, don't go hysteric on me or I won't tell you."

My mother swallowed hard and said quietly, "Tell me, I won't get upset, you are here now."

"Okay. So, where I was stationed was safe at first but the Egyptian forces were gaining ground so I had to be evacuated. A helicopter came to get me, I was the last one to be airlifted because the previous chopper filled up with the soldiers who needed to be elsewhere."

My father paused here, pushed his empty plate and lit a cigarette. I watched my mother closely. Her mouth was slightly open and her eyes wide, almost popping out. My heart raced in anticipation.

I watched my father light and then take a long drag of the cigarette. He stared at the kitchen green tiles that matched the avocado green table and chairs.

"Nu, what happened?" the pitch of my mother's voice higher.

"Calm down or I'll stop talking."

My mother leaned back and, with the open palm of her hand, motioned for him to continue.

"When the helicopter came for me and I got on, I heard the pilot receiving a message that injured soldiers nearby had to be evacuated and they needed all the space for them. He radioed that he was getting me out first, but I told him to evacuate the injured soldiers and come back for me later. The Egyptians were still far enough from me."

"And?"

"And, well, a few seconds after the chopper took off, it was hit by a missile and exploded."

My mother screamed like a wounded animal. I jumped back in my chair and began crying quietly.

"Stop! I'm okay, look at me, I'm okay," and my father put his arm on my mother's arm, squeezing it, as if he could squeeze the horror out of her.

"Look you are scaring Kooka," he said as if she was the one who had created my fear.

"What were you thinking, going there at all? You really are trying to make me a widow and your eleven-year-old daughter an orphan."

"Don't be silly. I am a journalist and I went to cover the war. You should be happy I'm okay and not behave like a mad woman."

My mother stood up, pushed her chair back, and threw her plate into the sink, shattering it. The sound of it, and her fury, pierced through my gut. She stomped down the hallway to the bedroom and slammed the door. My father got up slowly, gathered the broken plate into the garbage bin, and kissed me on the forehead before going to talk to her. They stayed in there for hours and I could hear my mother's sobs. I felt nauseous and hid in my room and doodled for hours.

In later years, my mother told the story to friends in a lighthearted way, referring to a guardian angel who protected her husband from his own irresponsible actions.

THE FIRE AT
THE TABLOID

While my father's series on organized crime caused a firestorm in Israel, there was that other fire, the one at the tabloid my parents had worked for. It happened in November of 1971, two months after the Shamgar inquiry committee published its report which denied the existence of organized crime in Israel.

I hadn't thought about the fire until 2019, when I learned that Uri Avnery, the past owner and editor of *This World*, had passed away the previous year. Sitting in my kitchen in Toronto, I Googled his name to see what people wrote about him. There were thousands of links, but the top one was an obituary—not your typical warm-and-fuzzy one, though. It was written by Nathan Zehavi, who worked for Avnery for many years. His name was familiar to me but lacked context.

What I learned from Zehavi's strange obit unsettled me for days.

My neck stiffened reading what Zehavi wrote about the fire at the tabloid—an incident I remembered from childhood. He didn't like Uri Avnery but didn't want to get into the reasons why. After the fire, Zehavi himself became a suspect. He wrote that one day he would make public details about what really happened the night the offices of *This World*, on Karlibach Street, were set on fire.

Who was he still afraid of, almost five decades later?

He continued, "I'll only say this, the arson at *This World* was in place of killing Uri Avnery and Ran (Wexler) Kislev due to the series of articles that hurt the business and honour of those who were considered at the end of the '60s, the heads of the underworld."[16]

Wait, what?

What did he say?

---

16. Source: https://www.maariv.co.il/journalists/Article-657350

My heart thumped through my skull, which turned into a violent hot flash. I walked out to our backyard deck to cool down in the chilly November air.

After I calmed and cooled down enough, I came back inside, slumped on the sofa and closed my eyes. I reached into my memory vault to see if there were any hints, any words I could retrieve that would have clued me in sooner that the fire was a deal to spare my father's life. I recalled hearing my mother tell my father repeatedly, "Fine for you to take risks but you don't seem to care that you are also putting me and Sara in danger." Now, I had a fresh perspective on her anger.

The line between courage and recklessness in my father had never seemed blurrier.

This discovery was a hole in the quilt I hadn't even seen.

Taking a deep long breath, I kept reading. Zehavi wrote that the first initial of the arsonist was the Hebrew letter *shin* ("sh" or "s" sound). This man was a member of the underworld who became addicted to narcotics and was later murdered by another drug addict. By 2019, those who placed the hit and later agreed to cancel it in exchange for torching the offices of the tabloid were already dead, too. *Shin* received three thousand liras as payment for the arson, a large sum of money in those days. "The life of Avnery and Wexler, who had moved to *Haaretz*, were spared."

I couldn't breathe.

Why hadn't my parents told me about this? Was it simply part of their pattern of keeping secrets in my family, or were they trying to protect me?

Then another thought entered my mind: what if my father never knew that the fire spared his life?

But he must have. The memory of the way my parents behaved after the fire, the whispers late into the night, the seriousness and tense body language told me all I needed to know.

Having entertained all possibilities and replaying fragments of memories from these years, I concluded that my father knew very well what and who was behind the fire.

When I had spoken with Jonathan, he mentioned Nathan Zehavi, too, since he had written a series on crimes in *Ma'ariv Daily* in the '70s. I recognized his name from my parents' conversations but it turns out he was both a journalist and a criminal. I looked online and found out he was caught once in Germany during a diamond heist. He was, according to that article, part of a diamond robbery ring. So, he had his feet—and hands—in both worlds. Maybe that's the reason he knew so much about the circumstances of the fire at the tabloid that spared my father's and Avnery's lives. I wonder if he was the one who had brokered the deal. I tried to contact him through social media, but he never responded.

In 1972, when my father published a second, nine-part series on organized crime in Israel, he named even more criminals. Did he not fear making new enemies and re-aggravating the old ones? Did he not worry that this time they wouldn't be so accommodating by agreeing to torch a building instead of his body?

Like the red wine sauce reduction my husband had been nursing in the kitchen all day, my anger at my father bubbled up and simmered once again, for days. It kept me up at night, too. But something my older daughter Sivan said helped to cool me down.

"Wasn't Saba Ran fearless about exposing the truth?" she said. "Wasn't his goal to point out what needed to be improved? It's called Tikkun Olam right?"

Publishing the follow-up series was my father's middle finger to his enemies and critics and yet another example of his relentless determination to speak the truth as he saw it, no matter the consequences. Taking a big risk was never an issue for him.

"There are causes worth risking your life for," he had told me more than once.

It gives me pause when I reflect on how my life's trajectory could have been derailed had my father been murdered in 1971. There was also the possibility that my mother and I could have been targeted and hurt as proximal forms of intimidation or revenge (Mickey wasn't born yet then). After all, I grew up with police protection and pistols in my parents' closet—a very unusual thing in Israel back then. If I'd infused humour into the story, it was only possible because we all made it out alive.

Was the risk my father put us and himself in worth it? Did he even achieve the goal of Tikkun Olam here, identifying a problem so it could be fixed? From what I read about organized crime in Israel today, I am not sure his articles made much difference.

What did happen, though unintended, was that the repeated denial of the issue by the Labour government contributed to its loss in the 1977 elections. It was the first time the left-wing party lost since the creation of Israel.

Is it possible that because of his early life experiences, escaping the Nazis, and surviving the dangerous life of a partisan while hiding the fact he was Jewish—a double whammy—wired his brain such that he no longer recognized danger? Had he acted that way despite fear, he would have been brave. Had he recognized danger to himself and others and chose to ignore it, he would have been reckless. I'll never know.

I'd like to think he was brave and defied fear and threats to do the right thing. That he followed his conscience, guided by a wish to achieve that elusive Tikkun Olam. But I am conflicted. I would have made different choices as a parent.

Yet, I'm glad he survived it all. That we all did.

ANOTHER INQUIRY
COMMITTEE

After the "commercial success" of the organized crime series, my father advanced from covering mostly crimes to writing primarily about politics and other social issues of his choosing. But his friend and colleague, the journalist Avi Valentin, picked up the subject and published a third series titled "Organized Crime—The Situation Today". The first instalment came out in *Haaretz* on August 5, 1977. The media, and probably the public too, expected the new government to properly investigate the issue, and indeed, on August 7, a new inquiry on organized crime was announced—the Buchner committee. Its members were all members of the police force.

Valentin obtained what became known as the List of Eleven. This document was born out of a meeting between Eliezer Shiloni, the head of investigation unit in the Tax Authority of Israel, and Moshe Tiomkin, the Chief Commander of the Tel-Aviv police. Since the police were unable to gather enough evidence about the criminal activities of the eleven people they suspected were key figures in the crime world, they used the American strategy of fighting organized crime by going after undeclared income and unpaid taxes. This strategy had worked well in the case of Al Capone and had been depicted in the 1987 Hollywood movie *The Untouchables*.

The List of Eleven was kept secret and was held back by the Tel Aviv district chief of police Yigal Marcus, who expressed concerns about the content. Someone from the inside leaked the list to Valentin.

Jonathan and I had spoken about the people named on the List of Eleven and he said that a couple of them turned out to be small fish. I once asked my father what he thought of the list in retrospect. He said he felt that number ten on the list, Yaacov Epstein, was small fish.

First on the list was the very person my father also claimed was the at the top: Mentesh. Second was Betzalel Mizrahi, a friend of the high-ranking army general Rehavam Zeevi, nicknamed Gandi, who was also a member of parliament. Third and fourth on the list were two members of the Kerem gang: Gumadi and Tuvia Oshri. Number eight was Munia Shapira, the person who hosted the first meeting between my father and Mentesh. Number nine was Raffi Shauli, a figure known in the entertainment industry, and one-time husband of Mandy Rice-Davis, who was associated with the Profumo scandal and the owner of the disco club my parents took Omar to.

Since my father was the first to write about organized crime in Israel, people wanted his opinion on the new series, and he gave interviews on radio and television. Once again, the tension at home rose.

I went back to my notes from my conversation with Jonathan. He had told me about his role in the third organized crime series by Avi Valentin.

"I prepared a report that was shelved, buried. Years later it was brought out and Yigal Marcus (the chief of police then) didn't understand a thing when he looked at it. He didn't look too deep into the content. He didn't have all the material."

Jonathan added, "The attorney-general Meir Shamgar heard about the file through Uri Avnery, but a high-ranking officer asked for it and made it disappear. Moshe Dayan got involved."

Scanning the pile of my father's articles, I looked closely at the piece he wrote after Mentesh's funeral in 1991. In it, he opined that, since the chief of police Yigal Marcus admitted to journalists that he was a friend of Mentesh, it was possible he prevented the investigation into the list of names the investigators gave him.

Such a tangled web.

I continued to review my notes from the meeting with Jonathan. He had said: "I advised Valentin not to publish some things as it could lead to lawsuits and to the burning of *Haaretz*."

There was indeed a failed attempt to set the offices of *Haaretz* ablaze.

"Ran based his articles on facts, Valentin on rumours," Jonathan commented.

That fit with how my father treated everything. Having studied some of his life's work, I saw that he approached his articles methodically, almost like scientific papers that he could defend.

"Ran had more sources. Publishing the List of Eleven was the biggest mistake anyone made." Jonathan was referring to the lawsuit Betzalel Mizrahi filed against *Haaretz* and won, almost bankrupting the paper.

Some of what Jonathan told me would have made more sense if I had the broader context in 2013. I might have asked him to elaborate in places. I would have loved to find out more about the clandestine meetings—was my father nervous? Were they scared of retaliation? Did anyone from the police-force suspect Jonathan was "the source"? What about Shem-Tov's murder? And was Abu ever re-tried and released, or did he languish in prison? What did Jonathan know about the fire at the tabloid? I wish I was more informed back then.

My biggest takeaway from speaking to Jonathan was how much, as a true insider, he respected my father and the way he approached his work.

Two Impossibles

In 1977, when the third series on organized crime was published in *Haaretz*, this one by Avi Valentin, the name Ran Kislev was in the news again. Although I was no longer in Geula and didn't have to worry about running into children of criminals, I picked up on nervous energy at home. I found myself looking over my shoulders often when I walked around our neighbourhood. My parents smoked more and slammed the phone on occasion, cursing the callers.

Barely three weeks after the Buchner committee was formed, it published its conclusions. Again, they saw no evidence of organized crime in Israel in the style of the American Mafia. They continued to miss the point.

I remember my father fuming. It was a scorching hot day in Tel Aviv. In his shorts that evening, he paced the apartment, lighting a new cigarette in each room. The whole place filled with blueish smoke. Our phone didn't stop ringing as friends and colleagues called to see how he felt about it. At one point, my father threw the phone down hard on the small stand, almost breaking it.

"This is a joke. I don't think they even examined the evidence in such a short time. Why are they focusing only on comparing it to the American Mafia? Obviously, Israel would have a different system," he said to my mother.

"They are stuck on your comparison to the American Mafia. But leave it. You've done enough. Let others pick up from where you left and do the fighting now."

There, at the kitchen table, it was clear to me that, for my father, denying the reality of what he uncovered was still a source of frustration. More than vindication, he wanted to see meaningful action.

"By denying it, they are allowing the problem to fester and grow and one day it will not be possible to control it."

The speed at which the Buchner committee arrived at its conclusion and the fact its members were all from the police force led to severe criticism that the police was investigating itself. Within less than a month, a new committee was set up, the Shimron Committee. My father's mood improved.

Irwin Shimron, a highly respected lawyer was once the Attorney General of Israel. He chaired the new committee; other members included a former head of the General Security Service known as the Shabach, the commander of the WWII refugee ship Altalena, a past head of the Tax Authority, and a professor of Criminology who was also a past head of the police investigation unit. They took a more thorough look at the subject, and therefore, their investigation took longer. Their mandate centred not only on the question of the existence of organized crime, but also on the ability of legal bodies to expose the activities of such syndicates and to prosecute effectively.

While committee members examined the data, the focus in Israel and the media shifted to a number of major events. Of all events during that time, what captured even my attention, aside from boys, was the historic visit of the Egyptian president, Anwar Saadat, who accepted Menachem Begin's invitation to come to Israel. On November 20, 1977, all of Israel and many around the world watched on television, in astonishment, as Saadat delivered a powerful speech in the Israeli Parliament—the Knesset—reaching out for peace. Another great speech by Menachem Begin followed. This ultimately resulted in a long-lasting peace between the two countries. My father praised them and believed that it was a sign of things to come—he felt that peace with all surrounding neighbours was imminent.

Today I consider Anwar Saadat the greatest political leader of all time. A man who put the well-being of his nation ahead of any religious or political grievances and did so knowing that he put himself at risk. He gave peace a real chance, and it cost him his life. My respect for such courage may have something to do with growing up under the same roof with a man who fought for contentious causes no matter the risk. But in those days, I didn't think philosophically about any of this, and most Israelis didn't even believe that the peace with Egypt would last.

But it has.

What seemed impossible was made possible. Twice that year.

On January 15, 1978, the conclusions of the Shimron Committee were published: yes, there was organized crime in Israel—not American style, but Israeli style!

The celebration at our home took many forms. The phone rang non-stop with congratulations. Gift baskets arrived daily, sometimes several a day. People stopped my father on the street to shake his hand. There was more laughter at home. My father was back to his old self, with fewer frowns and more singing and whistling to his favourite tunes. The dial of the mood-metre in our home shot up, way up. It was hard not to be swept away by the excitement, and I was glad to have my happy-go-lucky father back.

The following Saturday, my father put a Frank Sinatra record on the turntable in our living room and twirled me and my mother around. When he was in a nostalgic or romantic mood, he played "The World We Knew" and "Strangers in the Night". But after the Shimron Committee results were published, he put on "Fly Me to the Moon" and "The Best is Yet to Come" for us to dance to, while my three-year-old brother Mickey clapped and ran between us.

As we pranced in our living room, my father replaced the song lyrics, as always, with "dra-da-da-da" and "shoo-bi-doo-bi-doo's."

On that day, we weren't bothered by my father's deficiencies and flaws. It was a great day for our family, and it was easy to pretend that all was well on Nine Bialik Street, third floor to the right.

A Never-Ending Story

S adly, my father was right when he warned about the perils of ignoring the reality of organized crime in Israel. I found online episodes on the topic as part of an Israeli documentary series called "Light Unto the Nations," which was aired on the Kan 11 channel in 2008. I smiled when they played "Woke Up This Morning,"[17] the theme song of The Sopranos. The second episode started with my father's articles and had interviews with him as the person who first sounded the alarm. But, as they argued in the series, in the early 1970s, Israeli officials preferred to stick their heads in the proverbial sand. By 2008, the documentary confirmed, both Jewish and Arab organized crime gangs proliferated. Their level of violence was unbridled—shooting each other in public places, in broad daylight, blowing up cars of rival gangs.

An article published in *Ynet* on August 7, 2023 was titled, "This Story Will Never End", The Chronicles of Organized Crime in Israel."[18] I chuckled—if more essays on the subject kept popping up, the writing of my book would never end. The journalist, Mor Shimoni, referred to my father's articles as well as others. She quoted my father several times, most importantly his warning about Israel's mafia in 1971: "although it already exists for several years, the Israeli organization is still in its early stages. It is possible that today it can be easily eliminated. But it is also possible that in a year or two, we will reach the situation that American society has reached: the Mafia in the United States can't be eliminated."

Shimoni also interviewed Avi Davidovich, the same criminologist who wrote on the subject and argued that my father's series and the denial of organized crime contributed to toppling the Labour government. Davidovich told Shimoni that in response to my father's articles, everyone went on the defensive because it "indicated not only the failure of law enforcement in dealing with organized crime but also allegations of corruption that spread among its ranks. In other words, not only are you impotent—you are also partners in crime." Police

---

17. "Woke Up This Morning" is by Alabama 3, a British band, from their 1997 album Exile on Coldharbour Lane.

18. https://www.ynetnews.com/magazine/article/skgmhc8tn

spokespersons worked overtime to deny the allegations raised in my father's reports and blamed the situation on "lack of resources".

It was also shocking to read how long it took for the police to take the issue seriously. Davidovich told Shimoni, "In the early 2000s, the Israeli authorities finally began to realize that they could not continue like this, and that instead of these idiotic disputes over the existence of organized crime, they needed to do something."

By that time, organized crime in Israel was completely out of control, just as my father had warned.

Mills of Injustice

I used to think politics was a boring subject.

Not anymore.

As of 2023, the Israeli coalition government—made up of the right-wing nationalistic Likud (ironically meaning Unity in Hebrew) and the Orthodox and Messianic political parties, with Bibi at the helm, have begun what they call, a "judicial reform." It involves giving the government almost absolute power to pass new laws and cancel old ones they don't like, or which limit their power. These include imposing religiously based laws that limit the freedom of secular people. Protests have erupted and criticism from leaders around the world, as well as from Jews and Israelis in the diaspora, poured in.

My father's words reverberate in my head, "Just because some people are wearing a yarmulke or a black coat and hat, and study or teach the Torah all day, doesn't mean they are good people."

From as early as the 1970s, my father had been calling out the Rabbinic court's practices. Over the years, he penned many critical articles on the various ways that religious parties controlled the lives of secular Israelis and about what he saw as their excessive power and privileges.

In a 1973 article, he referred to the leaked blacklist of the Rabbinic court, naming those who were not allowed to marry according to Jewish law. Reasons named included a man who was not circumcised, an intended spouse who was Christian, and so on. In 1975, he followed this up by reporting that there were almost ten thousand names on these lists. In time, he'd be delighted that my brother Mickey chose to marry only in a civil ceremony, even though it meant the extra expense of flying to Cypress to do so.

Among his many articles on religious topics were two series published in 1984. One centred on the state-funded yeshivas that engaged in what he described as the missionary practices of converting secular Jews to orthodoxy—Hassara Betshuva—the Jewish equivalent of being born-again.

A bone of contention between secular and religious groups in Israel had been the special rights of Yeshiva students. These are religious young men who study the Torah. Taxpayers' money (garnered mostly from secular workers) funds the Yeshivas, most of whom do not go into army service, work, or pay taxes. For secular Israelis, both men and women, who complete the mandatory army service and pay taxes once employed, it feels exceedingly unfair.

The last article in the series examined the cost of bringing secular Israelis into the fold of the prayer shawl and the good book. He provided the staggering cost the government paid for each yeshiva student, which was higher for those leaving secular lives behind. My father made an interesting observation, a committee that was set up two years earlier to investigate the issue of cults in Israel faced a tough challenge: how to define a cult without including in it the various groups that engage in converting people from secularism to religiosity or orthodoxy.

The other series my father wrote in 1984 was titled "The Rabbinic Justice Mills". He covered legal matters like the unfair barriers women met when wishing to receive a Gett, a decree of divorce, if the husband refused to give one. He lamented the failure to consider the best interest of the child when one parent decides to convert to orthodoxy, and the shoddy and disrespectful way cases were dealt with inside the courtroom. Decision makers joked around and even left the courtroom or the building to deal with personal matters while cases were still being heard. In this series, my father described egregious violations of basic human rights in decisions, most of which favoured men.

For my father, the right to personal freedom was a central value—freedom of opinion, lifestyle, marriage, and religion.

It was the fact that religious bodies have so much power over people's lives that bothered my father, not their beliefs or lifestyle. "If they want to live in a shtetl in a modern country, it's their prerogative, but I'm not interested."

My father was not moved by the argument that practicing certain religious customs and commandments—like keeping kosher or the Sabbath—helped to ensure the continuous survival of Jews as a distinct people. Or as the secular Jewish thinker Ahad Ha'am (Asher Ginsberg) wrote "More than the Jews kept the Sabbath, the Sabbath kept the Jews." No one was going to make Ran Kislev do something he didn't want to do, and he fought hard to ensure everyone else's basic human rights were protected too, including Arab Israelis and Palestinians.

My father wanted Israel to be the best version of itself that it could be. I watched him click-clack with two fingers on a typewriter for decades, and later on a computer, as he fought with the weapon he had sharpened so well over the years—his words.

A Preacher at
the Gate

In 1960, on the tenth anniversary of the tabloid *This World*, the owner, editor, and main contributor Uri Avnery said, "I believe that a real newspaper has to take on the role that past prophets took, of preachers at the gate, manifesting the national conscience, whipping the tyrants and defending the helpless."[19]

My father spent at least half of his journalistic career writing about politics. As an adult I understand why it was important. One of my father's concerns was that Israel's orthodox political parties could drag Israel in a similar direction to that of Ayatollah's Iran, to religious fundamentalism and the erosion of human rights.

On April 5, 1996, my father published an interview with Shulamit Aloni, who in 1973 established the Citizens Rights Movement, known as *Ratz*. Her electoral platform centred on separation of religion and state and on human rights. She also pushed for dialogue with Palestinians hoping to achieve lasting peace. Her views aligned quite well with my father's. In 1996, she retired from politics and my father sat down with her to reflect on her career. What she was most concerned with, she said, was what kind of society they lived in. "We are at a crossroads. We are done fighting for survival. Both in Israel and in the diaspora [she was optimistic]. When you are done fighting for survival, you have to give some thought to meaning and identity. Our democracy is very fragile."

Aloni went on to say, "We are facing a stunning phenomenon. On the eve of WWII there weren't so many yeshiva students in the whole world as there are now in Israel. They are raising an entire generation of people who live on the public coffers, are brainwashed and are becoming an electoral power." She added that they weren't contributing to society and were creating a ghetto within Israel.

---

19. Erel Nitza, *Without Fear and Prejudice*. 2006, Magness Press.

Memories of my father bad-mouthing organized religion re-surfaced as I read this interview. He had seen the danger where others were indifferent. I didn't understand then what bothered him so much about the Haredi way of life, not realizing some of the haredi and orthodox leaders were working towards changing my way of life as a secular Israeli.

In an article published on February 16, 1999, my father wrote about a protest of Haredi Jews against the supreme court and against secularism. After the supreme court finalized the decision to maintain the separation of religion and state, he noted that two hundred fifty thousand Haredis showed up to protest in Sacher Garden in Jerusalem while only fifty thousand secular Israelis showed up. My father criticized Ehud Barak, the prime minister then, for not recognizing the importance of being present. Barak justified it by saying that the struggle for democracy doesn't go through Sacher Garden but through the voting booths. My father wrote about the right to protest as a basic right in democracy and that the two protests highlighted the real issue, the rupture in the population and that it should not be blurred out. Reading what he wrote in that article, it's as if he foresaw what took place in 2023.

It appears that the goal of the judicial reform was, essentially, to eliminate government oversight. The first step was to pass a measure preventing judges from striking down government decisions based on their "unreasonableness." Other parts of the "reform" would allow a simple majority government to overturn the supreme court decisions and to have a final say in selecting judges. This, some argue, opens the door to corruption of every kind, including firing and making improper appointments to powerful positions in government, municipalities, and various organizations. Many positions, government ministries, and committees have been filled by numerous religious or Haredi MPs, resulting in almost total control over budgets and policies. These steps have created a deep divide within Israeli society.

In the 1999 article, my father wrote, "This is not an artificial rupture that politicians create for political gain. Israel is amid what is called a 'cultural war' and what is in fact a political struggle between two opposing views about the image of the country: a country ruled by democratic laws, like most western countries on the one hand, and a theocratic state, a sort of Jewish version of Iran. In this war, the Haredi-religious camp is the aggressor, even though it pretends to be the threatened side. The threatened side here is the secular, even though it is the majority."

I paused here to reflect on the fact that since 1999 the orthodox community has significantly grown in Israel. In 2025, less than fifty percent of Israel's adult population defined itself as secular.

My father continued, "Israel is still ruled by law, but a theocratic state is not necessarily created through Khomeinistic[20] revolution; it can be built using the salami method, slice after slice, until the point of no return. That is exactly how the Haredi-religion leadership operates. With much talent it takes advantage of the democratic structure, like the Knesset (parliament), in fighting democracy."

He finished the article with, "It is no coincidence that this war takes place mostly in front of the supreme court, in which the Haredi leadership sees the biggest obstacle to its ambitions. But this time they went too far. The slice they want to cut from democracy is too big and it stands out. With their protests the Haredi leaders wanted to scare the supreme court's judges, and let's hope they didn't succeed. But they managed to scare the public. Maybe they scared it enough so that it would stand on its hind legs and fight."

What had happened in Israel in 1999 should have been a wake-up call. My father saw the writing on the wall and warned about how cleverly the Haredi/Orthodox/Religious parties were slicing away at democracy. The supreme court was at the center of it all then, as it is now.

Unlike the small numbers that showed up to protest in 1999, the numbers in 2023 were consistently high and included a cross-section of Israel's population—secular, religious, right, left, and center politically; people with various levels of education; Israeli Arabs and Druz; people of different sexual orientations and all ethnic groups.

When I visited Israel in June of 2023, the dominant subject of conversation among friends and relatives was the anti-democratic judicial reform. I experienced the charged atmosphere first-hand when I joined pro-democracy protests at the Kaplan-Azrieli intersection, which is now called Democracy Square. I am sure that if my father was alive and well enough, he would have joined the protests. Ehud Barak, Israel's past prime minister, spoke on one of those nights. I think about how he missed the mark in 1999 when he failed to encourage protests. My father would have scoffed at him. Barak and others like him slept at the wheel.

In a way, the articles I was looking at served as the calls of the prophet or preacher at the gate. I just wish people had taken his warnings more seriously back then.

---

20. In reference to the Ayatollah Khomeini, the religious leader of Iran who led the revolution against the Shah in 1979 and instituted strict Sharia law.

I trace precursors to today's troublesome events in my father's articles, not only on the issue of organized crime but also on the topic of separation between religion and state, and all matters religion. My father made stark warnings. He criticized the growing power given to the Rabbinic courts in matters of personal freedom and rights such as marriage, divorce; medical matters like organ transplants; access to public transportation on the Sabbath; sale of non-kosher food; women's rights; rights of non-Jewish Israelis; deciding what is an acceptable process for conversion to Judaism; the definition of *a Jew* (in the context of the right of return and matters); and more.

Finally, in one of the small brown envelopes in *Haaretz*, I found a tiny news piece from March 29, 1970. The heading was, "4 Are Demanding to Erase their Jewish Nationality from their ID". Following a change in the way nationality was recorded, four Israeli citizens requested an injunction against the Minister of Interior Affairs demanding the removal of "Jewish Nationality" from their IDs and next to their names in the census. They hired a lawyer, and the case was argued in front of three judges. Their request was denied. The names of the four were: Zigi Shtreman, the artists Levana and Moshe Gershoni, and the journalist Ran Kislev.

I wouldn't be surprised if bringing the case had been my father's idea.

Collateral Damage

It turned out that I wasn't the only child affected by the articles on organized crime.

After Mentesh's funeral in 1991, Done'el Fisher, a journalist from the newspaper *Hadashot* (News) wrote a piece with the headline: "They Called Him The Godfather" and a mouthful of a subheading: "Was Mordechai Tzarfati the Head of Organized Crime as Ran Kislev Argued Or Was it All a Journalist's Imagination. Exclusive Interviews with Munia Shapira, Shimshon Danoch and the Son Yoram Tzarfati About the Secret of Mentesh's Power".

The position my father took in the interview was predictable. He still believed in the narrative he put forward in his series. One of the points he made, in support of his theory that Israel had organized crime, was the fact the phone threats stopped just before the police began surveillance on our phone. Predictable, too, was Munia Shapira, who stuck to defending his late friend, as did Danoch. Mentesh, they said, was someone who helped those in need, including people who strayed, but he didn't break the law, at least not knowingly.

What caught my attention most in the article was an interview with Mentesh's son, Yoram. Ironically, Yoram is also the name of my father's son from his first marriage. The other interesting fact is that Yoram Tzarfati was thirty years old in 1991, which makes us almost the same age. I was fascinated to read his account of the impact of the organized crime series on his father and on him as a child. Yoram Tzarfati's sentiments felt strangely familiar.

We were children of the same age, on the opposite side of the same story.

Yoram Tzarfati shared that when the first articles came out, his home was in upheaval, but he didn't quite understand what was happening. When the List of Eleven (from Avi Valentin's series) came out, he was older and understood more. Seeing how upset his father was, he couldn't look him in the eye and felt helpless. Yoram explained that his father didn't have money, as he gave it all away. All he had was his reputation and honour, and the articles (my father's and later Valentin's) ruined it. He talked about the people who were guests at his home, from actors, singers to politicians and army generals, including several that my father had mentioned, like Shimeon Peres and Ezer Weitzman.

Until I read this article, I hadn't given much thought to how my father's articles may have affected the children of the people he named as criminals. As a child, I was either oblivious or later, in Geula school, scared of what they might do to me if they knew who my father was. Whether the accusations about Mentesh and others were true, partially true or false, the words in the articles written by my father, Avi Valentin, and others, hurt innocent people too, especially family members of the ones fingers were pointed at.

We were all collateral damage.

A Partial Tikkun

For my father, being a watchdog and informing the public was not enough. He needed to achieve Tikkun Olam. On a grand scale. It never occurred to him that his daughter needed repair, too.

In my psychology practice, when appropriate, I encourage clients to have meaningful conversations with their parents before it's too late. I emphasize the fact that what remains unsaid can haunt a person long after their parent is gone. Whenever possible, it's best to bring out to light what has been swept into the shadows. If done from a respectful place, these vulnerable and often difficult conversations can lead to a repair of past ruptures for both sides. I've had many clients share their surprise at how therapeutic such conversations have been for them.

I didn't get a chance to achieve that with my mother, who died when I was thirty, but my father lived long enough for us to enjoy this process. We covered several areas but not all, in part because I was not yet aware of some secrets, such as the fire-instead-of-assassination at the tabloid.

Over the years, my father and I talked about politics. When Yasser Arafat walked away from the Camp David negotiations initiated by Bill Clinton in 2000, refusing an offer by Israel that was very close to his demands, I asked my father if he still believed in a two-state solution and whether he thought peace in general were possible.

"Yes," he said. "It is possible that Arafat is simply not the right person."

"Yes," I said. "He is no Anwar Saadat, that's for sure."

After the failed Camp David talks, many left-wing supporters moved to the center. Some said that Arafat sent a clear message in the name of his people that they are not interested in peace.

After October 7, 2023, the idea some held that one day a kumbaya-like situation would exist between Israel and all its neighbors, appeared to be out of reach. I imagine my father's reaction would have been something along the lines of, "Maybe the right leader has not been born yet. On both sides. And as I write these words, the situation in the region keeps changing daily so who knows how things would evolve or devolve.

I ache for all the innocent people who suffer or die because their leaders cannot do the right thing. And I am glad my father didn't live long enough to grapple with that.

But there were other issues we did have a chance to sort out.

Until my fiftieth year, I quietly carried resentment towards my father for not supporting my wish to pursue a career as a visual artist. It was my calling, after all, and I had the right to try and fulfill my dream. Wasn't my happiness more important than money and prestige? That I'd likely end up a "starving artist" was bullocks, told by a snobbish father who didn't care about his daughter's happiness, only about status. That's what I had told myself for years. After all, he had chosen to pursue a low-paying profession, then he carved out a name for himself and ended up succeeding and earning well.

I had never let go of the dream to make it as a visual artist and over the years have taken classes in photography, sculpting, and various painting techniques. I'd paint on weekends in our kitchen or garage and in early 2011, I was accepted as a tenant into the Artscape Distillery Studios in Toronto. This meant I was recognized as part of the artists' community in Toronto. Two or three days a week, I switched identities. I spent full days at the studio and participated in group shows. My section in the studio had a large window and my shelves were full of art supplies. Although the cost of the studio rental and materials almost offset the income I made by selling my art, I was pleased with where things were going. On a visit to Israel, I showed my father images of some of my paintings and surprisingly, he asked for a reproduction of one of them—the biggest compliment he could have given me.

At the end of 2011, a health crisis forced me to stop working for several weeks. I stayed home and painted here and there but for the first time in my life, I realized that I missed working with my clients.

I had never stopped working long enough to discover fully what my work as a psychologist meant to me. There is a strong creative component to it and an even stronger sense of meaning when you help people and change lives. After my health stabilized and I resumed seeing clients, I knew I had to share my very late-in-life insight with my father. On a 2012 visit, my father was quite frail. While sitting in a wheelchair in his sunny living room in Tel Aviv, surrounded by art he had bought over the years, I said, "Aba, I have something important to tell you."

"What Kooka?" he continued to call me Kooka until the end, but only if no one else was around.

"You were right to trick me into going to university."

"What do you mean?"

He must have forgotten that he had promised to pay my tuition then rescinded after one semester when he saw that I was hooked. So, I reminded him.

We laughed.

"Yes, that was clever, wasn't it?"

"Sure was. I don't think you realize I resented you all my life for not encouraging me to pursue my passion for art. All these years I thought I would have been happier if I was an artist even if I had earned very little."

"You mean starve …"

We chuckled.

"Somehow, my brain never computed the fact that I truly loved what I was doing until I had to take a break to deal with those episodes of high blood pressure."

"Well, I am very happy to hear that."

We sat quietly together for a long time, both of us probably pondering different aspects of my confession. My mind flashed to the blistering hurt I had felt in my teens when he told me my abstract art was not good enough because, "A real artist needs to know how to draw a cow."

"But I don't want to draw cows…" I had said then, fighting back tears as another reason for resentment was born.

I also remembered how, years later, he framed one of my abstract oil paintings and hung it in his living room. This was one of only a few oil paintings I made. I wanted to bring it to Canada, but he refused to give it back to me. He hung it between reproductions of Picasso and several Israeli painters. He also framed a charcoal drawing I made of an old building and another acrylic painting inspired by Achziv, a place in northern Israel, where he took us many times during my childhood.

"What do you like about my oil painting?" I asked.

"It has a lot of movement, and I like the colours and textures."

"So, I'm a real artist now?" I asked him.

"You've always been," he said.

"But I still can't draw a cow," I said and laughed.

"You are good. Just maybe not good enough to make a living off that," he said.

I didn't appreciate the underhanded compliment, but in 2012 when he asked for a copy of my watercolour painting, he had nothing but praise for the composition, subject matter (Dreaming), and the colours. Maybe in the past he had feared that I'd give up my day job if he complimented my art without reservation.

During that conversation, I also couldn't resist bringing up his two-year-long stubborn refusal to pull strings and get me out of Geula school where I was bullied, beaten, and scared for my life.

"I wish I wasn't so idealistic in those days," he said.

Whoa.

For a moment I stared at him, then allowed myself a reconciliatory little smile. Even so, it stirred old pain.

"Is that an apology?"

"Maybe..." my father said, his mouth curving up a little. "I was quite stupid, considering the corruption that was going on all around me. I should've taken you out of that school before you even started."

"Well, I'm not sure about that. But it would have been nice if you did that at the end of the first year when I came home from school black and blue, and my grades plummeted."

His face lost colour and the room was enveloped in darkness. What was the point of making him feel bad now? This is the same dilemma my clients present when they consider difficult conversations with elderly parents. But it's a judgement call in each case. My father was resilient, and I trusted that he could cope with my feedback. And he was highly skilled at putting things behind him. Still, I regretted my harsh words and said, "Well, I survived and did okay in life."

Looking away, my father was quiet for a long moment and finally said, "I am sorry and there is no excuse. Parents should keep their children safe, and I failed you," and I noticed tears in the corner of his eyes. My eyes filled up, too, and we both reached for the tissue box between us on the coffee table. I wanted to hug him but feared we would both end up sobbing and he'd be embarrassed. We laughed afterwards, and as always, steered the conversation to safe and happy subjects—good movies and books.

We turned to humour and joked about the clunkers he drove us around in, like the one that had no floor. We reminisced over the beloved 1962 yellow Ford Consul, or was it the Vauxhall, that could only make right turns. It ended its life stuck in a pothole in Gaza and stayed there because it wasn't worth towing or fixing. And we chuckled about how upset I had been with him that he didn't bring home my sand toys from the backseat. The baby-blue Studebaker Skylark came up, too, and we reminded each other how lucky we were to survive that terrible accident when the brakes failed.

While revelling in nostalgic memories such as these, I asked my father about the risks he took with these clunkers, the frequency with which cheques bounced, and about the unpaid utility bills.

"Oh, the cars were fine," he said and immediately swiveled away to the topic of the cheques.

"The truth is I always thought we'd have the money by the time the vendors would cash them or when bills were due. Besides, life is to be enjoyed now because you might not be here tomorrow."

"Que sera sera, right Aba?"

He laughed.

"Enjoy life now" was his motto for sure. Although, most people practicing this motto did not spend money they didn't have or drive around in floorless death traps.

I wasn't going to get more from him without causing a fight, so I began gathering into my purse my glasses, phone, and a Paul Auster book he gave me.

"Well, no harm done at the end," my father said after a moment of contemplation.

"Actually …" and here I stopped myself from launching into psychological analysis. What good would it have done to lecture him on the impact his irresponsible driving and spending had on my life? My passenger anxiety with male drivers resisted all psychological interventions. But was the fact I developed an aversion to overdrafts and over-spending that harmful?

My oil painting in his living room.

Two more of my pieces in his living room.

Self-portrait (or a selfie) with an old-school film camera.
An unfinished oil painting in the background. 1981.

THE WRONG STORY

In the autobiographical documentary Stories We Tell, the viewer follows the talented Sarah Polley's journey as she tries to figure out who her biological father was. I related to her story on several levels. The lies told in my family about who my biological father was and later the affairs my father had, especially with the journalist Dalia, came to mind. I understood Polley's need for the truth. Her courage to examine the past of her flawed parents is inspiring. There are certain things a child does not want to look into about their parents, such as their infidelity. Sarah's vulnerability and courage to ask difficult questions awakened something in me and I found myself going back to the affair that tore our family apart.

My mother had a hard time understanding why her husband would cheat on her, a former fashion model who spoke eleven languages, so well read, and a published author[21]—a woman whom my father supposedly considered the smartest person he knew, after himself of course.

After my father confessed about the affair and the child, and moved in with Dalia, my mother told me, "Can you believe this? He had *me* all to himself at home, and he went and screwed this ugly-ass woman, this lowly talent-less journalist that probably got the job at *Haaretz* because she..." and I stopped her there.

She was so angry, and yet later, when my father wanted to come back, she accepted him. In those days, I could not understand her or forgive him.

My mother's modelling photo from the early 60's, around the time she met my father.

---

21. My mother published a short story collection titled *A View From Above* in 1984, with Akked Publishers in Israel.

But I no longer see my father's affair through that moralistic lens, nor my mother's forgiveness as a failure.

Out of all the perspectives I'd heard about affairs, Esther Perel's resonates with me the most. Perel, a world-renowned psychotherapist and author, provides a fresh, non-moralistic view on extra-marital affairs. She says that people don't have affairs because they look for another person. Rather, she says, "We go elsewhere because we are looking for another self. It isn't so much that we want to leave the person we are with as we want to leave the person we have become."[22]

Perel's perspective got me thinking about how my father's unique experiences and possibly his genetic makeup resulted in, among other things, an excitement and thrill-seeking personality. The predictability of married life, the routines, waking up and going to sleep with the same person for decades, are the opposite of that. And as Perel said in an interview to Slate in 2014, "we don't divorce—or have affairs—because we are unhappy but because we could be happier."

Perel argues that it might look like infidelity is about the person you met but it's more about you. She argues that recurring affairs are about avoiding intimacy—it can also be that the partner at home is avoiding or unable to offer intimacy. I believe that my mother had problems with intimacy as a result of childhood trauma. She was separated from her father when he left for America in 1939 and tried to bring his family from Europe to safety. They reunited in 1951 when she travelled to New York with her mother, and the relationship with her father was never good. All indications are she experienced his leaving as abandonment. She admitted to having "daddy issues" and I always saw her marrying my father, who was ten years older, in that context. My mother had a history of affairs, too. In fact, she began the relationship with my father Ran while still married to my biological father Yoav. Her first marriage failed; the second was doomed from the start. But I didn't have insight into the psychology behind all of that when I was growing up and even in my twenties when my father left my mother for Dalia.

During a workshop I attended in Toronto, Perel argued that affairs are not about sex, they are about desire, about attention, about reconnecting with parts of oneself you lost or never knew existed. It's about longing and loss. Affairs are also erotic plots: about what makes you feel alive, vibrant, engaged. The danger

---

22. https://slate.com/human-interest/2014/03/esther-perel-on-affairs-spouses-in-happy-marriages-cheat-and-americans-dont-understand-infidelity.html

of being caught may have made my father feel more alive. Maybe that's how he felt when he joined the partisans during WWII.

As Perel noted, the American discourse around affairs is framed entirely around betrayal and trauma. It has been the same in Israel. My mother and I experienced my father's affair with Dalia and fathering a child outside the marriage as deep betrayal and trauma. Today, I can see his behaviour from both the younger self perspective, validating the sense of betrayal that I experienced as a child, but also from the mature adult and psychologist's perspective. The adult me understands the complexity of human behaviour that applies to my family as well, and not just to my clients' lives.

After watching Sarah Polley's documentary, it occurred to me that I never looked closely at who Dalia actually was. Was she the lowly journalist my mother claimed she was? In 2021, I Googled her (real) name for the first time. While she wasn't pretty, she was not a talentless journalist. In fact, she was quite remarkable and accomplished.

It's possible that my father wasn't just after the excitement of an illicit affair. It's likely that he appreciated Dalia's intellect and passion when it came to important social issues that both of them cared about.

Tsipora and Ran, on their wedding day. 1966.

Back in 1986, none of that mattered to me. What did matter was the cowardly way the renowned journalist Ran Kislev waited until I was away in Europe to confess to the affair and to fathering a child outside the marriage. And it mattered to me how immediately after confessing he moved in with his lover, abandoning my mother and brother—it was both shocking and devastating. After that, I stopped talking to him for a second time and had no intention of ever reconciling with him, even after he returned to my mother. He did that, too, while I was out of the country, after I moved to Canada. I am sure he wanted to avoid my scorn.

Eight years later, after my mother passed away, I chose to maintain a relationship with him and as a result, my daughters had a fun, loving and generous grandfather. And I believe the story I told myself all those years about his affairs was wrong.

Fighting Shadows—
Vera's Story

Of all the revelations about my father, the one that had the greatest impact on me had to do with the sad Polish singer Vera Gran—the one who had given me a Polish doll and autographed records to my father. It was heartbreaking to learn what this magnificent woman with a velvety voice asked of my father when she visited us in 1971, and how impossible it was to help her. Only in 2013, after reading my father's articles about her from 1971 and 1972, did the disturbing story emerge. I also came across many articles, documentaries, and a book about Vera by the Polish biographer and poet Agata Tuszynska titled, *Vera Gran: The Accused*.[23] The author coaxed the eighty-seven-year-old Vera to tell her story in 2003, four years before she died.

Vera Gran Fighting the Shadows was the title of the detailed exposé my father wrote about her, published in the weekend section of *Haaretz* on December 3, 1971. I wonder why he chose the word "shadows". Probably, he wanted to allude to dark forces, yet I can't help musing about the way it also reflects his life work, which involved exposing Israel's collective shadow as well as individuals' shadows.

In the exposé, my father began by explaining that a few months earlier, several newspapers published ads announcing that the singer Vera Gran had arrived in Israel and was booked to sing at two of the biggest concert halls in Israel.

These and other planned shows never happened. Posters which had been printed were never displayed.

The reason: a certain phone call by Mr. Pesach Burstein, the Secretary of the International Organization of Jewish Fighters, Concentration Camp Prisoners and Victims of the Nazis. According to my father, Burstein demanded, in the name of thousands of Holocaust survivors, that the performances by Vera Gran be cancelled and declared he had proof that she collaborated with the Nazis. If they would not agree to his demand, Holocaust survivors would show

---

23. The original was published in Polish in 2010, in Hebrew in 2012, and in English in 2013.

up on the evening of the performance next to the venue wearing concentration-camp striped uniforms.

In 1971, many Holocaust survivors were still alive. Such a serious accusation and macabre threat meant no one wanted to take a risk. All of Vera's shows were cancelled, but the matter itself did not go away. The rumour about the cancellations spread and reached the ears of many who still remembered the singer. My father wrote, "Thus, the black-haired woman who still maintains her exotic beauty, returned to the bench of the accused where she is accused of the worst crime for anyone, especially for a Jewish woman. She tried to defend herself but was met with deaf ears. She was told this issue was too sensitive. She attempted to meet with her accusers, but they refused to meet with her."

It took just two phone calls from Burstein to draw a verdict with no chance of an appeal. My father wrote, "In Israeli society and with the justified sensitivity regarding the Holocaust, the meaning of this verdict—public death."

My chest felt heavy as I read this. If Vera was a collaborator it was a horrifying story, and if it wasn't true, her story was still undeniably tragic for her. As if the Holocaust, the darkest expression of humanity's shadow, wasn't horrible enough, another aspect of society's shadow was potentially coming to view.

Vera's second visit to our apartment must have been soon after the cancelled concerts. Vera was different then, sad and sluggish. Now, as I read my father's article and other sources of information about Vera, the memory of her visits makes sense.

In the 1971 exposé, my father presented the broader picture—a tapestry he stitched together from interviews with Vera. He also spoke with people who knew her or claimed they did.

"Warsaw of the late '30s had the nickname 'Little Paris' where cultural life and entertainment flourished," my father wrote. "Jews in those days, despite antisemitism, occupied a respectable place. In 1937 a new star rose: a black-haired young woman with a low voice, warm and sentimental. Within a few months, she secured a regular spot on Polish radio. Her records flooded the market. Several of her songs became best sellers." The woman was Vera Gran.

Years earlier, while still a high-school student, Vera began performing as a dancer at the famous nightclub, Paradis, on Novi Shwait Street in Warsaw. Her dancing career was cut short following a car accident which caused complicated fractures in her leg.

Someone in Paradis discovered Vera's voice. Initially, she sang with an orchestra while hidden from the audience. Visitors thought it was a publicity stunt. The real reason was simpler: seventeen-year-old Vera (whose name at birth was Dwora Grynberg) was too shy to appear as a soloist in front of an audience. In addition, her leg was still in a cast. Within months, she became well known and her salary increased from five zloty an evening to two hundred for each performance—an amount equal to the monthly salary of a clerk in Poland at the time. Her first two records were released under the name Sylvia Green. In 1938 she had a part in the last movie in the Yiddish language filmed in Poland before the war. She played a femme fatale who captured men's hearts when she sang longing tunes in a café in New York. The song "Beloved Mama, Don't Cry" was a tear-jerker. She played alongside a famous Polish actress and became a star after that. At the end of 1938, she took part in the traditional satirical Polish Christmas show where she was called "Marlene Dietrich of the Greenberg House." Later in Paris, she earned another nickname—The Polish Edith Piaf.

MYSTERIOUS
ACCUSATIONS

In 1939, Vera's career expanded internationally when she was invited to perform in Paris. The season started in September but on the first day of that month the war broke out and Vera stayed in Warsaw. During the first eleven days, through heavy and deadly bombing by German Junkers planes, she continued performing. In October, after Warsaw was occupied, she escaped to the east side German/Aryan area. At that point, Vera moved in with her future husband, a well-known Polish doctor, Dr. Kazimiesh Jazirski. His father was Vera's mother's physician. She met the son when he was a medical student and came to hear her sing in Paradis.

When life became more dangerous for Jews, Kazimiesh, who did not look Jewish and could hide in plain sight, offered to take Vera with him to a village in Northern Poland where he worked in a hospital. He said they'd be able to escape to Latvia or Sweden from there, and she wanted to believe him, so she agreed. They fled in cold weather, crossing a frozen river and taking trains. They stayed within the Polish borders. Her intention was to prepare a safe haven for the escape of her whole family, finding a suitable place to bring them to. But it didn't work out.

In the summer of 1940, Vera came back to the Warsaw area with her physician husband. At first, she hid in Krakow, but after the Warsaw Ghetto was closed, and with all her relatives inside, she began sneaking back into the ghetto. Her husband stayed outside.

The Warsaw Ghetto was the largest among all the European ghettos. At its height, as many as four hundred and sixty thousand Jews were imprisoned there, in an area of 3.4 square kilometers, with an average of 9.2 persons per room. Food supplies were scarce. Conditions were appalling.

Life in the Warsaw Ghetto was a tragic paradox between horror and illusions of normalcy, my father wrote. Vera tried to continue to entertain and sang the same songs that had made her famous in pre-war Poland: sentimental songs about the last letter locked in a secret drawer and one about the rain that sings with its drops like a love song. At the same time, in newsreels around the world, images from the ghetto appeared showing street beggars, hungry children, Gestapo Aktsias (mass transports), and starving people.

After returning to the ghetto, Vera began performing regularly at Sztuka Café on Leszano Street. It was run by the top Jewish entertainers in Warsaw locked behind the walls. Among them was Wladyslaw Szpilman, the Jewish piano player who accompanied her. Roman Polanski's 2002 Oscar winning movie *The Pianist* was based on Szpilman's biography published in 1946—Adrian Brody played Szpilman.

Vera continued to sing her pre-war hits in Polish. The place filled to capacity every day. Anyone who could afford it grasped at anything resembling a normal life. My father commented on this, "Today, retroactively, maybe these illusions can be understood differently. It's possible they were dangerous illusions that even blocked the resistance movement in the ghetto." An unsettling thought indeed. He added another perspective, "It's possible that these substitutes to normalcy gave many the strength to endure their suffering and not lose their humanity." However, he explained, this was not what Vera was accused of during the ghetto years. The accusations came years later.

As I read this, I tried to create a mental picture of Sztuka Café, but there was nothing in my experience that allowed me to imagine such a place in the hell that the Warsaw Ghetto was. In *The Pianist*, Szpilman wrote that Sztuka was the biggest café in the ghetto and that it had artistic aspirations. They had a concert room where music performances were held. There was a bar for those who were more interested in food, and they could enjoy chicken cutlets or beef stroganoff.

The banality of it all boggles my mind. And yet, it was a form of resistance the ghetto residents exercised, not letting the Nazis crush their spirit completely—a little bit of light in a hidden corner of the murky shadow of humanity.

Indeed, despite the situation on the streets, my father wrote, the starving and diseased masses and the vermin everywhere, both the bar and the concert room were always full or nearly full.

In *Life Strictly Forbidden*, Antoni Marianowicz wrote that the café became quite popular thanks to Vera Gran's acts. She was accompanied by a fine piano duet: Władysław Szpilman and Adolf Goldfeder and her greatest hit was her and Szpilman's 15-minute interpretation of Różycki's Casanova, called *Her First Ball*.

In *The Pianist* Szpilman wrote that, thanks to being able to perform in Sztuka Café, he managed to earn a decent income and support his family of six. Between musical numbers, the musicians enjoyed socializing with their friends. He went on to name people he performed with and named only one female singer, Maria Eisenstat—not a single mention of Vera.

And there was a more significant omission. In *The Accused*, Vera recalled Szpilman approaching her when she was already singing at Sztuka Café and asking her to help him get a gig there. "He accompanied me before the war sometimes. 'Help me, I don't have enough to live on,'" was how she remembered him pleading. Vera convinced the manager to bring other musicians. She came up with the idea of singing with two pianists Szpilman and Goldfeder. They placed two pianos on the small stage facing each other and she inserted herself in the middle. "The audience almost sat on their knees."

None of this was in *The Pianist*.

Other performances took place in the ghetto during the war. These were arranged by the *People of the Thirteen,* an organization that supposedly fought black-market scalping and was located on 13 Leszano Street. In reality, it was a collaborators' group vying for control of the ghetto which also infiltrated the Jewish resistance within the ghetto. Rather than fight the black market, it collected large sums via racketeering and extortions. Many of the Jewish members in this organization were connected to the Gestapo.

The *People of the Thirteen* occasionally organized private balls to which they invited Jewish dignitaries and artists to perform in front of them. Vera was invited once to one of these balls. Witnesses stated that she initially refused but ultimately agreed, and no one blamed her for that. Those who knew ghetto life well knew that refusing the *People of the Thirteen* meant only one thing. Death.

On September 1, 1942, a mass expulsion took place from the ghetto to a death camp, but Vera managed to escape to the Aryan side with the help of a Polish police officer who used a fake arrest warrant to take her through the courthouse that had entrances to both sides of the city. She was unable to help her family escape the ghetto and eventually lost them all.

For two weeks, Vera hid in several apartments until she moved to Avitza, a village in the Warsaw countryside where she lived until the end of the war as the "Christian" Polish wife of the respectable "Christian" doctor, Dr. Kazimiesh Jazirski.

INVESTIGATIONS

The material I unravelled about Vera was increasingly more disturbing. I found myself sinking into a dark place as I learned her story.

"You are looking unwell," Roni said to me one evening when he saw me reading *The Accused*, surrounded by my father's articles.

"I'm feeling so sad for this woman. I met her when I was a child and knew there was something tragic about her. But I had no idea, how terrible."

"You should take a break and watch a sitcom with me. *The Big Bang Theory* maybe?"

"I can't, I need to know what happened, but I'll make myself tea."

I went back to the book and to my father's exposé. I learned that immediately after the liberation of Warsaw, even before the end of the war, Vera returned to the stage. Jewish and Polish friends and audiences accepted her with open arms. Soon after, rumours began to fly. The stories implied that not all was kosher with Vera during the war. Claims were made that she had connections with people known only to the Germans, that she wore fur coats when keeping a fur coat in the ghetto meant a death sentence. Some said she walked without the mandatory yellow Star of David on her sleeve, in and out of the ghetto. Others said she did so while wearing the yellow star.

The worst accusation that surfaced against Vera was that she collaborated with the Gestapo and gave up Jews who were hiding in Warsaw. It is by far the most horrific crime a Jew could be accused of.

"There is nothing harder than fighting rumours," my father wrote. It required her proving the negative, or as they say in Israel, "Someone said your sister is a whore. Now go prove she isn't."

Attempting to clear her name while still in Poland, Vera sought the only remedy available—she contacted the Polish general prosecution office and told them what she was accused of and asked that they investigate. The stories had also reached a more dangerous organization—the Security Forces of Poland, which had Communist Jews among its ranks. Their focus was mostly on

Nazi collaborators, and the general attitude was that it was better to punish someone whose guilt was in doubt than to let a guilty person go free.

And so, in May of 1945, Vera was arrested by the Warsaw Security Forces. She was interrogated for two weeks and released. In *The Accused*, Vera spoke of the humiliation she suffered.

"Anyone who knew the situation in Poland of 1945, knows that this release is as good as total exoneration," my father wrote. He was one-hundred percent certain that Vera was innocent.

Investigations didn't end with Vera's release by the Security Forces. The Polish prosecutor's office and the Stage Performers' Guild checked all the performers who lived in Poland during the occupation. Later that year, the guild announced that Vera Gran's civic behaviour during German occupation "was without blemish" and closed the file.

Case closed?

Not yet. There was one more institution that had not yet conducted its own investigation—the Citizen's Court of the Central Committee of Polish Jews. It represented all the Jewish political parties of Poland. At the head of this organization was Adolph Berman, a left-wing Zionist, and this court was most strict. Some compared its trials to those of the Spanish Inquisition. Unlike the torture and grisly executions perpetrated by the Inquisitors, the most severe punishment by the Citizen's Jewish court was ex-communication from the Jewish community. And any guilty verdict by that court automatically led to the launch of legal action by the Polish Federal Court.

The Jewish Public Court became interested in Vera after receiving a letter from one David Shneyer. He wrote, "I noticed that the artist Vera Gran has been performing lately in concerts in Warsaw. I declare here that Vera Gran was a Gestapo snitch in the Warsaw Ghetto and I demand that legal action against her be taken immediately."

Shneyer gave a statement at the Jewish Public Court claiming he heard that Vera was connected to the Gestapo and to Jews who were known to be Gestapo agents. He alleged that Vera performed at the Britania Hotel where orgies involving Germans and Jews took place. According to him, she was connected to the Jewish Gestapo agents Kohan and Heller, and he argued that Vera has been given a death sentence by the Jewish Resistance. Shneyer claimed that, already in 1941, he read in the resistance newsletter about several people who had relationships with the Gestapo, among them, Vera Gran.

The pre-trial investigation lasted one year, and twenty-three testimonies were placed into the case file. Vera was indicted. The indictment stated that during the German occupation, from September 1941 until 1942, inside the Warsaw Ghetto and on the Aryan side, Vera maintained social relationships with individuals who were known (Jewish) Gestapo agents.

The trial began in October 1947 and lasted a year and a half. The court consisted of five judges representing the key Jewish political parties. Dozens of witnesses gave testimonies—some of whom repeated Shneyer's accusations, with additional details. Several witnesses testified that "after her performances at Sztuka Café, Vera sat at the tables of individuals suspected to be Gestapo agents; that she came and went out of the Ghetto as she pleased; that after she left the Ghetto she performed at a specific café, with the dancer Franceska Mann*, whom they alleged was a Gestapo agent as well."

The accusations against Vera included a claim that she was seen taking the train in the streets of Warsaw in 1943 with the known Gestapo agent Kohan. Yet, Kohan was murdered in 1942.

All the witnesses had one thing in common: none of them knew Vera Gran personally. When questioned in court, each testified they heard the stories about Vera from other people. Many mentioned one person, Jonas Turkow, as the one who warned them about her. In contrast, other witnesses—people who knew her in person, seeing her almost daily during her stay in the ghetto—disputed unequivocally claims that she was seen in the company of suspected Gestapo agents and collaborators. They insisted she never performed in unacceptable places, only in Café Sztuka and similar places. (An unacceptable place would have been where *People of the Thirteen* or other Gestapo collaborators hung out.)

Another witness, Tarkovsky, the head of the Polish Composers Guild had the task of looking at those suspected to be Gestapo collaborators. He testified that Vera Gran never appeared on his lists. Other notable figures offered similar testimonies.

The most important testimony was that of the couple who shared the two-family home with Vera and Kazimiesh in Avitza. They said they knew her as the doctor's wife. She was blonde then and always wore sunglasses, so they didn't recognize her as the famous Vera Gran. Although they didn't know her personally, they suspected she was hiding and the only time she left home was to go to the village's church. The couple said she gave birth to a daughter and, due to complications, was taken to a hospital in Warsaw and this was the first instance when she went to Warsaw. Later the daughter died, and Vera didn't leave the house after that. In *The Accused*, Vera spoke to the author about an infant she lost in the ghetto. She referred to the infant as a male and said he died at three months due to starvation. Did she lose two babies, a boy and a girl? So many traumas and losses.

Trauma often destroys a marriage. My mind wandered to thoughts about my parents' failed marriages. Each had different types of traumas and very limited resources to deal with them. All their major traumas started during childhood which overlapped with WWII. Their ability to love well was severely compromised by multiple losses and other extremely stressful experiences.

It is not surprising that Vera left her husband after the war when she left Poland.

Once the Citizen's Court of Polish Jews finished hearing all the hearsay, rumours, innuendo, and direct testimonies, it was time to decide. On April 28, 1949, it ruled that there was no evidence of guilt when it came to Vera Gran's behaviour during the war. This was the final step needed to clear her name.

Or so it seemed.

Franceska Mann was a Jewish dancer and before the war was considered to be one of the most beautiful and promising dancers of her generation. She was sent to Auschwitz with a stop at Bergen and there are several versions as to what transpired. According to the most popular version, Franceska was forced to perform a striptease dance for Nazi officers and, once stripped down to nothing but high heels, she took one of her shoes and stabbed one of the officers in the face "with the heel-piece, causing him to drop his firearm, which she then used to shoot the guards. One of them died from his wounds several hours later while the other was left with a permanent limp." It is said this prompted a revolt by the Jewish prisoners of the camp before she and the others were killed by gunfire. Wiera (Vera) Gran was among her friends.

(https://allthatsinteresting.com/franceska-mann)

THE CIRCLE CLOSES

V era emigrated to Israel a few months after the end of the trial. She saved all the documentation related to her trial and investigation.

These were challenging days for singers in the newly created Israel, especially for a singer who "people talked a lot about and whose past is vague," my father wrote. To combat the rumour mill, Vera went to the Israeli police, asking them to investigate her past so that any lingering doubt could be dispelled.

In the meantime, a radio station had a regular spot featuring Vera. Music managers arranged recitals for her that were very well received. She joined a satirical theatre and was considered their main star. But all of this didn't generate enough income to guarantee her financial security. So, in 1952, she moved to Paris and enjoyed huge success there securing a contract for regular performances in France. Occasionally, she went on a concert tour in Europe, the US, and South America—wherever there was a Polish or Jewish community. She sang in Polish, Russian, French, Spanish, Italian, and Hebrew. As she aged, my father said, her voice became deeper, maybe even better.

In the 1950s, Vera rose to stardom in France, winning over audiences and critics. She sang at Maurice Chevalier's Alhambra and collaborated with Charles Aznavour and Jacques Brel. Vera starred in Frederic Rossif's film *Le Temps du Ghetto* and recorded for Radio Free Europe and the Polish edition of Radio France Internationale. A music critic wrote about her "deep voice of a sensual tone, clean diction... With a varied scale of emotion, she sincerely expresses the outrage and indignation of a woman's spirit."[24]

In 1965, Vera returned to Poland for three months, taking part in concerts and recording another album. She and Szpilman recorded a new version of "Her First Ball". In the summer of 1969, the summer of love, Vera sang at New York's Carnegie Hall.

Following her international success, Vera returned to Israel to again explore the possibility of settling there permanently. She was booked to perform

---

24. https://culture.pl/en/artist/wiera-gran

at big venues, and that was when Pesach Burstein called to demand they cancel the show. The horrors she suffered during the post-war years resurfaced.

In *The Accused*, Vera told Tuszynska, "I could have just taken the suitcase and returned to Paris but I didn't want to give in." Instead, she flew to Paris and brought all the documents she'd saved. She knocked on the doors of her accusers asking them to right the wrong. Jonas Turkow, her key accuser, refused to open the door for her.

My father tried to break through the closed circle around Vera Gran, which began to look more like a noose. He called Pesach Burstein who told him, "I was the representative of the organization, I don't know her. I wasn't in the Warsaw Ghetto even. But I know she had relations with Germans," he added. "Hundreds of people approached me including Adolph Berman, and the main witness who knew her best, Jonas Turkow."

When my father contacted Adolph Berman for a response he said, "We don't accuse her of being a snitch." But, he claimed, she lived and had affairs with Nazis. "And if I say Nazis, I mean German Gestapo and SS. She had intimate relationships with these people, and she doesn't even deny it."

"She does deny it. You bet she does!" My father wrote, exclamation mark and all.

Berman clarified, "I personally had no connection to her. In the ghetto I didn't even hear about her. Contact Jonas Turkow, he knows everything about her." He added, "She can live in peace for the rest of her life, but to perform in public—we won't let her!"

My father followed the trail and contacted Jonas Turkow, who repeated the same stories, as stories he heard from others. He added that he read in the resistance publication a warning about Vera Gran. Turkow also wrote about this in his book *Once There Was a Jewish Warsaw*, for which he received a prestigious literary prize in Israel. He told my father he tried to find that publication in an archive in London but couldn't locate it.

I gasped. The only piece of possible evidence Vera's key accuser claimed to have had, he couldn't corroborate. Yet, he included it in his book despite the fact all courts and investigative organizations found no evidence to support this claim.

"The accusations against Vera Gran evolved over the years, from claiming she had intimate relationships with Jews linked to the Gestapo to accusing her of having intimate relationships with the Gestapo people themselves," my father wrote.

Not letting up, my father challenged Turkow to offer one name of a direct witness whose testimony against Vera was not based on hearsay, but from personal knowledge. The accuser gave my father the name of a woman who lived in Tel Aviv. She asked to remain anonymous and told my father she heard a story from another person who was close to Vera. That person said, "Look, there behind the fence Vera Gran is walking with a German." She admitted she didn't know Vera.

In Toronto decades later, I felt nausea as I followed this web of rumours, innuendos and possibly blatant lies that Vera had battled.

My father concluded the exposé with this: "That's how the circle closed. From a public perspective, Vera Gran does not exist. She was condemned to death by a lynch mob trial in which the principles of justice had no place. The words 'I heard' carry a huge weight in this trial, which can cancel facts—if the facts don't fit with the rumour."

As Vera told Tuszynska, "Fate has made me pay dearly for having survived the Jewish Holocaust." She stopped singing as a result.

MARKED

Both Vera and Szpilman survived the war, yet their fates were remarkably different. One was vilified and the other celebrated.

In *The Accused*, Vera said that when the war ended, she went to Szpilman, who was then the director of Polish Radio. "You are not dead!?" he exclaimed when he first saw her. She asked him to hire her, but he refused, telling her of the accusation that she had worked for the Gestapo. This is odd considering he did record a song with her after that. Once Szpilman told her of the accusations, Vera began seeking out all avenues to clear her name. For the rest of her life, she believed it was Szpilman who had it in for her and that he was the main source of the heinous and ruinous rumours.

As I followed the tragic tale, it was becoming clear that there was no court in the world that could have removed the stain that stuck on Vera Gran.

A wave of sadness rippled through me for the woman who first came to our house with a cheerful disposition and later sat slumped on our sofa with streaked eye make-up, sobbing. The psychologist in me who has worked with many trauma survivors is in awe of how much Vera endured, during the war and after. How strong a person has to be not to give up or curl up into a ball of sorrow and shrivel in the face of such horrendous and relentless accusations. A part of me is also deeply disturbed by the maliciousness of the people who attacked Vera, even though she was unequivocally cleared by every possible court and organization who investigated the kind of crimes she was accused of.

Over the years, I heard my father mention Vera's name a few more times. I know they also spoke on the phone, long-distance, and my father always looked gloomy after these calls. I saw him tear up when he listened to her records until he stopped playing them altogether. I now understand why.

Following the cancellation of the concerts in Israel because of Pesach Burstein's actions, Vera sued him, Adolph Berman, and Jonas Turkow for libel. She asked the courts to award her damages.

A short follow-up article my father wrote was published in 1972 on June 25, my father's birthday, coincidentally. It was about Vera's legal claim and the headline read, "The Accusations of Collaboration with Nazis Caused her Financial and Emotional Ruin". My father reported that, following the exposé he published several months earlier, the newspaper received letters from readers in Israel and around the world that disputed the claims made against Vera.

In her court claim, Vera's lawyers argued that, as my father wrote, "The libelous claims against their client caused her financial ruin as her only source of income is public performances around the world. After these claims were published her reputation was damaged and this caused her intolerable suffering and grief. There is no doubt that a long time would pass before the complainant (plaintiff) could recover from the cruel blow inflicted on her by the defendants."

After filing the lawsuit, Vera returned to Paris. There were delays in the hearing of the case. Finally, when a hearing took place in 1975, it was conducted in Hebrew and Vera, who flew in for that, could not participate. Although Vera sang in Hebrew and other languages, she was unable to speak most of them.

I found two letters to the editor published in *Haaretz* about my father's exposé. Both were supportive of Vera. One reader wrote that she knew Vera personally in 1941 and saw her daily at the Warsaw Ghetto. They worked at the Sztuka Café, and she went as far as saying she took full responsibility when stating Vera had no personal connections with Germans or with Jewish agents of the Gestapo. "Her behaviour in the ghetto was without blemish," the woman wrote. Another reader said he was pleased to read the article that was based only on direct eyewitnesses, facts, and documents referring to the period in question. Any objective reader, he said, could clearly see "the depth of injustice done to Mrs. Gran by several irresponsible people." He noted that he was a lawyer in the prosecutor's office in Warsaw and could fully guarantee that if there was even a shred of doubt regarding Gran's collaboration with the Nazis, they would not have dismissed the investigation against her.

It didn't even matter that Simon Wiesenthal, the most famous Nazi hunter sent her a letter confirming her innocence, saying, "your name does not appear among those who have collaborated with the Germans."

In 1977, the Polish Weekly *The Right and Life* published a letter by Jacek E. Wilczur, which Tuszynska described as "a pitiless and hateful attack on Vera Gran." The language used in the letter, she said, was reminiscent of language used in classic Nazi Propaganda. After reading it, Vera suffered a heart attack. More delays with her defamation suit in Israel occurred, and when Vera was called again to testify, she could not appear due to her poor health.

By 1981, Pesach Burstein and Adolph Berman had died and Turkow was old and ill. The lawsuit was dismissed. Not only was Vera Gran assassinated in the court of public opinion, even her lawsuit on that very matter was erased.

Decades after his articles came out about Vera, my father continued to defend her. When interviewed for *The Accused*, he told Tuszynska, "I have no doubt: Vera Gran was innocent. The Germans, despite appearances and rumours, did not willingly sleep with Jewish women. They risked being punished for it. It could take place in the camps, but not in the ghettos. They had their own women, who suited them, and they only slept with Aryan women. And if there was someone in the ghetto who would ask to make an appearance for the Germans, it was Mrs. Turkow, Diana Blumenfeld, rather than Vera Gran."

My father felt that it wasn't Szpilman who was responsible for the relentless persecution of Vera; rather, he felt it was Jonas Turkow. He said, "His wife wasn't a great shining moral example and the dirt about her stuck to Vera. In fact, I think that Vera Gran attracted rumours more than anyone. Perhaps we should ask why."

In a letter that Vera wrote to a publication called *Law and Life* in 1977, she argued that Jonas Turkow did very well in the ghetto owning a performance agency. His wife, Diana Blumenfeld, performed three to five times a week at private parties of Gestapist (Gestapo collaborators) and balls her husband organized. This was doubly profitable, as his wife received five hundred zloty per performance, while Vera was paid far less. She explained, "My only crime, which Turkow announced to the world during and after the war was: that one and only time I was forced to sing for the Gestapist Shimonovitch. Turkow was the first to know about it, not just as a visitor or critic. But due to the five hundred zloty his wife was losing."

In *The Accused,* Tuszynska described Vera's descent into life as a recluse in a dark basement of her apartment in the 16th Arrondissement in Paris. She lived in a cluttered and dusty space, surrounded by piles of newspapers, memorabilia, documents she saved and other things she hoarded. Tuszynska wrote that Vera had become paranoid and suffered from a persecution complex.

But she *was* persecuted.

After losing all her battles with forces driven by the human shadow, Vera' defenses crumbled.

As the psychiatrist Tomass Szasz wrote in *The Myth of Mental Illness,* "Insanity is the only sane reaction to an insane society."

Vera Gran died in 2007 and thirteen people attended her funeral, among them four nuns and two rabbis. On the day of her passing Marcin Przybylski

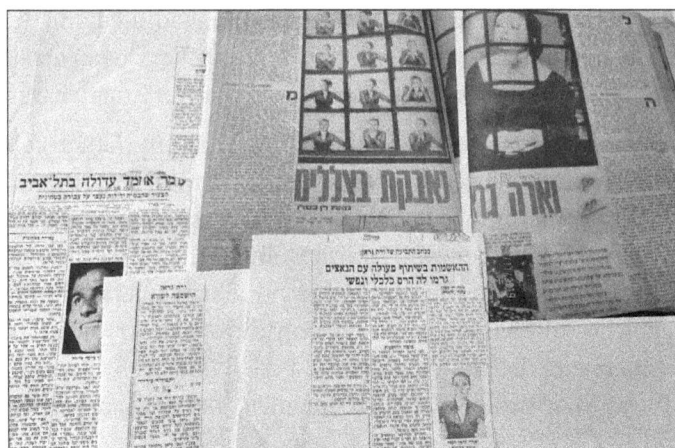

Ran Kislev's exposé about Vera Gran, Haaretz, 1971 and letters to editor. On the left, the article about Omar from 1969.

read on Polish Radio a selection from the novel *Bądź moim Bogiem / Be My God*, inspired by the life of Vera Gran.

I found online an interview my father gave for a 2011 documentary[25] about Vera. Still, after all those years, he defended her in that interview. It may have been the last filmed interview he gave. Based on how skinny and frail he looks, I believe it was done after the devastating stroke he suffered in 2010.

Like a fading candlelight in the wind, hope for justice for Vera vanished in 1981 when her lawsuit was dismissed. I ached for both Vera and my father. He had tried to achieve Tikkun Olam for Vera but was unable to correct the injustice. Vera spent the rest of her life with the mark of disgrace on her forehead.

---

25. Wiera Gran, 2011, reż. Maria Zmarz-Koczanowicz.

THROUGH HER EYES

My father's belief that Israel already had organized crime in the seventies and his suggestion that Mentesh was the (first) Godfather of Israel's organized crime was as passionate as his insistence that Vera Gran was falsely accused.

Something occurred to me as I reflected on everything I'd learned about his career, especially his relentless defence of Vera Gran.

My father spent his journalistic career pursuing facts and fighting to expose truths even if uncomfortable, even if resulting in death threats. But what he was up against with Vera's story, aside from destructive gossip, possible malice, and jealousy, was what lawyers, judges and juries often struggle with—the unreliability of memory. As a result, my father's wish to achieve Tikkun Olam for Vera failed, although not for lack of trying.

A chill ran up and down my spine when I read Tuszynska's words in *The Accused*, "I had two meetings with the journalist Ran Kislev, who had always defended Vera and the survivors. She considered him as the only Just Person on this earth."

I gasped and stopped reading.

Vera recognized his efforts as genuine and knew that at least one person believed her fully and tried his hardest to help her. I hope that knowledge offered her solace.

I put the book down as tears rolled down my face. A sob came out of me, emotions that caught me by surprise.

For the first time in my life, I could see my father through the eyes of the people he tried to help. I saw a side of him that was not always visible to me. In that moment, I also understood why it was imperative to him to never back down from fighting for truth and justice, no matter the cost.

I wish I could have told him how proud I am of him. I am proud of him in a way I was not when he was alive. While it was extremely unpopular to support anyone accused of being a Nazi collaborator in Israel, he demonstrated mettle and courage to do the right thing. And I can't help but feel shame for my transgressions, especially for punishing him so harshly—not speaking to him for almost two years because he didn't stand up to me against my teacher, and later, after his affair blew up, a matter between him and my mother.

He was imperfect in many ways, but who among us can cast the first stone?

How insignificant my grievances seem now, from the distance of a life lived.

THE PAST RETURNS

After processing what I'd learned about Vera Gran, how bravely my father defended her, and after recovering from what she had said about him, I was ready to look at the interview he gave to the *Virtual Shtetl* website. I finally felt prepared to read what he shared about his life in Europe before emigrating to Israel.

My heart softened a little.

While my father never talked about his sister Genia (Golda), I knew of her. She was four years older. In the interview for the *Virtual Shtetl*, my father explained that, upon his sister's graduation, she was immediately sent abroad. There was the risk she'd be arrested, together with many of her classmates, for being involved in Communist activities. She reached Belgium and later moved to France when WWII broke out, married a Frenchman and died in 1956. I remember hearing from my mother that Genia committed suicide as a result of a broken heart. My father didn't mention suicide in the interview, nor that his sister had a son. I knew he made no effort to find and connect with his nephew. The past was in the past, after all. His inclination to leave behind family was a side of his shadow I had a hard time accepting.

In the interview, my father explained that when he was twelve, on September 1, 1939, the Germans invaded Poland, signalling the start of WWII. At that point, his parents decided that they had better distance themselves from the German border and made their way to Radomsk, about thirty kilometres east of Chestohova, where his mother Rivka was from. Looking for safety in those early days of the war, my father and his parents knocked on the doors of Rivka's relatives and were turned away. From there, they continued to Warsaw. I can imagine the horror and desperation when doors were shut in their faces and the ensuing frenetic scramble to find safety.

On the third day of September, the German army seized Chestohova. And just days after their arrival in Warsaw, they heard a rumour allegedly originating from the mayor of Warsaw that it would be best for women and children to leave the city. Heeding the warning, the family escaped eastward until they reached Kovel (situated today in Ukraine). Three days after their arrival, the city was taken by the Red Army. The father, Moshe, was appointed director of a textile manufacturing plant in Sokal and they were sent there. My father believed that his father got this job due to his connections with Jewish Communists.

The town was divided between the Russians and the Germans. Initially, the Wexlers led an uneventful and peaceful life. That is, until one night in July or August of 1940, when three people arrived—a civilian and two soldiers—and told them to get out of their apartment, loaded them onto a truck and drove them to the railway station. They boarded a train that transported them in locked carriages to the Volga River. Upon their arrival, the carriages were unlocked, and the prisoners were given food to break the hunger they suffered during the journey. Afterwards, the train kept going until it stopped somewhere at the boreal forest of Sibirskaya Oblast, the Siberian region.

From Sokal to the closest point in Siberia, with a stop anywhere along the Volga River, the commute today involves several days. Surely back in 1940 it would have taken much longer and in harsher conditions. How terrifying it must have been—locked in a train car for days with no food, water, or facilities and not knowing where they were being taken.

Their final destination was a gulag.

IN THE GULAG

U pon the arrival of their detachment, some prisoners were transferred to another place while my father, his parents, and the others who travelled with them took their place. The gulags were constructed by Russian political prisoners starting in the 1920s. The camp was considered a "special settlement," which meant it was populated by families, and they were allowed a certain freedom of movement in the vicinity provided they did not venture too far. There were three camps in the area, about six kilometers apart. One camp was in the boreal forest, where its inmates were employed to fell trees. These were transferred by tractors to the river. Another camp was situated near the river and its prisoners oversaw preparing the trunks for transportation down the river. The third camp was in between, and it was responsible for the maintenance of the tractors that dragged the trees to the river. Moshe Wexler worked there as a mechanic.

Inside the camp were barracks for about twenty families each; the Wexlers were the only Jewish family in their barracks. Quite a few Polish children, the same age as my then-adolescent father, lived in that compound. One of their favourite pastimes was to gather in one of the rooms and listen to my father tell stories from the Sienkiewicz' Trilogy. While my father loved to read and share with me his favourite books until his last days, he never mentioned this trilogy, so I looked it up. The series of novels by Henryk Sienkiewicz, written between 1884-1888, is known simply as *The Trilogy* in Poland. It covers the lives and adventures of a group of fictional Polish and Lithuanian nobles starting with the 1647 Cossack rebellion[26] and continuing to dramatize wars, invasions, and other famous events in Polish history. This historical fiction, which was meant to "lift the hearts" of the Polish people, won acclaim outside Poland, too, and its author won the Nobel Prize in Literature. My father's ability to re-tell these stories to his peers in an engaging way was a precursor to his future journalistic storytelling abilities.

---

26. My father may not have known that the rebellion was no other than the Khmelnytzky Uprising, which was the worst pogrom in Jewish history (until the Holocaust) in Eastern Europe.

Very little food was available in the Siberian gulag, and they were hungry most of the time, my father explained in the interview. The children used to look for food—fish from the river and pick potatoes from the nearby kolkhoz (collective farm).

My father visited me in Toronto, in 2005, with his Polish common-law partner Magda, whom he had known since childhood in Chestohova. After my mother passed away, they began seeing each other and eventually moved in together. On the second morning at my house, Magda began telling me about the past my father had kept sealed. Before he came down for breakfast, in those few stolen moments, I learned interesting facts. She said their parents were friends and neighbours in Chestohova and ended up escaping the approaching Nazis together. Along with thousands of Jewish refugees they walked east in the nights and hid in the daytime, fearing the Nazi planes would spot them. The two families ended up in the Siberian gulags. Magda told me that she and her family were prisoners in the barrack adjacent to my father and his parents.

I don't know why I imagined my father and his family escaping only by cars or trains. Maybe it's a generational thing. Escaping by foot and walking many kilometers at night is a very different thing.

"Did you know we were so hungry in the gulag and we walked around with swollen stomachs?" she said in her thick Polish accent, while I fried bacon and eggs for them. I stopped and turned to look at her.

"No, I did *not* know that."

"Yes, and Henyek, the skinny and small *mamzer*[27] escaped at night to try and find any food scraps he could get his little hands on. He'd crawl under fences and bring us some of it, too, and probably saved our lives."

I gasped.

This story stunned me into silence.

Why didn't I hear about it?

At that moment, my father walked into the kitchen.

"Why are you talking about the past?" he scolded Magda. "The past is depressing. Talk about happy things, like what we are going to do today," and he shut the discussion down.

---

27. In Hebrew, this word means "illegitimate child", but in the Yiddish version it is also used to describe a person who "pulled one over" on you.

My husband offered to drive them to Niagara Falls, as I had to prepare for a presentation at a conference. For the next few hours, I struggled to focus as my mind played scenes of the skinny Herman Wexler, the daredevil teen who snuck out of the gulag's barracks to steal food, risking horrible punishment or death.

In the interview for the *Virtual Shtetl*, my father said that, on one occasion, he and his mother were caught gathering ears of corn. They were apprehended and taken to the main camp; Rivka was detained and he was allowed to leave. About half an hour later, a policeman came and released her, too. As it happened, a Russian parole committee arrived in the camp, acting on behalf of the agreement that was reached between Russia and the Sikorski's government in exile to the effect that Polish citizens who were detained or exiled, would be pardoned and allowed to settle in certain areas.

My mother told me once about this incident in the gulag's jail, which adds a bit of colour to what my father described in the interview. In my mother's version, "Rivka made a ruckus in her jail cell, banging, screaming and swearing so loud they had no choice but to let her go before these dignitaries arrived. The guards feared the visitors would think they couldn't control their prisoners."

According to my mother, no one could control Rivka or make her do anything she didn't want. She was a difficult woman and not particularly motherly, which might explain my father's insatiable need to rest his head in women's bosoms.

I remember Rivka as a small woman with white hair and glasses speaking languages I could not understand. She spoke only Polish and Yiddish, while I spoke Hebrew and English. The only thing I have left of her is a little brown leather-bound Yiddish-Hebrew dictionary she gave me, thinking this would help us communicate.

In the last few years of her life, it became impossible to communicate with Rivka in any language, and I wasn't allowed to see her. According to my mother, she talked to little green men she saw everywhere and often yelled at them, sometimes pushing them out of her apartment all the way to the street. My father could not cope with the change in his mother and so my mother took the bus from Tel Aviv to the city of Holon two or three times a week to cook for her mother-in-law and bathe her. Rivka had help from other relatives who lived nearby, as well. My father felt it was sufficient. She died in 1978 when I was sixteen and her funeral was the first one I ever attended. I remember my father's voice cracking as he said *Kadish* over her, but I didn't see any tears.

A Village in Uzbekistan

For a year and a half, the young Herman Wexler and his parents remained in the camp until they moved to Uzbekistan. Moshe found employment as a mechanic in a research institute that was established by Americans in Yangi Yul, a settlement not far from Tashkent, the largest city in Uzbekistan and the political center of Russian Turkestan. This village was built at the end of the 1930s and both the institute and accommodation for the staff were built using American methods of construction. When the war broke out, the Americans left and Uzbeks took their place. All the inhabitants worked in the fields growing crops, mostly corn, and the produce was distributed among themselves. Corn and all things made of corn were the staples of meals during that time, and that's where my father developed an extreme aversion to it.

During my childhood, I thought he was just being a controlling prick because he didn't like the smell of corn, the same way he didn't like spices on his food other than salt. I didn't know about his wartime experience in the Uzbek village, and I had no grasp of how trauma works on the psyche to produce such a profoundly disturbed response. Various cues, especially smells, can evoke the strongest emotions. Odours are the most efficient in activating autobiographical memories stored in the limbic brain and hippocampus. The neuroscientist Rachel Herz explains the smell-trauma connection, "In fact, what's known as the amygdala-hippocampal complex—which is where emotions, memories, and associations take place—is also the primary olfactory cortex."[28] The amygdala is the fear center and the hippocampus is where long-term memories are stored, the filing cabinet of the mind. Hence the intense emotional response when a smell triggers memories, good or bad.

My father finished high school while in Yangi Yul. The children had excellent teachers who arrived there as refugees from Ukraine after it had been attacked by the Germans. My father had learned the Russian language in the

---

28. In Herz, Rachel. *The Scent of Desire*, 2008.

gulag and graduated with very high grades, attaining a five out of five in all subjects and a grade of four out of five in Russian.

I paused reading my father's entry on the *Virtual Shtetl* and recalled that my brother Mickey once asked my father to tell him about his time in Siberia. My father's response was, "I had a dog there. I don't remember much else."

Obviously, he did.

I wasn't surprised that he infused the story with a great number of historical details, compared to the way other individuals told their stories on the site. I recognized it as a way of intellectualizing experiences, a coping strategy that keeps one away from emotions. It worked well for him. The only time I'd seen him express negative feelings other than anger was when he watched sad romantic movies. Casablanca always comes to mind. He often teared up and immediately lit a cigarette to kill the feeling.

From the interview, I learned that while still in Yangi Yul, my father became a member, and later a guide, in the Komsomol, a Communist youth movement. Its formal goals were to engage the members in health activities, sports, education, publishing, and various service and industrial projects. They were officially called the All-Union Leninist Young Communist League. During the war, these activities were put to good use when they became the youth arm of the underground resistance and were better known as the Young Avengers. It appears that my father dedicated his free time to resistance activities. In Yangi Yul, he was no longer locked in a gulag barrack so this had to be the period when he engaged in Partisan activities. I was finally able to connect the scattered dots of my father's personal history and sew more patches into the quilt.

My father's report card from Uzbekistan.

275

A Young Avenger

M*y Father, the Young Avenger* could be the title of a low-budget super-hero movie. But it would not be a Marvel comic or a blockbuster movie. My young father was a member of that youth movement during one of the most horrifying and terrifying times in history. The origin stories of certain Marvel superheroes involve childhood trauma during the Holocaust and, like Stan Lee (Stanley Martin Lieber), many of the creators of superhero comics were Jewish.[29]

I can't help but smile at the thought of my father wearing a cape and flying like Superman over enemy lines. Only, the father I knew would be holding a cigarette, with a typewriter strapped to his back.

The kind of activities the real-life Young Avengers engaged in were no laughing matter.

Typical covert missions included stealing weapons from the Germans, spying on German troops, and learning to operate and use weapons in a variety of sabotage missions. A famous young partisan in the Komosmol was Zinaida Portoova. Born in 1926, she was only a year older than my father. She participated in several missions, such as attacking German patrol squads looking to round up resistance fighters. In August 1943, when my sixteen-year-old father was probably active as well, Zinaida infiltrated a German garrison in Obol and poisoned its soldiers. She managed to escape but was caught in 1944. During her interrogation, she grabbed the pistol of the Gestapo interrogator, shot him and two more Nazi guards, and escaped the camp. She was found along the nearby river and, after being brutally tortured, was executed at gun point in the forest, one month before her eighteenth birthday. Surely my father heard about her exploits and maybe even crossed paths with her. Her heroism and courage were recognized and in 1958 she was the youngest female to ever be awarded (albeit posthumously) the title of "Hero of the Soviet Union." Later, she also received the Order of Lenin. There are numerous plaques and monuments in her honour throughout Russia.

---

29. https://jweekly.com/2005/10/21/cover-story-jews-and-the-invention-of-the-american-comic-book/

I had a difficult time visualizing what it was like for my father to be a partisan until 2022, when I saw the documentary *Four Winters*.[30] In it, Polish and other Eastern-European Jewish men and women speak about their experiences as partisans during WWII. It is estimated that there were about twenty-five thousand Jewish partisans, many of them teenagers, who escaped into the forests. They carried out clandestine activities such as blowing up bridges and derailing trains bringing supplies to the German forces. Interviewees said they occasionally came across Nazi soldiers and killed them. To avoid capture, they were often on the move hiding in forests. In the summer, it wasn't so bad sleeping under the stars, but winters were harsh, and they'd light fires, put them out, and put reeds on the still-warm wood to sleep on it. They knew they were in imminent danger all hours of the day and there was quite a bit of physical intimacy between these young men and women who thought they might not live to see another day. For subsistence they foraged and ate tree barks, grass or any animal they could catch. Sometimes, they stole food from local farmers.

Many partisans who lost their loved ones were motivated by revenge. Others by a simple drive to survive, knowing that Nazi forces and their collaborators wished them dead, and their homes were no longer safe to return to. At one point, Russian partisans connected with those from other countries and shared resources and information. The people interviewed for the documentary spoke about battles in which they lost friends and about the friends who were caught by the Nazis, tortured, and murdered.

How close did my father come to being caught, tortured, or killed? Or should I ask—how often? He chose to gloss over this period and kept us in the dark about this time in his life. It might have triggered painful memories—the loss of his comrades and stories he may have heard about their grim fate in the hands of the Nazis. Zinaida's story is one of many such examples. Every day could have been his last; a comrade could have broken down during torture and revealed their location. What may have felt like an exciting adventure could have ended in a slow and painful demise, as it did for many of those who were caught. I wonder if my father's attitude to life was born the moment he left his home in Chestohova, escaping the invading Germans and everything that happened after. Quite possibly, the chronic imminent danger he was in over many years wired his brain to operate as if every day could be his last. If that's how things are in life, what's the point of saving money? Why worry about unpaid bills? Why plan anything? Why not spend every minute and every shekel in your wallet on what gives you pleasure now?

---

30. https://fourwintersfilm.com

Daily, my father manifested his hunger for pleasure and excitement *now*, and a refusal to revisit the painful yesterday or worry about tomorrow.

Out of this history, he also developed the need to contribute what he could to achieve Tikkun Olam.

When talking to my brother about our father's history, he added another fact I did not know—that our father spoke German. All these years, I thought he only spoke Polish, Russian, and Hebrew, as opposed to my mother, the polyglot.

"How do you know?" I asked him.

"I discovered this while in Austria on my Bar-Mitzva trip with mom and dad to Europe. I heard both of them speak German there," he said.

Speaking German would have been useful when spying on the Germans with the partisans. I also found out that my father's last name Wexler means moneychanger in German and this suggests that our father's paternal side of the family may have had German roots.

Maybe his father, Moshe, was a descendant of that first recorded Jew, Mosiek (Moshe), who loaned money to the *Council of the City of His Royal Highness* of Chestohova.

In 1946, at the end of the war, my father and his parents made their way back to their hometown. It was then that they learned that Rivka's family in Radomsk and the whole Hasidic Dynasty perished in the Holocaust.

God apparently abandoned them.

A Final Patch
for the Quilt

Surviving the Holocaust by exile, by escaping to USSR-controlled territories, including enduring the harsh conditions in gulags and/or becoming a partisan, is a different category of Holocaust survival. As I have learned over the years, there is a "hierarchy of suffering" in which making it out alive of Soviet gulags ranks lower than surviving concentration camps. It's as if the world wasn't ready or willing to consider that perhaps Stalin's forced-labour camps were as brutal as Hitler's concentration camps. Starvation, religious persecution, torture, and executions were rampant in the camps, and all of that took place in the harsh tundra of Siberia.

I recall my father's claim that the Soviets were worse than the Nazis and can only imagine what he witnessed and experienced. But it is not a competition, and one does not need to silence any group of Holocaust survivors. Levi Bridges, in his article, "The Ultimate Guide to Siberian Gulags and Soviet Exile Sites", wrote, "The gulags quickly became infamous for their harsh treatment of prisoners. Gulag prisoners were packed into train cars on the Trans-Siberian Railroad and shipped to far-off camps in freezing cold. The long train journey was an excruciating prelude to the gulag. Once in the camps, workdays lasted as long as twelve to fourteen hours. Prisoners were given meager rations and often slept on bunks made of wooden planks. Some told of going without blankets even in the depths of winter. Guards exercised ruthless control over the camps, shooting inmates who tried to flee and killing others for petty offenses just to instill fear in the others." Nine in ten prisoners died of starvation, disease, or violence.

Three months after returning to Poland, having survived by exile, my father moved to Lodz to realize his parents' dream for him since the day he was born. They wanted him to study engineering at the Lodz Polytechnical Institute and subsequently work at the family factory. This, despite the fact his parents' factory no longer existed in its former status. Upon their return to Chestohova, three times Moshe Wexler received licenses to set up small factories and three times they were nationalized and confiscated by the Communist government.

From his time in Lodz, my father remembered "the Bourse" which was home for the educated young Jewish intelligentsia and the numerous young people who survived the war and the camps.

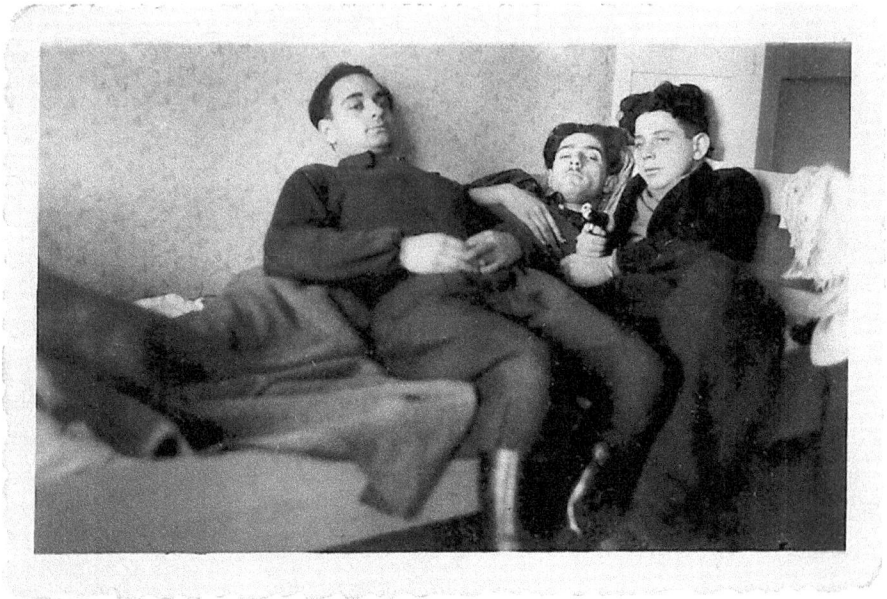

At the Lodz "Bourse" with friends. My father, on the right, pointing a pistol.

It was also in the Polytechnical Institute in Lodz where my father met Halina Plotek, his first wife. She was born in Lodz and was a concentration camp survivor. At the end of the first year in the polytechnical, my father passed the final exams with flying colours but decided to leave. He told my brother once that, as part of their program, he had courses on nuclear physics, a new field of which the professors knew very little. He was disillusioned by their lack of knowledge and decided to quit the program. The young Herman had always been drawn to journalism and took a course which led to a job as a censor for the Communist press—an amusing fact, considering how vocal my father would become against censorship in journalism in Israel.

During his visit in Toronto in June of 2005, I took my father to see the downtown campus of the University of Toronto where I attained my Master and Doctorate degrees in Psychology. I thought he'd enjoy the scenic footpath called Philosopher's Walk and the circle of buildings that include architectural marvels like Convocation Hall—a domed rotunda, built a hundred years earlier. Since he had an ankle injury and couldn't walk very far, I parked nearby. On that warm and sunny day, we strolled arm in arm on King's College Circle.

He stopped in front of the old University College building and gawked at the structure built in 1859. The brick and stone building has a mix of architectural styles and features. Most striking is the repetition of the semi-circular arches and small columns along with numerous carved motifs of nature, animals, and mysterious creatures.

On St. George campus, University of Toronto, 2005.

"I feel like I travelled back in time. Some of these buildings remind me of the Polytechnical Institute I went to in Lodz," my father said as he supported himself on my shoulder and I wasn't sure if it was because of his injury or the memory.

We sat down on a nearby bench, and I waited to see if he'd add anything. Several thoughts swam inside my head and I was trying to form a question, but before I came up with one he said, "Let's go eat at the place you told me about, it's there right?" He pointed towards another historic building on the campus called Hart House, where I said we'd be having lunch. There, between bites, he admired the dark wooden furniture, the architecture, the high and arched ceilings and Gothic style windows.

True to his style, my father made it easy to live in the moment but shut down any possibility of conversation about the past. He quietly carried the shadow of his past and that of a faraway land.

After marrying Halina in 1949, they moved from Lodz to Wrocław, where there were vacant apartments to rent. In 1951, he was hired by the Polish news agency, PAP, then moved on to become a reporter

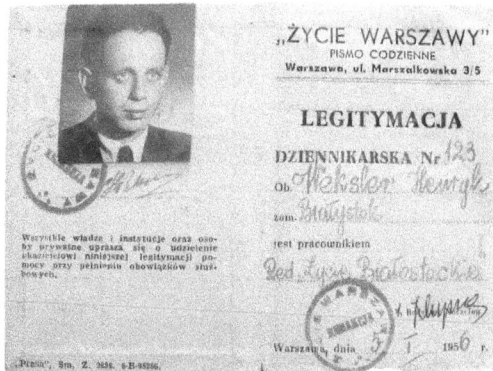

Journalist ID card from "Life of Warsaw", 1956.

281

on Lower Silesia for the newspaper Życie Warszawym (Life of Warsaw), and he later became the editor of Życie Białostockie (Life of Bialystok). His daughter Irit and son Yoram were born in Poland.

Mickey told me that he asked our father once why they didn't emigrate to Israel right after the war, like most Jews who survived the Holocaust. It never occurred to me to ask this poignant question and the answer he gave my brother revealed an interesting detail.

"We were Bundists, not Zionists," my father told him.

Bundism was a secular Socialist Jewish movement which manifested as the General Jewish Labour Bund in Poland, Lithuania, and Russia. It started in Russia in 1897 and was an important participant in the Russian Revolution of 1905.

The Bund was both a political party and a trade union, the avantgarde of the Jewish workers. The Jewish Labour Bund did not advocate ethnic or religious separatism. Unlike the Zionist movement, they emphasized culture, not a state or a place. "There, where we live, that is our country,"[31] was their motto. They condemned the proclamation of the Zionist State, Israel.

The family chose to stay in Poland, obviously hoping to resume a peaceful and normal life while re-building their business and livelihood.

While my father settled into his post-war life, the years 1955-56 marked the beginning of the first period of rebellion against the Soviet Communist rule and a new government was formed. After a short period, the people's freedom and liberty and the spirit of liberalization were once again limited by the government. According to my father, sometime later, one of the Wrocław newspapers published an article against him, claiming that he used to stand over the workers in his father's plant with a whip in his hand, and that he had been a capitalist.

The whip accusation was absurd and vicious.

A few days later, the article was reprinted in *Polityka*, the main political newspaper published in Warsaw.

In the *Virtual Shtetl* interview, my father explained that this was when he decided to move to Israel. This revealed another hole in the quilt that I hadn't seen.

I paused here and reflected. Could the fact that he had been falsely accused, and that claims were published in newspapers that he was abusive to workers in his father's factory, have made defending Vera more personal for him? Was he

---

31. https://www.jewishvoiceforlabor.org.uk/article/my-great-grandfather-the-bundist/

trying to repair the unrepairable in his life, through helping Vera and others? Viktor Frankl wrote in *Man's Search For Meaning*, "In some ways suffering ceases to be suffering at the moment it finds a meaning."

I believe that the tipping point for my father was more likely what my brother and I learned from people who had known our father in Poland. Following the war, the young Herman Wexler became a member of a secular Jewish movement. My brother thinks it was Beitar, a Zionist-Revisionist movement. While active in this movement and already married with one child, he had an extra-marital affair. That's when he most likely fathered the son I learned about after his stroke, the son he never mentioned to me. The expectation of high moral integrity (Tohar Midot) from members of the movement did not allow for such a lapse in behaviour and there were threats to expose his affair publicly. The possibility of being exposed as a philanderer may have been the proverbial last straw. And so it was that sometime in 1956, my father, Halina, Yoram, and Irit emigrated to Israel. His parents followed two years later.

Despite the negative consequence of his adulterous behaviour in Poland, my father continued with his philandering in Israel.

These were the final patches of the quilt that was my father's life.

Out of His Shadow

In June of 2013, I embarked on a quest to get to know my father more fully. As would be expected from a daughter of an investigative journalist, I did my best to research my father's story thoroughly, to gather facts, and to maintain an objective point of view. In the process, I shone light on aspects of his personal shadow and that of Israel, some of which I hadn't known before. But still, I cannot decide if he was more brave than reckless.

Like a quilt with different patterns on the front and back, I see my father's personal life as one side and his professional life as the other. Collecting the pieces for both was painstaking, but one I was determined to complete.

As this project concludes, I find that my father's shadow fades. I am more aware of his light and how it has illuminated my own life's journey.

As Jonathan, "The Source", said, my father was a man of life. He chose to leave the dark days of the past behind and to live as if each day might be his last. It is a common trauma response among Holocaust survivors. He turned existential dread on its head. Every day that he was still breathing and able to do what he loved was a good one in his mind.

I benefitted from being exposed to his deep appreciation of nature, art, literature, music, beauty, and food. In some ways, I followed his example; but, being a rebel, I did so more responsibly.

People who worked with my father or knew him professionally described him as a brave, hardworking, prolific, and brilliant journalist. Friends said he was fun to be around. His women friends told me he was a great dancer.

As for Ran Kislev the husband, I leave that opinion to those who are qualified to have it. My experience of him as a father was different than those of his other children. In the context of his time, and of my life, he tried to be a good father to me. I never forgot his heroism in the mine field, the gifts he bought me even though he couldn't afford some of them, and how he tricked me into giving university a try.

The sting of our conflicts has long faded, and in some instances what stings more is my nastiness. My past judgements and resentments have diminished to barely audible echoes.

Ultimately, I had to confront unpleasant aspects of my own shadow, too—such as my cruel and unusual ways of punishing my father for his transgressions. These were painful to face as they piled up on typed pages. I am disappointed with myself for the assumptions I made about him. I harshly judged his choices and flaws, as if I was in any position to cast the first stone. Despite my training in psychology and trauma, until recently I did not fully consider how events of his early life shaped him and how they explained aspects of his shadow self. It was only after he entered a coma that I took the first steps to get to know him better.

Despite my father's obvious personal flaws and his long shadow, I believe he did everything in his power to achieve Tikkun Olam—the repair of the world, or at least of Israel. He rallied his talents and resources to help as many people as he could if he felt they were wronged.

Today, it is clearer to me why I have always been compelled to speak truth to power. Sometimes it came at a high cost to myself, as was the case during my military service. It is why I have chosen to advocate passionately for clients who have faced unfair practices by insurance companies or the military. My father had been my role model in this.

Something else occurred to me, too. By moving to Canada, I was able to step away from my father's shadow and discover who I was on my own terms. Any accomplishment since that time was mine, and mine alone. The good grades in university were mine. The merit scholarships I received during master's and doctorate programs at the University of Toronto were mine. All my professional successes were thanks to my hard work and abilities.

When my father learned that I had done media interviews on radio, television, and newspapers, and that I was invited to speak at conferences including keynote talks on the treatment of trauma and addiction, he said, "So now I am the father of Dr. Sara Aharon."

I felt taller.

My own hole-filled quilt is more complete now, too. I got to know myself better. Previously confusing memories are now full narratives, and my childhood, although still unusual, makes more sense to me and I feel at peace with it.

As I stitched together the last patches of my father's personal life, I admired the complexity of the patterns in the quilt. Some had been either suppressed in my memory or were new revelations altogether. When I uncovered new patches, my emotions ranged from anger and sadness to awe and pride.

Mostly, now, there is pride.

Through writing this memoir and the difficult conversations I initiated with him late in his life, I achieved some personal measure of Tikkun with my father.

A part of me wonders though if my initial quest to determine whether my father was brave or reckless was the wrong question to ask. I think that the question I was truly trying to answer was: did my father deserve my love?

I believe that, as flawed as he was, he did.

BLUE

Blue was the Sea of Galilee, mirror smooth at sunrise when back in the tent

you tapped on my shoulder and said, time for a swim.

We tiptoed around mother, who preferred extra dreams while we created real ones
for one week, to relive every year and for years. We stood in awe, draped in the
vast open sky, inhaling the moment before

our feet swirled golden sand and we could no longer see the tiny fish and the shells

and the rocks that kissed our toes. When the sun caressed and

raised our hearts till we flapped our arms and

our strokes took us into the horizon and back

for an hour or for eternity—we were one with the sea

and the rocks and the fish and the sun and the wind.

I was closer to you than God ever was, and the blue of the sea was the

blue in your eyes when you closed them at last and ascended to the heaven

you never believed in.

I remembered that blue that you showed me,

the air that we shared, clear vision,

the touch of the water, the tickle

of fish as we swam

towards the

horizon.

(I wrote this in 2013 after my father became a memory)

Acknowledgements

Writing a memoir involves time travel. For the past twelve years I've been on this journey, going back in time, on and off, sometimes getting lost in the past but eventually returning to unpack the baggage. This book is like a travel diary but one involving many travel companions. I'd like to thank anyone who had joined me for any part of this trip whether your name is mentioned here or not.

Thank you,

To all my writing instructors and mentors. When I thought I might never be able to write a book, in my second language, it was Alyson Latta, in her course *Memories Into Stories* at the University of Toronto Creative Writing certificate program who had given me confidence and encouragement to keep going. I am forever grateful for that. Since then, I had quite a few wonderful teachers and mentors including Julie Hartley, Brian Henry, and David Bezmozgis. As to understanding the Jungian Shadow, I am grateful to Laurie Savlov in Toronto who helped me grasp the full meaning of the personal and social shadow, specifically of my father's, Israel's and mine.

Thank you,

To my writing peers. Feedback from professional peers had made me a much better psychologist and this applies to writing peers as well. In Brian Henry's advanced writing workshops, both he and the participants of his workshops had given me invaluable feedback. Having so many wise eyes and minds read excerpts had shown me what direction I needed to take when I got lost with so much information and too many stories. I am indebted to all of them for the time and thought they had put into my submissions: Tanya Bellhumeur-Allatt, Sarah Groundwater, Christine Michaud, Cynthia Stacey, Sheila Eastman, Jane Parker, Kristy Jackson, Margaret Ries, Larissa Thomas, Ellen Michelson, Victoria Hamilton, Deirdre Domegan, Jane Finlayson, David Bellerive, Hermine Steinberg, Penny Thompson, Roger Moore, and many others. Other writing peers who offered input and support include, Patricia Meyer, Susan Turk and Erdine (Dee) Hope.

Thank you,

To anyone who offered information and insight about my father, my brother Mickey Kislev, "Jonathan" (The Source), the criminologist Avi Davidovich, the journalist and author Avi Valentin and others who responded to emails and calls and answered my questions to the best of their ability.

Thank you,

To my life-long friends in Israel, Yonit Sinai, Orna Villeval and Shirley Algrably who had been a consistent source of support, sometimes working hard, together, to lift me from rock bottom. The showed up in the most incredible ways, whenever I needed them. Over the years, each of them contributed to this project in some ways, including sharing with me observations about my family. Emotional support from them throughout this very personal journey was crucial.

Thank you,

To the staff at the *Haartz* archive, especially Shoshi Mendelovitch who has gone above and beyond to help me locate articles, in person and via email.

Thank you,

To Alexandra Risen. I cannot express how grateful I am for the support and insightful critical feedback I received from this dear friend and greatest writing buddy. She had been the best sounding board anyone could have asked for, always making astute observations and suggestions and encouraged me whenever I wanted to give up on this ambitious project.

Thank you,

To the community of supportive friends, starting with Rachel Rodriges-Todd and her husband Bill Todd, my wonderful colleagues and friends, Ora and Isaac Prilleltensky, Maria Haarmans, and Marta Durski (who also translated material from Polish for me), as well as more recent friends from my writing life: Maria Ford and Virginia Wheatley.

Thank you,

To the excellent Beta Readers of my most recent draft, Annie Hadida, Virginia Wheatley and Michael Kaplan. They offered insightful and invaluable feedback and pored over my manuscript with a keen eye and generous hearts. And thank you to Michael Cooper for help with images.

Thank you,

There are of course friends who have been simply a wonderful source of support over the years and a source of light during dark times, Elizabeth Bush and Roni Boshari, Michael Kaplan, Pauline Abrams and Scott Allen and other members of my professional peer support group and book club including Ginny McFarlan and Bill Bishop.

Thank you,

To my brother Mickey who shared his perspective on our father and offered me small patches of the quilt that were missing. And to Shira, Mickey's other half who knew and loved my father and listened to some of our (often crazy) conversations about him without judgement.

Thank you,

To Maria Ford for doing the final edits and offering additional suggestions, and to Todd Coopee of Sonderho Press. Both Maria and Todd worked with me in a highly professional, patient and diligent manner to bring this manuscript to fruition.

Thank you,

My deepest gratitude, or - *the Oscar for Best Supportive Role* goes to my family.

Roni, my husband, had been my biggest cheerleader. Throughout the years, he had never stopped believing in this project and in my ability to reach the finish line.

My insightful and highly emotionally intelligent daughters Sivan and Maya offered unbridled support and made useful observations about their grandfather. You inspire me every day with your resilience and ability to milk life for all its worth, just like your grandfather.

None of this would have happened if not for the love and encouragement of my family.

Sara Aharon.

About the Author

D r. Sara Aharon was born in Israel and immigrated to Canada in 1987. In addition to being a writer and a visual artist, she is a practicing psychologist with a doctorate from the University of Toronto. Sara supports individuals facing health challenges, addiction and trauma. She has been interviewed for her work on television, radio and in written media.

Sara began writing creatively in 2013 and has had articles, stories and poems published in both online literary sites and in print. She also holds certificates in Creative Writing from the University of Toronto and Humber College.

My Father's Shadow is Sara's first memoir. She is currently writing a second memoir focusing on her mother—a teacher, model, journalist, translator, polyglot and published author who was at the centre of a highly publicized scandal during Sara's early childhood. Both memoirs weave together reflections on family, trauma, and identity with broader social and historical contexts.

Sara lives in Toronto and is the proud mother of two adult daughters.

BIBLIOGRAPHY

Christie, Agatha. *Murder on the Orient Express*. Collins Crime Club Publishing. 1934.

Davidovich, Avi. "*Organized Crime in Israel and Around the World: Theories and Reality.*" Jul. 1993. Paper towards a Masters degree in Criminology. (Quotes of Meir Shamgar and Minister of Police Moshe Hillel in response to my father's first series were taken from here).

Derogy, Jacque, *Israel Connection, la Mafia en Israel*, 1980, Paris : Pion. (in French, out of print).

Erel, Nitza. *Without Fear and Prejudice*. 2006, Magness Press.

Fisher, Done'el. "They Called Him The Godfather." *Hadashot,* 8 Nov. 1991.

Frankl, Viktor. *Man's Search For Meaning.* Washington Square Press. 1969.

Gran, Vera. (letter to publication) *Law and Life* in 1977, in Tuszynska, Agata. *Vera Gran, The Accused,* Alfred A. Knoff. 2013.

Herz, Rachel. *The Scent of Desire, Discovering Our Enigmatic Sense of Smell.* William Morrow Paperbacks, 2008.

Kislev, Ran. "Omar Ahmed Adula in Tel Aviv." *Haaretz Daily*, 22 Apr. 1969.

Ibid. "The Stolen Gems Return to the Bourse." *Haaretz Daily*, 12 Dec. 1969.

Ibid. "Gun Fight Between Diamond Robbers and the Ramat-Gan Police." *Haaretz Daily*, 19 Dec. 1969.

Ibid. "A Rising Wave of Violence" *Haaretz Daily*. 23 Jan. 1970.

Ibid. "The Trend of Mood-Altering Drugs Series. A Worrisome Development" *Haaretz Daily*. 30 Jan. 1970.

Ibid. "The Trip Not Everyone Comes Back From." *Haaretz Daily*, 13 Feb. 1970.

Ibid. "Organized Crime in Israel." *Haaretz Daily*, 15 Apr. 1971.

Ibid. "All The King's Men." *Haaretz Daily*, 18 Apr. 1971.

Ibid. "Home Made Mafia." *Haaretz Daily*, 19 Apr. 1971.

Ibid. "Mentesh (Mordechai Tzarfati), The Servant of Mapay and Raffi" *Haaretz Daily*, 20 Apr. 1971.

Ibid. "Connections at the Top—the Police, a Special Chapter in the History of Mentesh's Empire." *Haaretz Daily*, 21 Apr. 1971.

Ibid. "Mentesh About Himself—Connections with Ministers Namir, Rabinovitch, Officers and Members of the Party." *Haaretz Daily*, 23 Apr. 1971.

Ibid. "Kanner Doesn't Remember." *Haaretz Daily*, 25 Apr. 1971.

Ibid. "The War of the Stakehouses." *Haaretz Daily*, 7 May. 1971.

Ibid. "The Circle Closes." *Haaretz Daily*, 4 Jun. 1971.

Ibid. "The Organized Crime and The Violent Crime." *Haaretz Daily*, 27 Sept. 1971

Ibid. "Vera Gran Fighting the Shadows." *Haaretz Daily*, 3 Dec. 1971.

Ibid. "In Vera Gran's Lawsuit: The Accusations of Collaboration of the Nazis Caused Her Financial and Emotional Ruin." *Haaretz Daily,* Jun. 25, 1972.

Ibid. "The Ministry of Religions Made So far 144 Lists of Marriage Banned Individuals". *Haaretz Daily,* 19 Sept. 1975.

Ibid. "The Rabbinic Justice Mills." *Haaretz Daily,* Series 26 Sept. to 19 Oct. series. 1984.

Ibid. "About Hassara Betshuva." *Haaretz Daily,* Series from Mar. to Apr. 1984.

Ibid. "Death of A Godfather." *Haaretz Daily*, 8 Nov. 1991.

Ibid. "Lioness in Winter." (Interview with Shulamit Aloni), *Haaretz Daily*, 5 Apr. 1996.

Ibid, "At The Forefront of the Supreme Court." *Haaretz Daily,* 16, Feb. 1999.

Kosovska, Elzbeita. "Shattering Altars to Zionism." *Connections* no. 43, Summer, 2012.

Marianowicz, Antoni. *Life Gravely Forbidden.* 2004.

Przybylski, Marcin. *Bądź moim Bogiem.* (Be My God), 2007.

Puzo, Mario. "The Godfather." 1969. G.P. Putnam's Sons.

Rosen, Baruch. "Mentesh The Way I Know Him." *Haaretz Daily*, 11 May, 1971

Sienkiewicz, Henryk. *Sienkiewicz' Trilogy.* (1884-1888).

Szpilman, Wladyslaw. *The Pianist.* Picador, 2002.

Tau B. and Nevo, Raya. "Who Are You Ran Kislev?" *Ottot*, Nov. 1981.

Turkow, Jonas. *Once There Was a Jewish Warsaw.* 1969. Tel-Aviv.

Tuszynska, Agata. *Vera Gran, The Accused.* Alfred A. Knoff. 2013.

Valentin, Avi. "Organized Crime—The Situation Today." *Haaretz* Daily, 5 Aug. 1977.

OTHER SOURCES:
ONLINE:

Bridges, Levi. "The Ultimate Guide to Siberian Gulags and Soviet Exile Sites", 6 Jun. 2014. site: www.rbth.com https://www.rbth.com/travel/2014/06/06/the_ultimate_guide_to_siberian_gulags_and_soviet_exile_sites Searched October 11, 2022

Crabapple, Molly. "My Great-Grandfather the Bundist." *New York Review of Books,* 6th October 2018. https://www.nybooks.com/online/2018/10/06/my-great-grandfather-the-bundist/

Homberger, Eric. "Mario Puzo." *The Guardian*, 5 Jul. 1999. https://www.the-guardian.com/news/1999/jul/05/guardianobituaries

Laviv, Yigal. The Ben-Barka Affair and the Israeli Connection. 30 May, 2019. https://yigallaviv.com/2019/05/30/1065/ Searched April 27, 2020.

Jones, L. Thomas. "The Dying of the Light: The Joseph Valachi Story." *Online article from crimelibrary.org* searched on 27 Jun., 2022 https://crimelibrary.org/gangsters_outlaws/mob_bosses/valachi//mafia_2.html

Kowalczyk, Janusz R. "Weira Gran." *https://culture.pl/en/author/janusz-r-kowalczyk* Apr. 2013, updated Apr. 2013. Translated by Agnieszka Le Nart, Apr. 2013, updated by Natalia Sajewicz, Aug. 2018.

Perel, Esther. In Rosin, Hanna. "Why We Cheat. Spouses in happy marriages have affairs. What are we all looking for?" *Slate*. 27 Mar. 2014.

https://slate.com/human-interest/2014/03/esther-perel-on-affairs-spoeuses-in-happy-marriages-cheat-and-americans-dont-understand-infidelity.html Searched 15Aug., 2021)

Serena, Katie. *"The Nazis Sent Franceska Mann To The Gas Chamber, But She Had No Intention Of Going Quietly."* Published 19 Mar. 2018. Updated 28 Oct. 2020. Searched 16 Mar. 2022. https://allthatsinteresting.com/franceska-mann Searched 17 Oct. 2022.

Shimoni, Mor. "This Story Will Never End", *The Chronicles of Organized Crime in Israel. Ynet,* 7 Aug. 2023. https://www.ynetnews.com/magazine/article/skg-mhc8tn Searched 18 Aug. 2024.

DOCUMENTARIES

"Four Winters." Directed by Julia Mintz. https://fourwintersfilm.com Aspen Films. (2020).

"A Light Unto the Nations." Episodes 2: The Hebrew Crime. Aired 21 Feb. 2008 on Kan 11 channel.

"Wiera Gran." Directed by Maria Zmarz-Koczanowicz. 2011. https://chomikuj.pl/action/SearchFiles. wiera gran - składanka.mp3

UNNAMED AUTHORS:

Jews and the invention of the American comic book, 21 Oct. 2005, in https://jweekly.com/2005/10/21/cover-story-jews-and-the-invention-of-the-american-comic-book/ Searched 26 Apr. 2022)

"Moshe Dayan's Eye Patch." Stand for Israel, 22 May 22 2023 https://www.ifcj.org/news/stand-for-israel-blog/moshe-dayan-s-eye-patch Searched 2 Sept. 2023.

"Puzo, Mario, 1920-1999." Dartmouth Libraries https://archives-manuscripts.dartmouth.edu/agents/people/5993

Letters to the Editor, *Haaretz Daily*:

Re. Organized Crime series:

Fuchs, Moshe. 25 May, 1971.

Gindi Brothers. "Thanks to Mentesh." 7 May, 1971.

Halpern, M. "Silence is Admitting." 2 Jun. 1971.

Yitzchak Ziv-Av. "Not Asking for Forgiveness." 13 May, 1971.

Rubiner, Betty. 25 May, 1971.

Re. Vera Gran:

Victoria Boreido. "Vera Gran was Defamed." 12 Dec. 1971.

Oskar M. Baruch, 12 Dec. 1971.

Haaretz Daily articles without journalists' names attached:

- "4 Are Demanding to Erase their Jewish Nationality from their ID." 29 Mar. 1970.
- "S. Danoch is Charged with Threatening to Murder Ran Kislev." 28 Mar. 1972.
- "As Long As I Come Out a Real Man." 28 Apr. 1972.
- "Chief Commander Eli Lavi in Court: I Recommended Closing the File About Danoch's Words to the Journalist Ran Kislev." 12 May 1972.
- "Shimshon Danoch Acquitted from a Claim He Threatened to Murder Ran Kislev." 13 Jun. 13 1972.
- "Appeal of the Acquittal of Danoch for Threatening Ran Kislev." 18 Jun.1972
- "Appeal of the Acquittal of Danoch for Threatening Ran Kislev." 20 Jun.1972.
- "The Supreme Court Rejects Shimshon Danoch's Appeal Against Ran Kislev." 25 Jul. 1974.